You Might Remember Me

Also by Mike Thomas

The Second City Unscripted

You Might Remember Me

The Life and Times of
PHIL HARTMAN

Mike Thomas

ST. MARTIN'S PRESS ☙ NEW YORK

www.stmartins.com

Designed by Steven Seighman

Library of Congress Cataloging-in-Publication Data

Thomas, Mike, 1970–
    You might remember me : the life and times of Phil Hartman / Mike Thomas.
        pages cm
    ISBN 978-1-250-02796-2 (hardcover)
    ISBN 978-1-250-02797-9 (e-book)
    1. Hartman, Phil.   2. Actors—United States—Biography.   3. Comedians—United States—Biography.   I. Title.
    PN2287.H316T57 2014
    791.4302'8092—dc23
    [B]

                                                                        2014016901

First Edition: September 2014

10 9 8 7 6 5 4 3 2 1

For my parents

He has achieved success who has lived well, laughed often, and loved much; who has gained the respect of intelligent men and the love of little children; who has filled his niche and accomplished his task; who has left the world better than he found it, whether by an improved poppy, a perfect poem, or a rescued soul; who has never lacked appreciation of Earth's beauty or failed to express it; who has always looked for the best in others and given the best he had; whose life was an inspiration; whose memory a benediction.

—Bessie Anderson Stanley, "Success"

"I like my vagina."

—Phil Hartman as Charlton Heston, reading from Madonna's book, *Sex*

Introduction

For eight increasingly successful seasons Phil Hartman was an integral part of NBC's venerable sketch show, *Saturday Night Live*, so much so that colleagues there called him "The Glue." Fellow cast member Jan Hooks coined the term, and along with her, Dana Carvey, Kevin Nealon, Dennis Miller, Victoria Jackson, Jon Lovitz, and Nora Dunn, Phil helped save the show from almost certain ruin in the mid-80s. In the process, he joined a pantheon of *SNL* MVPs that includes John Belushi, Dan Aykroyd, Eddie Murphy, Carvey, and a handful of others. In fact, according to *SNL*'s creator and executive producer Lorne Michaels, Phil may well be the leader of that pack. As he once mused, "Phil has done more work that's touched greatness than probably anybody else who's ever been here."

At Fox's long-running animated hit *The Simpsons*, where he spent eight years from 1990 to 1998, Phil did such distinctive voice work for so many memorable episodes (53)—as dunderheaded shyster attorney Lionel Hutz, clueless D-list actor Troy McClure, and numerous other minor characters—he came to be regarded by the program's inner circle of writers, showrunners, and permanent players as an honorary member of their elite group. They revered him to such an extent that after Phil died, Hutz and McClure were retired in his honor. No one, *Simpsons* creator and die-hard Phil fan Matt Groening knew, could inhabit those roles in quite the same way. "He was a comedy writer's dream," Groening once wrote. "Phil could get a laugh out of any line he was given, and make a funny line even funnier. He nailed the joke every time, and that made all *The Simpsons* writers worship him."

NBC's witty workplace sitcom *NewsRadio* also benefitted tremendously from Phil's portrayal of the intelligent, arrogant, and aggressively self-centered broadcaster Bill "the Real Deal" McNeal. Executive producer and head writer Paul Simms created the character with Phil in mind, and Phil's sudden absence left a huge void that was never filled. "I can't count the number of times at table reads when they would first read that week's script with some line that was just filler, but Phil would get a laugh," Simms says. "I don't even know how. If I knew how, I would be a genius. He really could help even the silliest material. And as a writer, you find you want to write for the characters that make everything funny a little bit more."

And yet, Phil's *life* has long been overshadowed by his death. Which is only natural—after all, he was adored by millions and slain in his prime. But what happened in the early morning hours of May 28, 1998, when Phil's third wife Brynn shot him three times as he slept before taking her own life, should not supersede all that came before it. Like any human being Phil was a complex puzzle, and that tragic episode but one piece in a box of many.

While his work on *Pee-wee's Playhouse*, *SNL*, *The Simpsons*, and *NewsRadio* is well known, until now details of his earlier formative years have emerged only in dribs and drabs, and many of them not at all. His feelings of neglect and guilt while growing up with a developmentally disabled younger sister in Canada; his avid surfing and ceaseless spiritual questing; his visual artistry and rock 'n' roll road-tripping; his relationships with the women he loved and the reasons that love was lost—all of those subjects and more are explored in the pages that follow. So, too, are never-before-told stories from the set of *SNL,* accounts of Phil's frequent jaunts to his paradisaical getaway Catalina Island, and previously unpublished accounts of his final days.

In researching and writing Phil's story over the course of nearly three years, I tried to understand and present him as much more than a highly gifted and widely beloved comedic performer, or the still-mourned victim of a terrible crime. He was and is all of those, certainly, but he was also a deeply sensitive man who loved life and reveled in nature; an eminently approachable and even gregarious public figure who was privately reserved and enigmatic; a loyal friend and generous collaborator. As a friend of his once observed, "There is a small room in Phil that no one will ever get to."

This book is a key to—or at least a reverse peephole through—its previously locked door.

Judge: Mr. Cirroc [pronounced Keyrock], are you ready to give your summation?

Cirroc: It's *just* "Cirroc," your Honor. [He approaches the jury box.] And, yes, I'm ready. Thank you. Ladies and gentlemen of the jury, I'm just a caveman. I fell in some ice and later got thawed by some of your scientists. Your world frightens and confuses me. Sometimes the honking horns of your traffic make me want to get out of my BMW and run off into the hills. Or whatever. Sometimes when I get a message on my fax machine, I wonder, "Did little demons get inside and type it?" I don't know. My primitive mind can't grasp these concepts.

(Transcript courtesy of snltranscripts.jt.org)

I need no blessings, but I'm counting mine.

—David Gilmour, "This Heaven"

Prologue

O n hiatus from his NBC sitcom *NewsRadio*, Phil drove his white Mercedes coupe to a Holiday Inn at Sunset Boulevard and the 405 Freeway. Arriving around 11:30 A.M., he picked up good pal and fellow outdoorsman Britt Marin, and the two of them motored down to Schock Boats in Newport Beach to buy supplies for their Boston Whalers. Phil needed a cooler for the seventeen-footer he'd recently purchased. During the roughly sixty-mile drive, they smoked dope and talked about life. Death, too—ghosts, spirits, the hereafter. Phil said he believed in spirits and that some of them were too disturbed to migrate from here to eternity. He was sure, however, that his spirit would make the trip without a hitch. Reiterating something he'd mentioned a couple of years earlier, Phil reminded Marin that whenever the time came, he wanted his ashes to be scattered in fifteen to twenty feet of water around a natural monument called Indian Rock, located in California's Emerald Bay off the coast of Phil's beloved getaway Catalina Island. Marin made his own preference known as well: If he died first, Phil should place his ashes in a large gel cap and set it at the summit of Diablo Peak on Santa Cruz Island. During the next wet season, Marin reasoned, the gel cap would dissolve and Marin's remains would flow down into his favorite canyons below.

Phil asked him, "What makes you think you're going to die before me?"

Chapter 1

Phil, early 1950s, outside 225 Dufferin Ave. in Brantford.
(Courtesy of the Hartmann family)

There were already three children—a brother and two sisters—when Philip Edward Hartmann made his debut, all five pounds of him, on September 24, 1948, at Brantford General Hospital in Brantford, Ontario, Canada, then a barely century-old town settled by a collective of Iroquoian Indian tribes not far outside Toronto. Most famously the former home of telephone inventor Alexander Graham Bell and located on the banks of Ontario's Grand River, Brantford also produced *The Lone Ranger* actor Jay Silverheels, electron microscope inventor James Hillier, and several pro hockey legends, most famously Wayne Gretzky.

Until Phil (or Phippie, as he was also called) was nearly nine, the Hartmann clan lived in tight quarters at 35 Lancaster Street and then 225 Dufferin Avenue. The latter dwelling, a 100-year-old brick cottage on a street lined with chestnut trees, had a small living room to the left as you entered through the front door and two bedrooms on the right. A kitchen and dining room occupied the rear, and as offspring multiplied, Phil's parents Doris and Rupert built an addition with another bathroom and more bedrooms on the home's northwest side. The house was out of place amid its rather upscale surroundings.

"We were the poorest people in the neighborhood," Phil's older sister Martha says. Vacations were out of the question and everything, she remembers, "was kind of a financial struggle." But their mother and father always appeared nattily attired and even belonged to a nearby country club. "There wasn't a lot of money," Martha says, "but [they] always looked really nice. And I felt proud that they were my parents." Still, Phil's oldest brother John says attempts to appear "more affluent than we really were" probably fooled no one.

Beginning when Phil was very young, his parents dreamed of making a new start in the United States. Their aspiration to do so began in 1950, when Phil was around two and they received an exciting offer from Doris's great uncle Hubert Haeussler. A Detroit resident, avid University of Michigan fan, and successful businessman (in retirement, Haeussler would serve as a tour guide for and goodwill ambassador of sorts to his city's foreign visitors), he invited them to drive with him to Pasadena for the January 1, 1951, Rose Bowl matchup between U of M's Wolverines and the California Golden Bears. Thrilled at the prospect of vacationing, an expensive undertaking they never attempted with their growing brood, Doris and Rupert motored down to the Motor City from Brantford, joined up with Haeussler, and then headed west.

When the trio arrived in Pasadena, California, with its near-perpetual sunshine and easygoing vibe, Rupert and Doris were immediately smitten. Who cared (well, besides Haeussler) that U of M bested the Golden Bears in a hard-fought 14–6 victory? This palm-tree-lined paradise, they decided, was their future home. Or somewhere close to it, anyway. Getting there was just a matter of how and when. Exuberant, Doris and Rupert "came right back and took out their papers," Phil's oldest sister Nancy recalls, in eager anticipation of imminent relocation. And they talked up the Golden State to all who'd listen, spurring some to relocate there ahead of them. Then Doris found out she was pregnant again. Daughter Sarah Jane was born in late October, with son Paul following in December of 1953. Nearly four years passed before the Hartmanns migrated south of the Great White North to make a better life.

In a 1997 interview with *Hollywood Online*, Phil spoke of growing up in a family that "struggled to make ends meet." He went on to explain that his inability to shed excess weight during adulthood stemmed from scrambling for his share of grub during those lean early years. The craft services tables at his various television and film jobs would become a particular weakness, for he'd find it almost impossible not to partake of free meals. "Hot dogs, donuts—bring in the pizza and the fried chicken," he quipped. "I came from a family where you needed a fork in your hand to reach for some food." Oddly enough, according to Martha, there was a social upside to the Hartmanns's simple lifestyle: "The neighbors loved our family. They loved that we weren't spoiled and they wanted us to hang out with their kids so maybe something would rub off on them."

Those neighbors, the Taylors, had two boys named John and Tom (the latter was Phil's age) and a house that dwarfed the Hartmanns' cottage-like abode. As a youngster, Phil strolled into the Taylors' place at will, as no one in the low-crime area locked the doors of their homes or cars. Martha remembers that one day, as the Taylors were seated at their long table and silently eating breakfast, Phil wandered in and proclaimed, "Good morning, all you happy people!" He had heard the phrase on a local radio broadcast and it struck him as funny.

The neighbors "burst out laughing. It made their day." In another instance of Phil's scampishness Nancy was asked to check on him and his younger brother Paul (five years Phil's junior) outside. Doris sometimes tethered the boys to a clothesline so they wouldn't run off if left unsupervised. And it usually worked. But when Nancy went to look for them, she found only Phil's tiny swimsuit—still attached to the rope. Phil himself had wriggled out of it and ran off "stark naked" down the street.

When Phil was in elementary school, he nearly went blind, no thanks to brother John's errant Red Rider BB gun. "You'll shoot your eye out!" went the typical parental admonition, and in some cases it was true. "I had the scare of my life when I was shooting at a Popsicle stick that I had put on the windowsill of a little room Phil and I lived in with our brother Paul," John says. "The BB hit the Popsicle stick and ricocheted off it. Phil was walking up behind me and he screamed and had his hand over his eye. And I thought, 'Oh, my God, I've blinded my brother!' And I'm freaking out. He's screaming and crying and yelling, 'Ow! My eye!' and I run over and I pull his arm away and his eye was there. I'd anticipated seeing it shot out. It was like horror and relief in the same breath. Inhale and exhale."

Thinking quickly, John pulled Phil aside and whispered one of his earliest business propositions:

"Don't tell Mom about me shooting you in the eye."

"Yeah?" Phil wondered what came next.

"And I will take care of you for the rest of your life."

Phil pondered the pitch for a moment and said, "What if I die first? Who will take care of you?"

"Don't worry," John promised, "the big brother always dies first."

Another near miss occurred at the post office in tiny downtown Brantford. As Phil would remember it during a visit decades later, John shoved him inside the building's revolving door and gave it a mighty spin. Unable to match its velocity, Phil stumbled headfirst into a glass windowpane, which cracked as if smacked by a stone. Fearful they'd be tossed in the clink for damaging public property, both boys quickly split the scene.

A far safer haven was Brantford's only movie theater, where Phil first encountered such big-screen stars as the sultry Marilyn Monroe and Gregory Peck as the whale-obsessed Captain Ahab in John Huston's *Moby Dick*. The latter made such an impression that Phil and his best friend John Taylor acted out scenes from the film, pretending to harpoon the Hartmanns's dog, Mike, with a broomstick and feeding each other dialogue.

Behind the Hartmann house, beyond a patio and white wooden lounge chairs, was a long and grassy yard filled with tall mulberry bushes. On the other side of them sprouted a well-tended vegetable patch. The so-called victory garden was a holdover from the rationing days of World War II, when growing one's own produce not only aided war conservation efforts but saved money. As John recalls, the Hartmann plot yielded strawberries, carrots, lettuce, and green beans. "One of the agonies of our youth was that instead of running off and playing on the weekends, we had to go out and weed the garden," he says. Abutting the yard was a vacant no-man's-land where neighborhood kids dug holes and made underground huts for, as John puts it, "real and imaginary rivals" in an era when "war was the subtext of all life." There was, he says of those Hiroshima-shadowed days, "massive paranoia" about atom bombs dropping from on high.

Not far beyond the no-man's-land, at the foot of a long hill, was a potato field that belonged to the castle-like Ontario School for the Blind. Opened in 1872 and later renamed the W. Ross Macdonald School, the institution offered traditional studies as well as manual and vocational training to hundreds of students. In winter and on holidays the Hartmann children and other kids from the neighborhood sometimes went sledding and romped on its hilly grounds. During school breaks, they sneaked onto the premises at night to play in barns on the property. The bravest (or most foolhardy) mischief-makers scampered up and slid down the winding slides of rocket-shaped fire escapes. "We goofed around up there even though we knew it was off limits," Nancy says. "We never got caught, but we did come close."

Because he was too young to participate in such hijinks, Phil palled around with his brown teddy bear, Jackie, and proved exceedingly easy to care for. "He'd just hang out with you, whatever you were doing," says Martha, who became Phil's primary guardian when Nancy was called to other duties. Quiet and introspective, Phil increasingly longed to be noticed—most of all by Doris. As he'd confide to Martha in their adulthood, his younger years were spent vying for the attention and affection of their tough and entrepreneurial mother and to a lesser degree their traveling salesman father. Martha, it turned out, had always felt the same way. "When Phil and I talked, we were kind of on the same page about being raised not feeling important," she says. As Phil told late-night host David Letterman decades later, "It was pretty desperate. Couldn't get a lot of attention. That's why I'm craving it so much now." Despite his goofy grin and joshing tone, it was true.

"I have met people over the years who felt it was their destiny to be a star, and I never had the confidence," he'd confide to another interviewer. "I think it was just part of the insecurities that were engendered in me in my childhood, being a middle child in a large family." Being "so withdrawn and so shy" and "just, really, a quiet observer of the stars within our family," he also explained, "created a tension in me that made me need to be appreciated."

In the Hartmann clan, Martha says, "You had to be kind of a problem or really great to get attention." John filled the latter role and then some. Athletic, stylish, handsome, and popular with the girls—"He had a huge, huge ego," Martha says—he naturally attracted a good share of notice, matriarchal and otherwise. "I think my mother favored me in a lot of ways," he says, recalling how she surreptitiously gave him money despite the family's strained finances.

At the opposite end of the spectrum was Phil's younger sister, Sarah Jane. Born October 30, 1951, she was afflicted with a then unknown and long thereafter undiagnosed condition called Angelman syndrome. The rare neurogenetic disorder was first described in the mid-1960s by an English doctor named Harry Angelman and is characterized by hyperactivity, frequent laughing and smiling, stunted intellectual growth, and certain behaviors associated with autism, such as hand-flapping and language difficulties. While on vacation in Verona, Italy, Angelman happened upon a Castelvecchio Museum oil painting called "A Boy with a Puppet." Its subject's "laughing face and the fact that my patients exhibited jerky movements," he said, spurred him to write about the curious condition. But the title of his article, "Puppet Children," proved quite unpopular among parents. More disconcertingly, Angelman lamented, initial interest in his study waned quickly and it "lay almost forgotten" until the early 1980s.

Especially during the earliest years of her life, Sarah needed nearly constant assistance. Moreover, no hospital was equipped to properly care for her. So Doris made the decision: they'd keep her at home and do it themselves. That arduous undertaking lasted for a physically straining and emotionally draining half-decade, during which period Doris's energies were almost singularly channeled into Sarah Jane's care. Along with their mother, Nancy and Martha bore the brunt of Sarah's caretaking. Phil watched and listened and absorbed. "She was really a handful," remembers Nancy, whose Phil-sitting responsibilities were passed to Martha soon after Sarah's birth. "For a long time we thought she was just deaf." Her immune system was highly compromised, too. "She was in my room with me," Nancy says, "and every time she'd get sick, there would be a convulsion and a trip to the hospital."

Nancy suspects that Phil and eventually Paul "might have fallen through the cracks some days" because of Sarah's dire condition. She required two people to dress and feed her. And her food had to be specially prepared beforehand due to an underdeveloped swallowing reflex. Because John was older than Phil and better able to process the chaos, he found Sarah's disorder deeply disquieting. "It was a very, *very* hard thing to deal with. And I can't say I dealt with it very well. My sister, Nancy, was a saint about it. My mother was a saint about it, too."

Given the opportunity, Phil might have told Doris he was sorry.

"The only thing Phil ever said to me about Sarah Jane is he thought it was his fault," John says. "You don't know what it means when you're little and you're centered in your own universe, and he thought what was wrong with her had something to do with him."

The stress of raising Sarah without professional assistance took its toll most acutely on Doris. "She was run through the ringer," Nancy says, and eventually had "kind of a little breakdown and ended up in the hospital for a good long rest." That's when Rupert's brother, Rev. Edward J. Hartmann, leveraged his role as the family's "spiritual head" and demanded that Sarah enter a facility that was better equipped to address her various health issues. "We couldn't keep her well," Nancy says. "She picked up every bug that we'd bring home from school, and so she was in and out of hospitals all the time and she needed so much specialized nursing care. We just weren't able to provide it."

In later years, while married to his second wife, Phil occasionally discussed Sarah and the feelings of worry and shame he'd dealt with as a confused boy living with a sibling who was utterly helpless and seemed hopelessly damaged. Phil also lamented that because Doris kept having babies—daughters Mary and Barbara Jane came after Paul—throughout his high school years, Sarah's absence did little to re-focus her gaze upon him since she remained preoccupied both with child rearing and one moneymaking venture or another to help fill the never-brimming family coffers.

The daughter of a seamstress and a rogue father who split when she was young, Doris Hartmann (née Wardel) hailed from the working-class Canadian town of Port Dover, on the banks of Lake Erie, where her mother Ethel ran a boarding house for fisherman. Prior to that Ethel worked in Detroit at the Florence Crittenton home for unwed mothers, making layettes (infant ensembles that included gowns receiving blankets, bonnets, and booties) and maternity clothes. Later, while living with her grandkids, Ethel made most of their apparel and even their underwear. "She could look at a dress and make it without a pattern," Nancy says. "Just incredibly talented." Ethel's sister was similarly skilled. Their creativity was passed down to Doris.

A self-taught painter and sketch artist who always dressed smartly, Doris ran a beauty parlor out of the Hartmann home in Brantford using a converted space near the front entrance. Patrons sometimes bought her artworks, which she made during limited spare time and put on display. Eventually she relocated her business to a small building nearer to the center of town. Though never a gold mine, its profits nicely and necessarily supplemented her husband's modest income. "She was in charge," John says. "She was the one you'd consider tough." His ex-wife saw the same quality, albeit in later years, remembering Doris as "incredibly creative, artistic, bright—and, boy, you didn't want to cross her, because she'd let you know it and she'd tell you exactly what she thought." John, however, can't recall ever witnessing any overt friction between his parents. "It's not Canadian to fight in front of others," he says. "At the worst of times I never saw them fight or even argue. Doris ran the show and we all went along."

She had a softer side, too, particularly when it came to her treasured boys and cherished clients. "She was a river to her people," John says. "They came to her beauty parlor not just to get their hair done, but to get her advice and counsel and philosophical direction. She took care of a lot of people and got a lot of respect." Adds Paul Hartmann, "My mother was a real entrepreneur. She could turn a garbage can into art. People in our family were always real diligent, hard workers. They knew the meaning of a good work ethic."

Though Nancy and John (born in early 1939 and late 1940, respectively) were considerably older than Martha, Phil, and Paul, the Hartmann kids had at least one thing in common aside from shared DNA. They called it "Egg Latin," a nonsensical language that had become something of a fad in Brantford. Translating words from English involved placing "egg" in every syllable before the vowel and after the consonant. For instance, Phil became Pheggil and Hartmann Heggartmeggann. Phil and company found it especially handy for cussing around their parents without getting busted. "Fegguck yeggou! Eggat sheggit!'"

The *actual* words had no quarter in their staunch Catholic household. Doris (a formerly Methodist convert), Rupert, and their entire brood attended Latin Mass every Sunday morning at nearby St. Basil Church. On weekdays, the kids went to St. Basil Elementary and Brantford Catholic High School. Both were within walking distance. "We had a very prominent prayer life in the family," Nancy says.

The Hartmann clan's piety trickled down from Rupert, the son of a devout mother (Helen) who prayed fervently, often with rosary beads in hand. Reserved and stylish, with a pencil-thin mustache like Errol Flynn's and Brylcreemed hair that was often topped by a feathered fedora, Rupert was an Air Force veteran sans wings (he saw no combat due to peritonitis from a ruptured appendix) and possessed a dry but clever sense of humor. Born in New Hamburg, Ontario, Rupert traversed Canada as a beverage deliveryman for Coca-Cola and covered territories that included the Six Nations Indian Reserve. "He was not an aggressive salesman, but he was brilliant, so he could talk you into anything," John says. When it came to matters of discipline, a glance from Rupert and the mere words "Do you want me to get the belt?" did wonders to quell misbehavior. "My father was not a heavy-handed man by any means, and it was always just a threat," Nancy says. "He really had a very gentle nature. I recall very few times when I was disciplined that way and I'm sure the other kids would say the same thing. He was the type of guy who could give you The Look and you knew. Nobody wanted to get The Look from Dad, because we loved him and we didn't want to ever disappoint him."

"There was a different mind-set about how you treated children in those days," John says. "If you were bad, you got punished. You got beaten. And my father hated to do it, I know, but if my mother said that 'John was bad and he's got to have a spanking,' the spanking consisted of his leather belt across your butt. And it was a real beating. Today you'd get arrested for it; your kid would turn you in."

As far as Paul knows, Phil was whipped only once, after they'd moved from Canada and as the result of a baseball mishap. In general, he says, Phil steered clear of misbehavior at home, thus sparing himself lashings and groundings. "He never got in trouble for anything," Paul says. "He knew what he had to do to achieve what he wanted, and he adhered to the rules and conditions as much as possible and just did it. He never put himself in jeopardy. That was part of his philosophy. It wasn't necessary to do that to have fun."

Back to the baseball mishap: Paul was catching and Phil was batting. As he took his backswing, the bat struck Paul in the face, breaking his nose and knocking out teeth. The younger Hartmann went running home. When Rupert saw his bloodied boy, he was as concerned with Paul's wounds as he was with the cost of mending them. "Any time you got hurt and it meant going to see a doctor, that cost money," Paul says. "With eight kids, if everybody gets hurt once a month, that's X amount of dollars. That doesn't work out." Hence the belt. Typically, though, Rupert was a sweet soul who, as John puts it, "never let us down. He always had a job. He always took care of business. He always was there."

Unlike Doris, who came from modestly educated blue-collar stock, Rupert was raised in a clan of spiritually and intellectually enlightened overachievers. His sister the sister, Mary Andrew (Eugenia), was a respected psychologist and nun who taught at Ottawa University and later the Sorbonne in Paris. "She was a brilliant woman who was very prominent in her order," John says. Rupert's priest brother, Edward, was the dean of men at Assumption University in Windsor, Ontario, and a Royal Canadian Air Force chaplain during World War II. Another sister, Clarice, taught high school. Their father John, Phil's paternal grandfather, was a business entrepreneur who ran a popular tavern as well as the Alpine Hotel in Brantford. John Hartmann (grandpa's namesake) claims that during World War II, when one's German heritage was potentially problematic, their grandfather would perch outside his lodge, shotgun in hand, to keep potential marauders at bay. "He was a tough guy and a severe guy," John says. "You look at photos of him and go, 'Wow, this is a serious cat.'"

The low-key and traditional Rupert, who walked the line between humorousness and seriousness, was decidedly more laid-back. While he was often introverted in public and around Doris, others recall his coming alive in private. He especially liked to spend time with his boys. When Phil and Paul were younger, he toted them along on various errands. And since Doris never drove, Rupert frequently played chauffeur, shuttling his progeny to doctor's appointments, school, and wherever else they needed to go.

What few in his family or circle of friends knew was this: Rupert was a drinker, sometimes a heavy one, but he kept his imbibing largely hidden from view. John recalls seeing his dad inebriated only once, when he was fifteen or sixteen, in Canada. "Come with me!" Doris told her eldest son, leading him to the back of their house. "Open the bathroom window." So John pushed up the window and peered inside. There, passed out on the floor, was Rupert. "I freaked," John says, "and I started to cry. And my mother said, 'Oh, shut up! Just get in there and unlock the door!'" John did as he was told. Later on, Phil poked fun at Rupert's drinking in a sketch that depicted Doris as the stern taskmistress standing over a blacked-out Rupert, who clutched an empty bottle in his hand. Doris and Rupert both laughed and thought it was funny.

Years afterward, John came across a letter Doris had written in the 1980s telling Rupert in no uncertain terms that he was an alcoholic and she was tired of walking on eggshells around him. Now that their last child (Barbara Jane) had left home and Doris had fulfilled her duties as a mother, there was no reason they should continue living together. After Rupert promised he'd quit—by going cold turkey and without the benefit of drugs or Alcoholics Anonymous, John says—Doris gave him another chance. Rupert, John says, kept his word.

When Phil was eight, in March 1957, after a formal visa presentation in Niagara Falls the previous November, half of the Hartmanns— Rupert, Nancy, baby Paul, and Mike the dog—finally left Canada. Their first stateside stop was Monmouth, Maine, where they'd spend the summer. Doris, Martha, and Phil met up with them in June after the kids were done with school. Sarah Jane did not make the trip, and John stayed behind briefly to paint the house on Dufferin (a condition of its sale). "It was a sad parting," he told the *Brantford Expositor* of his family's uprooting, "but also an exciting adventure."

Chapter 2

Phil, age nine, St. Rose Elementary School in Lewiston, Maine.
(Courtesy of the Hartmann family)

aving taken a job selling roofing supplies for a company called
Ruberoid, Rupert settled his family into a rented four-
bedroom tract house on Cochnewagon Lake. The "incredible
little cottage," as John describes it, had a sink pump, no running water
and only the lake for bathing. It was there the Hartmann clan began
acclimating to their new country. "It wasn't even a one-horse town,"
John says. "It wasn't even a one-goat town. I don't even recall a store."
There was, however, a pea-canning factory whose runoff drained into
the lake, and a magnificent old Victorian building that housed the Gilbert and Sullivan Festival Theatre, where that summer Nancy worked
in the box office and John sold librettos.

In September, just before school started, they packed up again and
left for Lewiston, Maine, where Phil entered St. Rose Elementary

and the family inhabited a drafty old farmhouse just outside town at 866 Main Street. Most of the kids were felled by the flu that winter, and Mike the dog died after a car struck him on the highway. The Hartmanns remained pet-less from that day forward.

Next up for the nomadic clan: Meriden, Connecticut, and the bottom floor of a two-story duplex at 31 Wall Street. Its upstairs inhabitants—an Italian cop and his wife—fed their housemates hearty dishes from the homeland. But that stay, too, was short-lived. At long last, in early 1958, Rupert and his brood set off for California, where he had secured work as the western states sales representative for Whirlpool. As with the family's Canada-to-Maine trek, a few of the kids stayed behind to finish school and joined the early arrivers—Rupert, Nancy and Paul—later on in the L.A. suburb of Garden Grove.

One of the best things about their rented home at 7348 West 82nd Street—particularly for ten-year-old Phil and his five-year-old charge Paul, whom he watched over much as Nancy and Martha had him in Brantford—was that Disneyland in Anaheim was within walking distance and cost only a nominal fee for admittance. Sometimes it cost nothing, Paul says, courtesy of a family friend with connections. Knott's Berry Farm in Buena Park was close by as well, offering rides, live shows, and what Nancy remembers as "the best darn fried chicken west of the Mississippi."

Soon enough, the family outgrew its Garden Grove home and moved yet again—this time to a three-bedroom, one-bathroom cottage in Westchester, forty minutes or so away. There, in the shadow of an expanding Los Angeles International Airport, Phil and Paul attended St. Anastasia Elementary School. Fortunately, they were able to stay enrolled when the family transitioned to a larger ranch-style place at 8648 La Tijera Boulevard, where Doris set up her artist's easel on the patio or in one corner of the dining room and painted when limited time allowed. Featuring a walled-in backyard, a handsome patio connecting the house and garage, four bedrooms and two bathrooms, the dwelling and many others in its well-maintained middle-class neighborhood would one day be razed to make way for a new jet runway. Phil's sister Mary was born on La Tijera, in October 1960. The youngest, Barbara Jane (called Jane), came six years later. Until then, after much wandering, the family stayed put.

When twelve-year-old Phil began attending Westchester's Orville Wright Junior High in seventh grade, he befriended a kid named Jim Jones. Both of them were Boy Scouts. In early February 1960 the Crescent Bay Area Council made Phil a certified Tenderfoot Scout, and his Troop 77 spent weeklong summer stints earning merit badges, hiking, and sleeping in tents with wooden floors at Camp Emerald Bay on Catalina Island, twenty-six miles off the L.A. County coast. "Water was a big part of it," Jones says of their camping excursions, during which merit badges were handed out for mastery of sailing and distance swimming, among other disciplines. Jones can't recall if Phil was present when a group of boys sneaked off (inadvisably) to the nearby garbage dump, where packs of Catalina's indigenous wild boar population gathered to feast at night, but says that may well have been the case in light of his playful personality. "Phil wasn't a bad kid, but he was a jokester," Jones says. "He could entertain everybody and come up with crazy stuff, but not go too far."

By the time Phil was thirteen or so, with the help of Rupert's shuttling, he'd taught himself to surf and soon became a regular at several L.A.-area beaches, including Dockweiler, Ballona Creek, Hermosa, Rincon, and Malibu. It was at one of those locations where he first dispensed wave-riding wisdom to brother Paul and then set him on a board to have at it. Paul rode that maiden wave all the way to the beach, where Phil stood drop-jawed and obviously jealous. As Phil got older, secured his own transportation, and moved closer to the water, his love of the sport and its philosophical underpinnings only deepened.

Art, too, became an ever more time-consuming hobby as he grew more confident of skills passed down from his artistically inclined mother and grandmother. Looking back, Paul thinks his and Phil's semi-regular jaunts to Disneyland and the iconic characters they encountered there might have sparked Phil's interest in cartooning, which blossomed during his two years at Orville Wright. "Phil could draw anything," schoolmate Ettore Berardinelli says. Wright is where he got his first taste of theater, too, studying Shakespeare and Molière in drama class, where meeting girls was every bit as important as learning the stage classics. He also won the lead role in Wright's production of *Li'l Abner*. Appropriately enough for a budding artist, the musical (which had its Broadway debut in 1956) is based on Al Capp's long-running comic strip of the same name.

Grade-wise, Phil scored mostly B's and C's in English, social studies, math, "electric shop," metal shop, Algebra II, art, music, and senior drama, with only two A's—for physical education, in which he also earned a couple of C's—tossed into the mix. Marks for "work habits" and "cooperation" were almost all "Satisfactory" or "Excellent." The only classes for which he apparently was somehow uncooperative and thus earned an "Unsatisfactory" were mixed chorus during both semesters of eighth grade and social studies that same year. His work habits in the latter subject were equally underwhelming.

Upon exiting Wright with the class-voted title of "Happy-Go-Lucky Girl" (classmate and future Charles Manson disciple Lynette "Squeaky" Fromme co-won the category "Personality Plus" with another student), Phil entered Westchester High on W. Manchester Avenue, amid a thriving residential community that sprang from what had been acres of bean fields. Increasingly in need of cash to support his surfing hobby and other teen necessities, he earned extra scratch by tricking out his peers' trendy three-ring binders (they were clad in a blue denim-like material) with funky designs. He often sketched at home, too, on pads of paper and on far more expansive surfaces. In his La Tijera bedroom, part of one wall and the adjacent ceiling eventually bore a pencil sketch of Auguste Rodin's renowned sculpture "The Thinker." Phil jokingly described it to friends as "Oedipus contemplating the death of Rex."

Berardinelli, one of Phil's first pals in the area, lived across an alley from the Hartmanns in a house that cost around $33,000—average for those parts. The two met in art class and began hanging out. As Phil's comedic sensibility continued to evolve, Berardinelli remembers, he often staged small-scale private and public performances during which he mimicked popular comedians of the day. "I just had to open the gate, walk across the alley, and go over to Phil's house to be entertained," Berardinelli says. John Hartmann was also a witness. In 1961, struggling to make ends meet as an underpaid junior agent at the William Morris Agency, he briefly moved back home to La Tijera and bunked with his younger brothers. It was there that he began to truly appreciate Phil's humor. "Phil and I would collect material and try to crack each other up," he says. "The goal was to get my father pissed off by laughing. Phil made me laugh so hard that my father would pound on the wall and say, 'Stop that laughing in there!' I would be shoving a pillow down my throat and Phil would be laughing at the trouble I was in." Jim Jones saw it, too, in the imitations Phil often did. Walter Brennan, who played Amos McCoy on TV's *The Real McCoys*, was a favorite—made even funnier when Phil uttered things in character that were totally out of character such as "Goddammit, Lucas!" (as Amos addressing his son Luke). Or "Dag-nabbit, Pepenis!" (As Amos addressing farm hand Pepino). And so on.

But Phil wasn't all yuks all the time. His often hidden sober side emerged when he felt a close kinship with someone or shared a profound life experience. On at least one occasion a conversation with Berardinelli went beyond goofing and girls to pondering what then, during the height of America's Cuban Missile Crisis, seemed like the very real possibility of obliteration from on high. As the guys sat in Berardinelli's car one evening, they had a long heart-to-heart about life and death. "This was like the start of World War III," Berardinelli says of those tension-filled days. "President Kennedy kind of drew a line in the sand and it was a scary time."

Perhaps as something of an antidote to the gathering darkness, Phil's humor was nearly always on display. Far from being the "man of a thousand voices" he'd one day become, his stable of impressions gradually grew to include, besides Brennan, big-screen badass John Wayne. Stand-ups Stan Freberg, Shelley Berman, Bob Newhart, and Jonathan Winters entranced him as well, and he listened to their best-selling albums studiously. During get-togethers with friends, as in the bedroom with brothers John and Paul, Phil performed popular comedy routines verbatim. And while he admired the stammer-punctuated musings of Newhart and the improv-influenced stylings of Berman (who perfected the art of sit-down stand-up from his perch on a stool), the frenetic genius Winters was far and away Phil's favorite. Before long, he had Winters's improvised meandering and other-worldly characters down pat.

He must have been immensely pleased, then, to find someone who worshipped the great comic as much as he did. John Sparlan Holloway, nicknamed "Sparkie," had taken a liking to Phil's John Wayne impression in their homeroom class and soon they were palling around. An ROTC cadet and future firefighter, Holloway became one of Phil's closest confidants and remained so for decades to come. "We were devoted [Winters] fans, so once we got to know each other and found out Jonathan Winters was going to be on [a show], we would sit down and plan that out," Holloway says. "We'd even have a party and get offended that people were still talking when Winters was on."

They also spent long stretches lounging in cushy black La-Z-Boy recliners at Holloway's house, where they played records and watched television on his parents' RCA console. Just for kicks, they turned off the sound on old movies—Hitchcock flicks or *Casablanca*, for instance—and substituted their own silly dialogue. That Holloway was typically

game for playing along with Phil's theatrical shenanigans only strength-
ened their friendship. One memorable stunt starred Phil as then-
president Lyndon B. Johnson and Holloway as one of LBJ's stone-faced
bodyguards. Accompanied by several other school chums, they began
at Westchester's junior quad and made their way toward the senior one.
With Phil behind them, fake LBJ musclemen barreled through un-
witting students, shouting "Secret Service! Make way for the President of the United States!" Onlookers were baffled, Holloway recalls,
because Phil wasn't yet well known for his imitative abilities. When
they arrived at a small stage on the senior lawn, Phil and his sunglasses-
sporting cadre ascended a few steps and continued their guerilla performance. Surrounded by a grim-faced security detail, fake LBJ addressed
puzzled spectators in his heavy Texas drawl: "Ma fellow Amerrkins, we
do not want wohw. We just want to kill all the Nee-gruz." ("There were
a disproportionate number of blacks serving in the military and Vietnam," Holloway explains, "so it was satire.")

When they weren't disturbing the peace, Holloway and Phil bonded
over other mutual interests such as cigarette smoking (which they both
soon vowed to quit), fast cars (muscle car king Carroll Shelby's nearby
dealership was of particular interest) and their own version of Mad
Libs that involved stringing together random words from magazines
to form nonsensical phrases. A game called "squiggles" was popular
as well. Holloway drew a random squiggly line in red and Phil turned
it into a wacky drawing, complete with caption.

To earn cash for dating and smoking and surfing and driving,
both got jobs at different locations of a local fast-food chain called
Woody's Smorgasburger—Phil as a grill chef, Holloway as a bus-
boy. Phil also did a stint at Zaff's Marina Fountain, a surfer hangout
in upscale Playa del Rey. Outside of school and work during their
junior and senior years, he and Holloway cruised around in Phil's
two-tone blue 1952 Chevy coupe. (Far more devotee than tinkerer
when it came to automobiles, Phil never took his father's advice to go

into "body-fender" work. Reasoned Rupert, "People are always crashing cars.") A seventeenth-birthday gift from Mom and Dad, the Chevy's keys came hidden in a large but otherwise empty box. Phil jazzed up his mean machine with strips of window fringe called "dingle balls" and adorned its exterior with tiny moons. A chick magnet if ever there was one—not that he needed such bait.

"He could have gone out with anybody," says Berardinelli, who was more introverted and fared less well on the female front. "And he was a good-looking guy. But it was his personality. He was Mr. Personality. And he was entertaining; he could hold court anytime he wanted. People were drawn to him." Paula Johnston (now Grey) of Westchester and Kathy Kostka (now Constantine) of Playa del Rey were two of the beauties who caught his eye. With a litany of extra-curricular activities that included drama, cheerleading, and student government, and a boyfriend who captained the football team, Paula hung with the so-called "popular" crowd of which Phil was eventually a part, if only in a transient way. Initially something of a theater nerd, he began floating between disparate social groups with ease. One day he was shooting the breeze with jocks, the next he was rehearsing for a school play with fellow thespians. Besides drama, his extracurricular social circle expanded via his participation in art production, the *Westchester Comet* school newspaper (for which he drew cartoons), student government (the senate) and the Boys' League (whatever that was). "Phil kind of hung with the people that were going places," Berardinelli says. "I don't know if I'd call them ambitious. They were just people who kind of had their act together. And they dressed nicer, you know? But Phil could transcend any group."

Part of him, though, would have preferred to live in another era, and it was around this time he began channeling the rhythms and riffs of hard-bitten detective types from the thirties and forties—Philip Marlowe–esque characters who pondered crimes while slugging down bourbon in dark and smoke-filled offices. Who spoke in cynical rat-a-tat-tat phrases and cavorted with dangerous dames. They were every-thing Phil wasn't, which made them all the more appealing.

After an extended period as friends at Westchester High, Phil and Paula considered taking their relationship to the next level. The esca-lating intensity of Phil's feelings for Paula are evident in yearbook notes that range from praising her as "about the sweetest girl I have ever known" (1964) to hoping God made her "every wish come true" (1965) to, senior year, expressing "how jazzed I am on you" and his desire "to get to know you a whole lot better." Still, Paula says, "there wasn't a lot of chemistry there. It was the old high school 'let's kiss and see what we've got,' and nothing came of it."

Kathy, however, had a "crush" on Phil from the get-go as well as a stronger romantic bond with him. Phil even accompanied her and her family on boat trips to Catalina Island. Like Paula, Kathy was struck by Phil's charisma and his onstage prowess during school drama pro-ductions. And he seemed equally at home with material lowbrow or high. "He could do comedy, but he could also do Shakespeare!" she says. "And that just blew my mind." He was also the only person she knew in their age group who smoked dope. Self-imposed periods of dormancy notwithstanding, he would do so with ever increasing en-thusiasm throughout his life. The grade of weed got better, too.

A couple of times, in spring of 1965 and again senior year, Phil, Kathy, Phil's Lil' Abner co-star Judy Thompson, and some other friends appeared on the top-rated and nationally syndicated teen dance party *The Lloyd Thaxton Show*, which emanated from the studios of KCOP-TV in Los Angeles. To convey an idea of its tone, in one episode host Thax-ton opened the program perched on a stationary bicycle and lip-syncing (quite skillfully) to "Getaway" by Georgie Fame and the Blue Flames as he briskly pedaled to nowhere. During their appearances, Phil also lip-synced while grooving to the tunes of such famous guest artists as Don-ovan and Peter Paul and Mary. "If there was something theatrical to do, he would do it," Kathy says. "And this gave him a platform."

But Phil's constant questing for new experiences proved an impediment to his budding love life. In junior year drama class, for which Kathy signed up mostly to overcome her shyness, Phil fell hard for another girl. (He frequently fell, and often hard.) This frustrated Kathy, who had feelings for him and instead was relegated to playing chief consoler when Phil needed nurturing. "It went on and on and on, and he was always having his heart broken," she says. "But Phil always wanted what he couldn't have." He also liked the drama that invariably arose in those situations. And because he regarded the world with an artist's critical eye, she says, he was "definitely looking for perfection. And that's why I don't think he could ever fully land anywhere with anybody."

When Kathy and Phil had a go at dating their senior year, it proved more difficult than she had anticipated. He needed to be needed, she says, and he told her in no uncertain terms that she had fallen short in that department. Another impediment was Phil's ever-present veneer—an invisible mask he wore that made it hard to tell where his performer persona ended and his everyday one began. "Phil always liked getting outside of himself," she says. "He'd always get into a role and I'd lose the Phil that I knew. That was always very interesting for me. Because I knew him at a different level, where we talked and talked and talked. I kind of knew his heart and knew who he was, which I don't think a lot of people did." When Phil let his guard down, as he often did with Kathy in the absence of others, it all came pouring out. "He would tell me whatever he was thinking," she says. "His insecurities, his fears, his ambitions. He was deep and he was very serious."

Although the teenage Phil exuded ever more self-assuredness and possessed many enviable abilities, Kathy thought he seemed skittish in his own skin and always searching for the next best thing. "I used to call him the True Believer," she says, "because he kept trying to embody something else, and then he'd go for it all the way. All of a sudden he'd want to be a Zen guy, and he'd study that for a while and be really into it and just jump in with both feet." That would be his M.O. for many decades to come, whether in the realm of work, relationships, or hobbies: jumping in with both feet. It applied to his spirituality as well. Both early on and down the road, Phil's endeavoring to comprehend the universe and his place in it was ongoing and could quickly change course. "I don't know where he finally ended up," Kathy says, "but I never saw him really take something on and keep [at] it."

On June 17, 1966, Phil graduated from Westchester with (as per the description on his diploma) "a Major Sequence in Art—College Preparatory." That evening, he celebrated with fellow classmates at a formal dance on the Disneyland grounds. "As a senior in high school, I made the conscious choice to become an art major instead of pursuing acting," he said in 1991. "It was largely because my brother [John] had attempted to be an actor and I was exposed to the slimy underbelly of Hollywood life. It was important to me to make a living, because I wanted independence. I didn't want to get into a career that involved a lot of effort for no return, period." As he noted in a two-and-a-half-page yearbook inscription to Judy Thompson, he had also changed and matured. He'd experienced "bitterness and sorrow" but was salved by fond remembrances from their "awkward, innocent" past. If ever Thompson—whom he deemed "deep and mature in mind"—wanted to talk, Phil was all ears and ready to "give my thoughts and myself to you."

On the funny front and as something of a surprise to his mother, who had always pegged him as "serious," Phil and a female classmate were voted Westchester's Class Clowns. In a photo of the jesters, whose caption misspells his last name as "Hartman," Phil folds his arms over a puffed chest in a comically cocky pose. The dropped *N* and arch attitude prophesied things to come.

Chapter 3

Phil, late 1960s.
(Courtesy of the Hartmann family)

For many thousands of U.S. troops stationed in Vietnam and those waiting to be transported over, the summer of 1966 wasn't exactly a high point. But even as President Lyndon Johnson steadily increased America's military presence in that far-off jungleland (the draft didn't start until late 1969), life in surf-centric Southern California remained quite idyllic. The Beach Boys still held considerable sway on the pop charts, despite anemic U.S. sales that May of the group's experimental (and eventually lauded) album *Pet Sounds*. William Jan Berry, of the surf-rock duo Jan & Dean, was in the news after being critically injured that April in a car crash very close to Dead Man's Curve in Beverly Hills. Ironically, he and his musical cohort, Dean Torrence, had scored a hit two years prior with a tune of the same name.

Cruising around in Holloway's 1964 Pontiac GTO, Phil and Spar-kie did some "really insane things" of their own, such as straddling the running boards of their respective rides while tooling up and down Manchester Boulevard. Mostly, though, they hung out and smoked cigarettes. Or watched television. Or played "squiggles." Completed il-lustrations included a toothless old woman and a bleeding chicken flee-ing a blood-drenched ax. And, of course, there was surfing. With the craze in full-bloom, a new generation—of fad-following *Gidget* fans and die-hard disciples of surfer-rebel Miki Dora—was loading up its Woodies with Dewey Weber, Gordie "Lizard," and Greg Noll's "Da Cat" boards (named after Dora, who was nicknamed "Da Cat") and setting off to drop in, hang ten, and eat it courtesy of bodacious waves all across the Southern California coast. Phil and Holloway were among them. "Surfers always looked down on jocks because they were stupid enough to stay after school while we were at the beach," Phil once said.

Mornings were always best. On Friday and Saturday nights, after divesting themselves of their respective female companions, if there were any, Phil and Holloway regularly reassembled at a drive-in called Tiny Naylor's on the corner of Manchester and Sepulveda in West-chester. It was a social hot spot through whose large windows hangers-out could keep tabs on new arrivals and passersby could scan the clientele before entering. "We'd sit there and chew the fat and then decide, 'Oh, shit, let's go surfing,'" Holloway says. An hour or so later, after fetching their boards, they reconvened, loaded gear into a '61 Ford Station wagon Holloway had at his disposal, and headed out to a favorite surf spot near the Ventura County line. "Half the time we'd almost fall asleep and kill ourselves running off the road," Holloway says. Parking on the beach, they waited until the sun rose and then paddled out—Holloway on his stomach, Phil on his knees (a style that was considered much cooler). "Phil was actually good at it," Holloway says, "and I was just sort of there." As Paul Hartmann remembers,

Phil's repertoire of surfing techniques on his Dewey Weber board included walking the nose, hanging five and ten, cutbacks, and frontside/backside off-the-lips, to name just a handful. "You'd go every chance you got," Paul says.

For Phil and countless other SoCal surfers, however, riding waves was more than a sport or mere pastime. It went much deeper than that. As former *Surfing* magazine and current *Surfer's Journal* publisher Steve Pezman explains in David Rensin's oral history, *All For a Few Perfect Waves: The Audacious Life and Legend of Rebel Surfer Miki Dora*, "Some waves are too simple: not a drop of water is out of place, it's easy to ride. But the Malibu wave has different modes, and although it's dependable in some ways, it's never the same twice. It has enough complexity and variation to hold one's attention, almost like a human relationship. When you find a wave like that, you invest in it."

Hours before the surf was up, Phil and Holloway sometimes perched atop a lifeguard tower on the beach and gazed into the sparkling night sky. Topics of discussion were wide-ranging: How many stars were there? How big was the universe? Who was God? What did the future hold for humankind? "All the things you want to solve when you're seventeen or eighteen," Holloway says. And when Holloway told Phil that as a boy he'd seen four smaller spacecrafts emerging from an alien mothership, "there was no doubt with him that I'd seen what I'd seen."

"He was hopefully spiritual," Holloway says, "that there's got to be something more besides us."

That fall, around the time he turned eighteen, Phil enrolled at Santa Monica City College as a full-time student and commuted to classes from his parents' home in Westchester. Holloway entered as well and joined the football team. During his freshman zoology class, Phil kept a partially dissected rat in the freezer at home. One day Paul walked into the house and found Phil at his drawing board. Only he wasn't drawing. Instead, Phil had taped the rat's severed hind legs to his fore- and middle fingers and, employing the table as a tiny dance floor, was performing a soft-claw rendition of "Tea for Two."

With another sophomore named Wink Roberts, Phil also took a public speaking course. An early bloomer when it came to showbiz, Roberts had already filmed a movie with Jacqueline Bisset. "Phil was so envious," Roberts says, "and he was so talented and wanted so badly to get into the industry." For the time being, though, he polished his skills where he could. In their speaking class, Roberts says, Phil always added "a funny twist" no matter the topic of his presentation. "He could never walk into a room and be happy if he couldn't make people laugh."

Outside of classes, they skied together at Mammoth Mountain, located about thirty minutes from campus in the Sierra-Nevada range of Eastern California. It was there, during a visit to Mammoth's Hot Creek—a geothermal volcanic spring—that Phil gave a public performance Roberts still remembers vividly. On this particular evening, scores of gatherers parked their cars, walked down a long dirt road, doffed clothing, and hopped naked into the 100-degree water with their wine and beer and joints in hand. "The fog was so dense that you couldn't see the hand in front of your face," Roberts says, but the moon shone brightly. At one point, Roberts turned to Phil and said, "Do your Eric Hearble," a reference to the quirky 1964 short story by John Lennon. Phil obliged with a dramatic reading: "One fat morning Eric Hearble woke up with an abnorman fat growth a bombly on his head."

"I'm telling you that within thirty seconds, this entire creek was quiet," Roberts says. "He had all of these strangers in the palm of his hand, and all that they had was a voice in the dark and fog." Upon reciting the Lennon ditty, Phil went on to do movie star impressions, jokes—the usual. "And for two hours," Roberts claims, "he had this audience riveted to every word he said. Two hours where no one ever even saw his face or knew who he was." When Phil's set came to a close,

Roberts says he announced, "Ladies and gentlemen, that was Mr. Phil Hartmann, and someday he's gonna be a big star! Remember this night!"

Phil's other courses throughout his four semesters at SMCC included American Government, U.S. History to 1865, Beginning Drawing, Beginning Oil Painting and, oddly for such a die-hard aqua man, "non swim" phys-ed.

He repeated Reading and Composition during his first and last semesters, his evolving worldview and sense of humor coming through in disjointed and grammatically screwy essays that received mostly mediocre marks. In "Soul Reality," Phil explained how the soul imbues man with "an ability to sense truth beyond his own intellect, a reality too awesome to understand intellectually, yet so powerful we embrace it blindly as a babe." Philosopher Phil went on, if a bit incongruously: "There are no practical lovers. Love is not controlled, it controls. The soul literally takes us beyond ourselves, as does love."

In "A Harmony of Life" he mused about why men and women are attracted to one another, concluding that attraction goes "beyond social needs and the desire to be approved of, beyond overcoming guilt and beyond sexual gratification."

An uncommonly high B was awarded for his comedic essay titled "The 1969 Croceledillo Is Here," which purported to be "the first in a series of reports on America's greatest achievement in crossbreeding" involving a crocodile, an elephant, and an armadillo. The bizarre hybrid, he explained, weighed "some two tons" and was invented to replace the "Automobilis Americis"—cars. "The loss of air pollution alone," he reasoned, "will make the whole effort worthwhile."

In the tonally disparate "Why I Will Live After Death," Phil pondered the afterlife much as he did with Holloway on surf outings. "I guess each man looks for his own proof or disproof of life after death," Phil wrote. "My proof is simple. When I look at a star-lit sky, I am awed by its infinite beauty and mystery. I cannot perceive the phenomena [sic] and on the same [level] believe that man is the ultimate being in the universe."

Between essays and other coursework, Phil poured his aching and sometimes loopy heart out in letters to high school confidante Kathy Kostka, who'd begun attending Arizona State. In a doodle-filled missive dated January 14, 1967, he addressed her as "Kasha" and excitedly broke news of his split with a girl named Marilyn: "I guess it's about time. It was hard, sad, confusing—but final. It's all over now and I am back to my old self (unfortunately) as you can see. Are you coming home on semester break? Dear God I hope you are. The sunsets have been absolutely out of control!" Upon signing off ("Love forever, Phil"), he signed right back on. "Did you really think that was the end! Ha ha ha. I'm sorry, I will continue to bore you, on purpose. Kasha, I look at your picture as I write. In your eyes I see the beauty and passion of a human being full of soul and the love of life . . . I feel my mood changing from joking to something else." As the hour grew later, Phil grew goofier—confiding that he probably couldn't pen "such an offbeat letter to anyone else." At one point he simply began listing thoughts that popped into his brain: "Your face is beautiful, and warm, its warmth radiates around me." And: "I just want to look into your eyes again . . . and let them talk."

But Kathy knew that Phil's suddenly intensified romantic feelings for her were as much about the physical distance between them as anything else. "He liked the chase and the longing," she says, "more than he liked being in a relationship."

In the spring of 1968, a few months before Phil turned twenty, his brother John and a couple of business partners—music manager Skip

Taylor and future Los Angeles International Film Festival founder
Gary Essert—joined forces to open a cutting-edge live performance
venue they dubbed the Kaleidoscope. John had by then left his agent
job at William Morris, where he handled such acts as Buffalo Springfield, Chad & Jeremy, and Sonny & Cher. During the Kaleidoscope's
evolution, he booked shows for the rock group Canned Heat, whom
Taylor managed. John and his cohorts had tried to open the Kaleidoscope a year or so prior, but various roadblocks impeded progress. When
they finally secured the former Earl Carroll Theatre, at 6230 Sunset
Boulevard, work began to transform it into what John and his fellow
founders envisioned as the hippest joint around for jam sessions, dollar
film "orgies" (classics, current fair, cartoons, newsreels), and even wild
political events. With the help of hired hands—including a struggling
young actor-carpenter named Harrison Ford—they installed a dance
floor made from the planks of a nearby shuttered bowling alley, two in-
terconnected round and rotating stages, and a finely woven scrim onto
which overhead projectors beamed artist-swirled images of water and
oil. One especially crazy event, dubbed the "Independence Day Spec-
tacular," included a sketch in which comedian and mock-presidential
hopeful Pat Paulsen (who'd chosen the Kaleidoscope as his mock-
presidential campaign headquarters) played George Washington to
rock-folk queen Mama Cass's Betsy Ross. As John recalls it, Paulsen
made his entrance on a horse and the show ended with indoor fireworks.
Throughout the evening of "total insanity," Chad Stuart of Chad & Jeremy conducted a twenty-five-piece band, vaudeville acts (bell ringers,
fire-eaters) wowed the crowd, and someone coaxed a pachyderm onstage. Maybe it was fortunate the all-ages club served no alcohol.
"We wanted to keep it open to anybody and we kept the ticket price
very low," John Hartmann says. "We were probably, stupidly, hippies
in trying to keep it civilized and not expensive, but we had a great
time."

    So, too, did Phil on the handful of occasions he dropped by to chill and check out the acts. On any given night, the club's lineup featured Jefferson Airplane, the Grateful Dead, Canned Heat, Tiny Tim, Steppenwolf, Genesis, the Doors, and a host of other already famous or soon-to-be famous bands. When Holloway tagged along, hijinks ensued. If they weren't posing as roadies for the featured act, Phil was pretending to be an English gent and Holloway a deaf-mute. One time, Phil convinced a few girls that Holloway was a stuntman for Warner Bros. who had just appeared in an episode of *Bonanza*. The girls, as Holloway remembers it, were all agog.

Besides comedy, surfing and shenanigans, Phil and Holloway shared a common interest in cigarettes. But on February 28 and 29 in the leap year, 1968, both swore separate written oaths to kick the habit. Using a fine-tipped black marker, Phil elaborately stated his intent in neat cursive.

"I solemnly promise, upon my honored word, that I will quit smoking tobacco cigarettes down to the slightest, secret puff," it began. Penalties for breaking the pledge included: paying Holloway $10; letting him "slug" Phil in the arm twice; footing the entire bill for a double date; washing and waxing Holloway's car and putting gas in its tank; and purchasing for Holloway two cartons of cigarettes—his choice of brand. Phil swore to the truth of the aforementioned "under the God of my choice" and signed his name: Philip Edward Hartmann and Philip Edward John Hartmann/Future Unlimited.

Holloway approved the document by inking his own signature at 1:34 A.M. on February 29. Their respective contracts were folded up and stashed in an empty Newport Menthols carton. As for their mutual abstention, it lasted maybe a week before both parties admitted to cheating and the whole thing went up in smoke.

By the spring of 1968, tar and nicotine must have seemed safe in contrast to what Holloway's future had in store. He'd recently dropped out of Santa Monica College after injuring his ankle during football and being dumped by his girlfriend. While still in school, he'd received a couple of draft deferrals. Knowing he was unlikely to get another and aware that the Marine Corps offered a shorter enlistment term than other military branches—two years instead of three—Holloway signed up to serve rather than leave things to chance and the U.S. Government. Starting that June, he spent a couple of months at boot camp in San Diego followed by Advanced Infantry Training at Camp Pendleton (also in California) before heading to Vietnam. Stationed there at a heavily protected base outside Da Nang dubbed "Monkey Mountain" (Hill 647, officially) by the soldiers, PFC Holloway worked briefly in supply and pulled guard duty. Eventually he ended up in a financial role, handling multimillion-dollar military accounts.

That fall, around the time Holloway was settling in overseas, Phil earned a respectable (and higher-than-average) B for his English essay "My Point of Rebellion."

"No political situation merits more dissension than the intervention of the United States in the Vietnam revolution," he wrote, going on to blame greedy corporations and the greedy people who ran them for helping to fuel the war effort in a grab for profits. He also questioned what seemed to him an unnatural fear of Communism. As for America's meddling in a "sovereign nation," Phil concluded, it was entirely unwarranted—akin to if another country had assisted the British against the colonies during the Revolutionary War.

The many letters Phil and Holloway exchanged between the summer of 1968 and the fall of 1969, when Holloway returned home, were typically lighter in tone. Holloway's missives to Phil have been lost to time, but all of Phil's survived. At turns funny and poignant, they are rife with wisecracks and doodles and personal revelations. "Are they teachin' ya to kill?" reads the caption beside a goofy-looking G.I. character wearing a "Sparkie" T-shirt and clutching his rifle in proper military fashion. In another drawing, Phil adorns a peace sign with the words "Peace—Love—But Mostly Money." And in its center: "Ha Ha Ha Ha."

Phil went on to tell Holloway about his new 1961 VW panel van. Purchased from "a desperate guy" with money ($430) Phil had made from hawking his motorcycle (for $450), it "runs bitchen." As part of its interior revamp, Phil installed a twin mattress in back. He also mentioned his plans to attend SMCC for another semester "and then I'm gonna ski my brains out till I get drafted, I guess." The Kaleidoscope's temporary shuttering due to "legal problems" came up as well. And on the surfing front, Phil informed Holloway, seven-foot "miniboards" were all the rage. He signed off "The Real John Wayne," then added, "Why don't you send me a deep soul-packed letter, you crusty bastard?"

Although still a non-citizen, Phil's status as a U.S. National between the ages of eighteen and twenty-six made him fully eligible for the draft. According to Kathy Constantine (Kostka), he was ambivalent about going were his number drawn. They even discussed running off to Canada together. "He was just toying with getting out of there," she says. "He definitely did not want to be drafted." While the possibility loomed, Phil was free to find himself in the mountains of Mammoth and the waves off Malibu. Upon completing a fourth semester at SMCC, he also submitted an application to attend the University of Hawaii. Before shoving off, however, he planned to spend five months bumming around and, he hoped, cleaning up his act.

"Let me know how you're doing," Phil wrote to Holloway on November 30, 1968. "Do you have a lot of free time? Do you have access to a Bible? I know if I was in your boots ["shoes" is crossed out] I would especially be able to get right into it, Spark. But I do here too. There's a kind of war here for me. It's a war to make myself into a pure, clear thinking, clear acting and clear meaning person, and that means no 'kicks.' It is a war too because I am surrounded with 'freaky people' who make it hard to go straight. But I am overcoming this, as I will overpower everything. That's the way I feel now because I'm not depending on myself. My inspiration comes from outside of me. It is stronger than men. It made them. We've both got many things to do til we meet again Sparkie, but let's keep the letters going. It's good for both of us."

A couple of weeks later, Phil put pen to paper once again. He was enjoying his time on the slopes of Mammoth, he told Holloway, but a move farther north to live secluded in the Santa Cruz Mountains would be just the thing to extricate him from "this city and its corrupting influences." He mused about chilling out there and selling his landscape paintings to earn money. There were also a couple of colleges up in those parts, Phil continued, one of which was dotted with pine forest cabins. He was considering adopting a macrobiotic diet as well, though he admitted doing so was difficult with competition from his mom's cooking.

As 1969 dawned, Phil wound down his ski bumming and readied to cross the Pacific for school at the University of Hawaii—even though he had yet to be accepted. In order to partially replenish his ever-dwindling personal coffers before relocating, he put his van, Head skis, and acoustic guitar up for sale. "It's Hawaii for sure," he proclaimed in a letter to Holloway dated March 7. At the moment, he was preparing for his draft physical on which he would hopefully get a "1-Y," which meant he'd be qualified for military service only in the event of war or national emergency rather than immediately available to serve like those who received a "1-A."

Upon letting his hair grow long and bushy "like Jimi Hendrix," Phil decided it was a bit too extreme and chopped most of it off—down to an inch and a half. His facial foliage, however, was beginning to sprout anew, and soon he'd have another full-blown beard. But his scraggly, devil-may-care style blended in nicely with that of his shaggy new rock 'n' roll friends, several of whom played in a Malibu-based band called the Rockin Foo. Managed by Phil's brother John, the Foo took their handle from a Chinese symbol meaning joy, played what used to be described as "psyche garage country rock," and were on the cusp of recording their first album. Meanwhile, the guys gigged around town (they played on bills with Alice Cooper in March) and elsewhere, cultivating a wider following. He'd seen them a couple of times, Phil informed Holloway, "and they are just super bitchen." As it turned out, the Foo dug *him*, too.

By early May, Phil had sold his van for $450 and received a tax refund of $121.31—hardly a fortune but enough to get him to Hawaii. If he ever left. The University of Hawaii persisted in "giving me the runaround," he groused to Holloway, and the whole ordeal was making him anxious. He even reapplied, upon the school's suggestion, as a foreign student, but that proved fruitless since he was already a permanent U.S. resident. So he waited. And waited. Nothing. Phil aimed to be an art major with a concentration in photography, he wrote, "if I can just get in the fucker."

For a month or so Phil had been living with his brother John and the Foo clan—initially a trio made up of Lester Brown Jr., Michael "Raccoon" (Clark) and Wayne Erwin—in a small Hollywood house on North Fairfax, and traveling with them locally as one of two equipment managers. He also worked with college pal Wink Roberts at an advertising firm called the Boardroom, where Phil operated a stack camera and photo-typositor machine to create print ads for such clients as Telluride ski resort.

That same year, after Kostka got married, Phil came to terms with the fact that he and she would never be an item. Upon learning of her engagement, Phil had tried to persuade Kostka not to get hitched, but to no avail. And maybe that was just as well. "I have been relieved of that big sex hang-up that I had with her," he confided to Holloway, "and now we can be really close friends without my dick popping out of my pants. I realize now that's really how I've always wanted it. Her married, I mean. Not my dick poppin' out, you dirty jarhead." Phil hadn't heard from the draft board, either, so he assumed all was cool. It was about to get cooler.

In late May, he fired off another missive to Vietnam. "This letter is going to flip you out, believe me," it begins. On May 24, he'd made "a decision that will no doubt change my life." Instead of attending the University of Hawaii, which still hadn't approved his application and probably never would, he accepted an offer (a plea, really) from John to become a full-time Rockin Foo roadie. John was thrilled to have him on board and closer to home. When he first heard about Phil's Hawaii plans, John says, "I felt this incredible sense of loss. And I said, 'Don't go to Hawaii. You're just going to become a surf bum. Come with me—come and become a rock 'n' roll bum.'" So Phil stayed put.

It surely helped that he would earn a nominal fee for his toil, as the band had just received a $25,000 advance for their debut album on Hobbit Records. With part of the money, John leased a bigger home at 23758 Malibu Road. Featuring a yard, garage, patio, and detached front coach house, the three-bedroom pad was situated in the trendy and celebrity-dotted Malibu Shore Colony development and cost only $600 a month during the off-season ($1,700 during prime months). Originally constructed as a vacation home, it was poorly insulated and, Brown says, "built like a barn." On the plus side, it had a fireplace and the location was unbeatable. "Right on the beach," Phil wrote to Holloway, "a few steps away from the best surfin' spot in California. FUCK!!" Best of all, he'd have his own dwelling: a detached ten-by-twenty, two-room cabana in back that had previously (supposedly) been occupied by Brian Wilson of the Beach Boys and whose rear-facing picture window looked out onto the Pacific. Paradise. "I have a job . . . for people I love," Phil gushed in a late May letter. "In [re]turn, I get a house and a van and a beginning in the art field. Also all the thrill of really being on the inside of the rock scene. I'm a born long-haired man. That is the lifestyle I love. I have no qualms about the decision I made. It all seems like a dream, but it's really real."

When Kathy occasionally ran into Phil, she saw more than a wide-eyed rock 'n' roll wannabe. "He was acting like he was already hot shit," she says with a laugh. "And it was not the person I knew—down-to-earth Phil. He was somebody trying to portray a celebrity."

Well, there *were* groupies, and in one of his letters to Holloway Phil did a bit of good-natured bragging. "What is every kid's dream in America?" he asked rhetorically, teasingly. His answer, tucked away in the bottom margin: "I balled a Playboy Bunny. I won't give you the details in the mail, but pal it was beyond your imagination." Still, even as he revealed and reveled in that momentous event, another young and free-spirited chick sat beside him—one of the many "groovy groovies" who wandered in and out of the Foo compound. Before long, though, Phil's seed sowing would cease (for a couple of years, anyway) and he'd only have eyes for one.

Chapter 4

Phil, Malibu, early 1970s.
(Photo by Steven P. Small)

Malibu Colony in the 1960s was exclusive but unassuming in contrast to the pricey paradise it would become. There were stars and swell homes, as there had been since the 1930s, but far fewer of the behemoths that today occupy the area's private beachfront plots. For a while, in fact, the Colony was served by only one bank (Bank of America) and one diner (the Malibu Diner). During the period Phil called it home, neighborhood luminaries included Steve McQueen, Henry Gibson, and Richard Burton and Elizabeth Taylor; the latter two rented singer Bobby Darin's four-story house not far from Phil's little cabana. *I Dream of Jeannie* and future *Dallas* star Larry Hagman lived close by, too, often lounging in his large Jacuzzi and playing Frisbee on the sand. For whatever reason, Hagman took a shine to Phil. Often with other mates in tow, they attended the Malibu

Grand Prix together. They also spent much time soaking in Hagman's hot tub and smoking pot. Back then, ganja was available in abundance—at the Foo house, a cake pan was always stocked with choice weed and rolling papers—and Phil readily partook. Nevertheless, says Foo member Michael Clark, "Even in those wild years when we were tripping on acid and smoking joints every five minutes," Phil always demonstrated good sense and was "very much under control." Adds John Hartmann, "He was not vulnerable to the fuel aspect of [drugs]. It was a toy, sometimes a tool, but it was never a fuel."

Ever the seeker and always thirsty for knowledge, Phil's most recent spiritual discovery was the so-called *Urantia Book*, a copy of which he gave to Hagman but likely never read from cover to cover. (He was known to give people books that he himself had never read or merely perused.) Packed with more than two thousand pages, the dense tome—a mashup of science, religion, and philosophy—is said to have originated in Chicago between the mid-1920s and mid-1950s. Its 196 "papers" are divided into four parts and include "The Universal Father," "The Evolution of Local Universes," "The Mammalian Era on Urantia," "The Social Problems of Religion," and "The Mount of Transfiguration." Despite his growing spirituality, however, Phil was no holier-than-thou square. After all, this was the summer of '69. The summer of rock 'n' roll; the summer of peace and free love.

Throughout June, July, and August, Phil and his musical mates played festivals in Seattle and Oregon as well as several gigs in the L.A. area and one—in early July, with Eric Burdon and Lonnie Mack—at Bill Graham's famed Fillmore West in San Francisco. They motored to all of them in a dark blue Dodge van—Phil's lucky van. During an outdoor event in Ashland, Oregon, the vehicle was parked in back of a college football stadium. While the Foo rocked outside, Phil rocked inside. "He got laid in the back of that van," Les Brown says. For the rest of the day, Phil walked around singing a verse from the Doors' song "The End": "Meet me at the back of the blue bus."

Back in L.A., no injuries were sustained when Phil again stepped in to lend a helping hand (two, actually) during a Foo performance at Thee Experience. Owned by a Jimi Hendrix acquaintance named Marshall Brevitz, the short-lived venue regularly teemed with industry players and was a stepping-stone for many emerging artists (Burdon, Alice Cooper, Poco, Grand Funk Railroad, Joe Cocker) en route to packing arenas and stadiums. The building's façade sported a massive mural of Hendrix's head, with the entrance positioned over his mouth. One evening there, likely during the Foo's three-night stand in late June (they'd already done stints in March and April), Hendrix himself made an appearance and sauntered onstage to jam. "The place was just electric," Brown says. "Everybody's going nuts." Then drummer Buddy Miles, at the time a member of Hendrix's "Band of Gypsys," joined Hendrix and began thumping his bass drum with such force that its spurs broke. "Every time he hit the drum, it moved about a foot," Brown says. Devoted roadie that he was, Phil sprinted onto the stage, got on his knees, and held the instrument in place for the song's duration. Every time Miles whacked the drum, Phil's shaggy hair flew up and then flopped down. "I'm surprised he could hear after that," Brown says. "But he was so in awe."

In mid-August, when hundreds of thousands of revelers converged on Max Yasgur's farm in Woodstock, New York, to trip on acid and groove to round-the-clock jamming, Phil and the boys were otherwise occupied; there was plenty to keep them busy in California and elsewhere. Late that year they shared a stage with Janis Joplin, the Byrds, and other rock gods at the Palm Beach International Raceway in Florida. The Foo also had a musically tepid but nonetheless eventful stay in New York City, where Phil heroically (supposedly) prevented a colleague's potential incarceration. According to Brown, here's how it went down: Just out of record company meetings, Brown received a concerned call from John Hartmann. "We've got a big problem," John told him, and proceeded to explain that said colleague had been lounging in the lobby of his hotel when he became smitten with a pretty girl in one of the phone booths nearby. Naturally, then, he entered the glassed-in booth next to her and exposed himself. "The girl goes ballistic," Brown says, "and she's screaming and yelling." Once again, it was Phil to the rescue. Grabbing the offending party, he whisked him out of the lobby and up a set of marble stairs that led to the mezzanine. En route, Phil tripped and fell and knocked out his front teeth.

John Hartmann remembers the lost teeth but not much else. In the story he tells, there was no phone booth, no shrieking hottie, and no indecent exposure. "We had smoked a J in our hotel room," he says, "and dropped a lot of floors to the lobby [in the elevator]. The cannabis and the loss of altitude made Phil black out. We were walking out the door and he twisted slightly to his right and fell into the wall, then did a header face-first into the cement. I was really scared for a minute. When I turned him over I could see he'd lost his two front teeth and was bleeding." So they hustled up a dentist and got Phil some temporary caps, which he soon had replaced with artificial choppers. While all of this was going down, the band's hotel room was burgled. C'est la vie. Says John, "We were wild and lived in a fantasy land inside the rock 'n' roll bubble."

As Phil's digs in Malibu Colony were located some twenty miles from Westchester, the car-less roadie beach bum rarely went home to visit his parents. Besides, he was having too much fun spending hours each day surfing at the nearby Malibu Surfrider Beach, bedding female Foo fans in his tropical-themed bachelor pad (bamboo walls, oriental rug, colorful mosquito net canopy over a double bed), sketching in his ocean-view art nook, and schlepping amps to venues where he regularly encountered rock legends. "I have never been browner or healthier in all my days," he wrote to Holloway. Just for grins, Phil also began drawing bawdy and looney comic strips based on Foo members and their exploits.

More important to his budding career as a graphic artist, he designed cover art—a rustic rendering of the trio that resembles a wood etching—for the Foo's fall 1969 debut album. (The band's follow-up effort, after guitarist Ron Becker joined in 1971, also features Phil's handiwork outside and in. An included six-page comic strip booklet, titled "The Foo Story," tells a comical Genesis-inspired tale of the group's creation.)

"I feel like a real artist," Phil wrote to Holloway. "Wow. Sheeeaaaat!"

Only a few months into his Malibu dream Phil passed Gretchen Lewis (now Gettis Blake) and her pet poodle Noodle on the beach by his shack, where they struck up a conversation. Gretchen lived with her affluent dentist father—a "pothead" devotee of astronomer Carl Sagan and philosopher Alan Watts—and his young second wife only three or four doors down. Just nineteen and not long out of high school in Florida, she then worked at an upscale clothing store called I. Magnin & Co. on Wilshire Boulevard. A former member of her high school's men's track and field team, Gretchen had previously been engaged to a javelin thrower—a "nice Jewish boy" with whom she'd broken up for lack of chemistry.

After introducing themselves and making small talk, she and Phil grew more comfortable in each other's presence and ended up hanging out on an ocean-carved sand ledge until well past sundown. "I've never met anyone like him in all my years," Gretchen says. "You just felt like he was a lie detector. What you saw is what you got, but it wasn't in a bad way—like, 'take it or leave it.' He was a genuine guy." They parted ways that night without so much as a kiss. Upon meeting up the next day, however, "sparks flew." Phil reached over to kiss her, "and all hell broke loose." Almost immediately thereafter the two of them began spending virtually every night together in Phil's cabana, which he described to Holloway as an "invigorating and a truly beautiful experience. I no longer have any sex hang-up, which had built up . . . and was beginning to flip me out. My hang-up was that I'd never had a girlfriend who dug sex as much as me. Well, I've met my match!"

Gretchen had met hers, too. "I remember being in his [bed]room and things went on from a sexual standpoint that I didn't even know existed before," she says. "Just from the point of pure duration. I was a living bladder infection!" Before the year's end, Gretchen was pregnant. But because she and Phil were so young and nearly broke, not to mention unmarried, "we both realized that this couldn't happen." So she had an abortion—which was then illegal in cases unassociated with rape, incest, or the mother's health—with the help of her connected father. Phil, she says, seemed fine with it—or at least not distraught. "Whatever Catholic-ness there was [in him], practicality took over."

During the next several months, Gretchen sometimes accompanied Phil to Foo gigs that were close by. At home, they spent many hours together on the beach, in his oceanfront hut, and kicking around Malibu. The local Renaissance fest was a favorite annual jaunt, and they attended once as Robin Hood and Maid Marian. As he would in years to come, Phil made sure his costume suited the part, which in this case meant donning tights among other era-specific flourishes. "He was a masculine guy," Gretchen says, "but not afraid of his feminine side." She liked that. She *loved* him—for his supreme but easy confidence, lack of pretension, and laid-back outlook on life. For being everything she was not. "He saw something in me that I didn't know was there," she says. "I had a ton of insecurities; he had none. He was as unabashed all the time as a human being could be."

About six months into their relationship, Gretchen became acutely aware of how much those around him also loved Phil and gravitated toward him: the band, random passersby on the beach, her sisters, her father. His "organic" magnetism, bolstered by his ever-present sense of humor, drew them into his often-wacky orbit. People wanted to be around him and they frequently asked him to perform. Phil never needed coaxing. "Whatever he felt like doing, he'd do," she says of his public antics, which typically included celebrity impressions. "But it wasn't the kind of thing where you'd look at him and say, 'This guy's a loon.'" On the contrary, she says, he was "a gamin"—a "happy little character" who brought out lightness in others. "We were never around people who were miserable or unhappy or fighting. You couldn't be around us and have that happen."

On March 12, 1970, at the Malibu courthouse, Phil and Gretchen obtained a marriage license and exchanged vows in a no-frills civil ceremony. He was twenty-one, she twenty. A casual reception followed at her father's house (he thought the world of Phil), where guests dined, danced, and mingled outdoors and around a massive picnic-like table in the sprawling living room. Phil and Gretchen barely knew themselves, let alone each other, but here they were embarking on a new life together—one that initially played out "like a fairy tale."

Not everyone viewed their pairing so rosily. Being older, with more life experience, Les Brown had his doubts from the start. "The unfortunate thing is that Phil was infatuated with beauty," he says. "You get to a point in your life where the beauty becomes less important, but it takes a long time to get to that place. Let's be frank about it: At that time, with the free love and all that, you screwed enough beautiful women and you were finally like, 'OK, she's pretty. Big deal. So what,' and you start looking for people you can make some sort of connection with. But in order to make those connections, you have to be there. And that's difficult for some people, especially actors [or in Phil's case, aspiring actors], because they're always being somebody else." While he thought Gretchen was "a sweet girl," if "a little spoiled,"

Brown got the sense that "she wanted to take [Phil] away from the evils of rock 'n' roll. Of course, there was a never-ending stream of ladies going through that [Foo] house, which must have driven her crazy."

Though Gretchen says she grew accustomed to the scene, bearing witness to it certainly darkened her worldview. "Oh, my God! If ever there was naïveté that went sour, it was mine," she says. "I mean, the stuff I used to see go on in that house. Ultimately, you got used to it, but it was a constant revolution of women. Sex, drugs, and rock 'n' roll." In the process of trying to extricate Phil from that world, Gretchen encouraged him to get "a real job," which at first he was hesitant to do. But it was increasingly necessary for their survival.

With only meager sources of income, the couple lived a bare-bones existence, moving from Phil's cabana to a cramped one-bedroom apartment across the street and maintaining a fiscally conservative lifestyle with their white-and-orange tabby cat Russell (named by Phil after musician Leon Russell), black mutt Levi, and a king-sized waterbed. Still car-less, Phil shared Gretchen's red VW bug, which was eventually replaced by a blue-and-white VW van. And though they kept their circle of intimates tight—two or three couples at most—Phil continually attracted admirers. "He wanted to be a comedian," Gretchen says. "It was his passion. We had a lot of friends because he was so funny. People wanted to be around him, and they always wanted him to perform."

Together with a friend who managed a movie theater in Malibu, Phil got his first taste of improvisation when the two of them staged comedy skits on weekends before and after screenings with pals Wink Roberts, Mark Pierson, and others. "It was such a small community back then," Gretchen says, "that I'm surprised someone like Henry Gibson didn't wander in there and discover Phil."

Although the newlyweds were scraping by "paycheck to paycheck," Phil's ambition to succeed in showbiz outweighed his financial concerns. "Phil had such a strong desire to be what he wanted to be," Gretchen says, "but he wasn't going to prostitute himself to be that." The highly connected John Hartmann might have helped, she says, but Phil was reluctant to accept assistance from anyone. Not that John offered any. "It was interesting when I'd hear him say, 'I manage Sonny and Cher,'" she says. "But then the reality of it was, 'Well, where are they? Bring them over.' But that stuff just never materialized."

At the time, John says, he was struggling himself and unaware of Phil's dire circumstances, because Phil never said a word. Pride and principles prohibited him from doing so, as did a reluctance to make waves or put others out. And so, since freelance artistry was at best an inconsistent means of subsistence, Phil scored a design job with the Santa Monica ad agency Farrell-Bergmann, Inc. "It was kind of a low point," says Phil's attorney friend Steve Small, who at the time dated founder Bergmann's secretary and worked across the hall. Both men shared an interest in photography and talked about it when they could. The agency was small and Phil earned low wages doing paste-ups for print ads. He didn't last long there and was, Small says, happy to leave.

That June, Phil stood drop-jawed in front of a television as his former Westchester High schoolmate, Charles Manson acolyte Lynette "Squeaky" Fromme, staged a protest and answered reporters' questions outside an L.A. courtroom where Manson was being tried for masterminding multiple murders—including that of filmmaker Roman Polanski's pregnant young wife, Sharon Tate, in L.A.'s Benedict Canyon. A budding peacenik and an occasional participant in protests, Phil thought to himself, "Darkness is descending on the movement." Five years later Fromme was imprisoned on charges that she attempted to assassinate President Gerald Ford with a semiautomatic handgun. She spent more than three decades in lockup until her release in 2009.

———

In late September 1970, after a fierce Southern California wildfire (commonly referred to as the Malibu Canyon Fire) driven by 80-mph winds destroyed 150 homes, killed ten people, came a half-mile from idyllic Malibu Colony, and ultimately charred half a million surrounding acres, Phil and Gretchen moved from their badly smoke-damaged apartment and into a nearby condo. The down payment on it, $5,000, was a gift from Gretchen's father. He helped in other ways, too. But the monthly mortgage—which amounted to a couple of hundred dollars more than they'd paid to rent their previous pad—was a couple of hundred dollars too much. Still, they somehow made do and got along in the process, even taking on a roommate for a time. "There were never cross words between the two of us," Gretchen says. "I mean, we had our issues—like, we didn't have enough money. But we didn't live ahead of ourselves. Our life was really simple, kind of like in that Shirley MacLaine–Robert Mitchum movie *What a Way to Go!*"

Before long, though, stress—partly brought on by mounting bills—began taking its toll. To further complicate matters, Gretchen again became pregnant. Phil wanted kids, five of them, even back then—but not *then*. The timing, Gretchen says, was worse than before, and so she quietly had her second pregnancy terminated at a clinic in Beverly Hills. "Twice it was accidental," she says, noting that even the use of an IUD had failed to prevent conception. "And whatever smarts we had, we just knew we weren't bringing a kid into the world. We just weren't ready." Phil stayed cool and gave no hint of being upset. Gretchen admits, though, that if something bothered him, "certainly nobody ever knew—and that included me."

"He didn't have a lot of requirements," she adds. "He really didn't. And he definitely didn't expect anything of other people. My attitude is if I give out to you, you'd better give me something back emotionally. He wasn't that kind of guy."

That same fall, Phil transferred his credits from Santa Monica City College to San Fernando State University (now Cal-State Northridge), a four-year institution, where he took graphic arts classes but declared no major. He dropped out the following spring. A few months before doing so, in early February 1971, a massive earthquake registering 6.6 on the Richter scale rippled through much of Southern California and portions of neighboring states, causing $500 million in damage, killing sixty-five people and injuring two thousand more. Aftershocks, seismic and otherwise, continued for several more months.

By late that year, Phil and Gretchen had lost their spark and grown apart. Continuing money woes and Gretchen's most recent pregnancy were key issues, but even more detrimental was a "flirtation" she had carried on with a bigwig client from the dentist's office where Gretchen found work after quitting her bank gig. "It was exciting," she says. "I got to see a barber come into his office and give him haircuts, manicures, and cater to his every whim. But I was just a bystander caught up in it all. When it came down to the rubber meeting the road, I tucked tail and ran home to Phil. I told him everything, which was nothing, but I believe it did irreparable damage to an already fragile and strained marriage."

The end of their union was as inauspicious and unexpected as its beginning. As easily as they'd come together, they drifted apart. Steve Small handled the divorce proceedings, which were cut-and-dried since Phil and Gretchen had few if any assets to divide. "There was no drama to it," Small says. Gretchen agrees, calling the split "a real matter-of-fact kind of thing. I don't remember ever walking into a courtroom." By March 1972 their marriage was officially dissolved, though they stayed in sporadic contact and on friendly terms for the next quarter-century. "I take full blame for whatever didn't work out," Gretchen says. "I don't know that we'd still be married today, because fame and glory might have changed all that. But from what I believe and things I've read, Phil didn't change."

For the first time in a couple of years, Phil was a free man—a young, talented, good-looking bachelor in the casually amorous Age of Aquarius—and he took full advantage of his newfound liberation. "The guy was a frickin' animal!" Paul Hartmann says admiringly. "I'm sure he had a new [pickup] line for every occasion." Having moved to a first-floor studio apartment on Santa Nella Boulevard in Malibu, in a funky mansion-like structure where the swashbuckling thespian Errol Flynn was said to have dwelled decades earlier, Phil drew and surfed (though not typically near his place, where the waves were too small) and smoked weed and charmed the ladies. He also landed the role of River City con man Harold Hill in a 1973 production of *The Music Man* at Santa Monica's Morgan-Wixson Theatre. There he met a fellow aspiring actor named Floyd Dozier, who shared Phil's interests in wave riding, drama (the showbiz kind), and cars. They hit it off right away. "Everybody wanted to be his friend because he was an interesting guy," Dozier says. "Immediately when I met him, I sensed there was something really different about him. He was a true artist. He didn't really march to the same drum as most people, although there was a part of him that wanted to be perceived as normal. He went through life trying to find a character that he could present to the public that seemed normal and wholesome."

During their first hang session they surfed, then shared a joint. Canadian singer-songwriter Joni Mitchell's 1971 LP *Blue,* cued up by her countryman Phil, provided the soundtrack. There were also *Music Man* bashes on the beach with fellow cast members (Dozier was also part of the production). As ever, partygoers gathered around to watch Phil do impressions. And, as ever, Jonathan Winters routines were common. "Do Arnold!" revelers yelled, referencing a famous Winters bit called "Moby Dick & Captain Arnold" from the comic's hit 1963 album *Mad, Mad, Mad, Mad World.* Sometimes, on lazy afternoons,

Phil and Dozier watched old black-and-white movies on television. Phil, Dozier says, was encyclopedic in his knowledge of actors and the characters they played. John Wayne's were among his favorites.

Phil and Dozier talked religion and philosophy, too, much as Phil had with Holloway back in high school. Though still a fan of the *Urantia Book,* Phil had lately become intrigued with another mystical tome: the ancient Chinese Book of Changes—or *I Ching.* It contains a so-called divination system that is essentially used to foretell events and solve problems. "Throwing the *I Ching,*" as the parlance goes, involves tossing three coins (Chinese ones, pennies, etc.), then multiplying the number of heads by two and tails by three. The sum total of those numbers becomes the basis for interpretation via the symbolism of sixty-four different "hexagrams."

Phil frequently threw the *I Ching* for others and himself, as he was deeply curious about his own fate—and, if possible, redirecting it to better align with his aspirations. When Paul came across Phil's *I Ching* years later he found scraps of paper inside, and on each scrap variations of Phil's name (Philip Hartmann, Phil E. Hartman, etc.) in Phil's handwriting along with calculated "destiny" numbers. In numerology, each letter has a value and each value a meaning. The name "Phil Hartmann," for instance, has a "destiny number" (or "expression") of 8, a "soul urge" of 11 and an "inner dream" of 6. Which meant, in short and in part, that Phil was an ambitious, practical, materialistic, spiritual utopian who envisioned living a happy-go-lucky family life, with doting children and a devoted wife. Merely dropping one "n" would change his destiny number (and thus, to Phil's way of thinking, his actual destiny) to an even more desirable 3—the height of artistic fulfillment.

In an attempt to help bolster Phil's artistic pursuits, Dozier bought his buddy a new drafting table, where Phil spent many solitary hours sketching, cartooning, and working on freelance graphic art projects as they came his way. "You know how some artists have an ego about being an artist?" Dozier says. "He wasn't like that. But he was real serious about his craft. He'd get cranky if you were interfering with it." But freelance work was spotty, and Phil's money was typically tight. What he really needed was another salaried job, though a return to the ad world at Farrell-Bergman was entirely unappealing.

Fortuitously, John Hartmann and his music business partner, Harlan Goodman, had just settled into swanky offices at Hollywood's Crossroads of the World complex on Sunset—formerly Alfred Hitchcock's headquarters. Its walls were paneled in redwood, gray gabardine, suede-leather and tartan plaid. "H&G" (for Hartmann & Goodman) was etched into a small window above the entrance. With high-profile clients like Crosby, Stills & Nash, America, and Poco, John and Goodman needed someone to design album covers. Phil was a natural choice, and before long he set up shop on the second floor of the ship-shaped structure's bow.

As a jack-of-all-trades, doing everything from layout to printing and the preparation of artwork, Phil came into the office almost every weekday and was busier than he'd ever been—not to mention earning some coin for his efforts. Although his monthly stipend of $750 plus a small per-album fee (based on the amount budgeted for graphic art, which was generally $7,500) wasn't much to live on, Phil was again tight-lipped about asking for help. "Quite frankly, he wasn't happy with John," Small says. "John would screw him monetarily, and it caused some ill feelings. I had conversations with my wife and Phil when he was debating whether he should stay and do what he was doing or go in another direction."

John, though, says he was never aware of Phil's situation until years later, when Phil admitted that he'd gone through a tough stretch while working at Hartmann & Goodman. "Phil was a very strong character," Harlan Goodman says, "but such a sweetheart, such a beautiful soul, that there was this great internal struggling [because] he didn't want to be a burden. So he wouldn't tell us."

Goodman also witnessed Phil's ongoing search for a concrete identity. "He was constantly trying to figure out who he was. Some days he was a cowboy, some days he was a surfer, some days he'd come in with a jacket and a tie." A used Porsche 924 and a pickup truck were among his modes of transportation, and Phil's outfits were always vehicle-appropriate.

Ongoing money issues aside, Phil's long H&G tenure—which lasted from 1973 to 1980—saved him from further corporate boredom and provided him with a wealth of professional experience, beginning with his conjuring of cover art for Poco's 1974 album *Seven*. Often clad in faded OshKosh overalls, H&G's newest employee—a one-man art department—could usually be found tucked away in his always-tidy alcove. Besides *Seven*, other album artwork included a now-famous cover painting for *History: America's Greatest Hits*, the minimalist horse sketch that fronts Poco's bestselling *Legend* LP and a logo for Crosby, Stills & Nash that is still used as a stage backdrop when they tour.

After attending band meetings to get a sense of what each group envisioned artistically, Phil regrouped with John Hartmann to hash out further details. Before creating an initial mock-up, he did deep research and sought out other works for inspiration. Things he witnessed in everyday life—people, places, objects—were catalysts as well. His image for Poco's *Legend* was spurred by black-and-white Asian brush paintings of horses with dust swirling around their heads that Poco member Rusty Young and his wife came across one day while shopping for furniture. "When I saw that artwork, I thought it was just providence," Young says. Excited, he phoned Phil and they made plans to meet at the store so Phil could see the paintings for himself. Once he had, the wheels began to turn. Instead of aping the artist's style exactly,

Young suggested, why not omit the dust and draw a single horse using as few lines as possible? Phil loved the idea, retired to his studio, and before long he'd produced a dozen different versions. Young and Phil chose the winner together.

Done in an entirely different style, Phil's portrait of America was loosely based on the work of enormously popular American illustrator and painter Maxfield Parrish, who plied his trade in the first half of the twentieth century, was revered by Norman Rockwell, and was fond of rich colors. Parrish, too, was a darling of the rock 'n' roll set. One of his paintings appears on Elton John's *Caribou*. Another was adapted for the Moody Blues' 1983 album *The Present*. "[Phil] would *always* come back with way more than I had even imagined and blow us all away," John says. "Each situation was unique. With *America's Greatest Hits*, he did it all on his own. He came with what he presented as roughs for the cover. The band immediately said, 'That isn't the rough; that's the cover.' He probably knew that was going to happen, but was being modest."

But it wasn't all toil at H&G, described by John as "an extremely happy place." Says Goodman, "We really believed in the people that we worked with. We cared about them a great deal and they cared about us. You couldn't call it a job." As befitted H&G's rock 'n' roll environment, a steady stream of groupies flowed in and out of the offices; pot was plentiful ("There wasn't a time that I walked into that office that someone didn't offer me a joint," rock photographer Henry Diltz says) and corporate bullshit minimal. In keeping with the spotlight-loving side of his bifurcated personality, Phil served as a sort of in-house jester. On one occasion, Diltz recalls, Phil trotted out a comedy bit he'd been working on starring a German John Wayne. And when, toward the end of Phil's stint, a young aspiring actress named Daryl Hannah stopped by to be photographed by Diltz (he snapped her early publicity stills), Phil suddenly popped into the frame wearing a curly red fop wig. Hairbrush in hand, he proceeded to affect the voice and mannerisms of a fey and fussy English hairdresser. "It turned into this half-hour bit,"

John Hartmann told Larry King in 2004. "Everybody in the office gathered to see Phil do his thing." Goodman likens Phil to a comedic gunslinger: "If you weren't careful, he could drop you to your knees, convulsed in tears."

Phil had been at his H&G drafting table for only a couple of years, though, when he began to grow creatively if silently restless. He was constantly under the gun to meet deadlines and cooped up inside when he preferred to be out. Consequently, as stir-craziness worsened, he began searching for what he later termed a "psychological release." As luck or fate would have it, one awaited him just minutes down the road.

Chapter 5

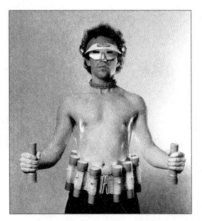

Phil as Lightman, Groundlings, late 1970s.
(Photo by John H. Mayer)

By the mid-1970s Phil had established himself as a top-notch graphic designer and was making a decent living at it. He'd conjured fanciful album art for Poco, America, and Crosby, Stills & Nash. He'd even bought himself a little house on Norwich Avenue in Sherman Oaks, where he hung John Wayne's first studio portrait on his bedroom wall and planted azalea bushes that never grew quite right. Besides his work for Hartmann & Goodman, he began tinkering around with ideas for a comic strip based on the exploits of a masked aviation hero named "Don Patrol."

But the long and solitary artist's hours wore on him. Despite his introspective nature, Phil craved more frequent human contact and feedback from a live audience, be it on a beach or in a theater. He also yearned for creative diversion—"a social outlet" that would enable him to expand his artistic horizons, ideally while meeting available females. And if it led to bigger things professionally, that was all the better. "I didn't want to wake up at sixty and discover that life had passed me by and I was still doing the same thing," he later said. "What's the good of having big dreams if you're afraid to see where they lead?"

And so he searched and finally found. One weekend night in 1975, his future was made clearer during a birthday party for Phil's friend Steve Small in East Hollywood. Revelers packed all thirty basement-level seats of the Oxford Theatre, a tiny and rather rundown venue that housed a nascent improvisation group called the Groundlings—a nod to those cretins in Shakespeare's *Hamlet* "who for the most part are capable of nothing but inexplicable dumbshows and noise." Having begun life as the Gary Austin Workshop in 1972, the Groundlings was officially established as a nonprofit in early 1974 and quickly became known as a training ground for up-and-coming talents—and a poaching ground for showbiz scouts from Hollywood and New York. Prior to launching *Saturday Night Live* in October 1975, the show's executive producer Lorne Michaels hired Groundlings member Laraine Newman for his first cast. Besides Phil, the many others who followed in decades to come included Jon Lovitz, Julia Sweeney, Will Ferrell, Chris Kattan, Cheri Oteri, Will Forte, Chris Parnell, Maya Rudolph, and Kristen Wiig.

Before the birthday show, Austin was backstage prepping for the performance when laughter wafted in from out front. Curious as to who might be causing it, particularly since the show hadn't started, a couple of his associates went to find out. Their reconnaissance report: a guy from the audience, whom they later learned was Phil, had hopped onstage to tell jokes and do impressions. Granted, the crowd was comprised of friendly faces, but Austin sensed that Phil was garnering genuine guffaws. And Phil surely knew it, for the sensation was by now a familiar one after his many gut-busting shtick sessions on Malibu beaches and elsewhere.

Right after the show, Phil approached Austin and asked how to join the troupe. It wasn't difficult. At that point, and for the next few years (until the Groundlings School of Improvisation was formed in 1978), just about anyone could participate in workshops as long as they paid the $25 monthly dues. "We even had two hookers who joined and then got into a fight," Austin says. "They left and never came back, so it was a crazy, bizarre circus."

Singer and actress Jaye P. Morgan accompanied Phil to the birthday show and ended up joining the company as well. "It wasn't an audition, per se," she says of the tryout process. "They wanted you to come in and just riff on an idea and see how far you could go, so we both did that. It wasn't that hard for me, and so it was amazingly easy for him." Tracy Newman was wowed as well with Phil's early improv acumen and self-assuredness. He was one of those people "who walked into the Groundlings ready," she says. But there were still plenty of rough edges to smooth, so Phil happily immersed himself in weekday workshops while dutifully dressing stages or cleaning up after weekend revues at various venues around town.

"Laraine Newman was in the performing company and I was just dazzled by it," Phil recalled of his first Groundlings experience. "I couldn't believe the intellectual challenge of making something up as you went along. And I thought: 'I've got to join that workshop.' Also, I knew it was a way to meet ladies—I had taken acting class in high school for the same reason. So I joined." He redesigned the Groundlings, logo, he said, in lieu of paying tuition.

Although the Groundlings had relocated in 1975 to bigger and better digs at 7307 Melrose Avenue, across the street from a porno theater, it took four conflict-laden years to resolve parking and building code issues with the city—issues that legally prevented the ninety-nine-seat space from opening to the public. Consequently, Austin's growing gang performed in a number of venues, including the Improv on Melrose, where the group was in residency for several months,

and the rickety White House theater on Pico Boulevard, where mush-
rooms sprouted from the carpet when it rained. Out of financial neces-
sity Phil retained his position at Hartmann & Goodman, where on
many Fridays Groundlings came to hang out with staffers and which-
ever rock stars happened to be on the premises. "It was pretty festive,"
Goodman says. "The whole place was pretty much rockin'."

At some point during Phil's first couple of years with the Groundlings, he became disillusioned or bored or both and (not atypically,
other Groundlings say) dropped out. It's been fun, he told Austin, but
I don't want to be an actor. (He'd have several more bouts with self-
doubt before his tenure there was up.) Austin, though, was chagrined;
he knew Phil's potential. "We were all very disappointed," he says.
"Because we knew he was very, very good and he was getting better
all the time."

Months went by during which Phil continued his graphic design
work, began doing voice-overs for local radio spots and even recorded
a comedy album, *Flat TV,* with the assistance of Small, musician pal
Chad Stuart (of the musical duo Chad & Jeremy, John's clients), and
fellow Groundlings Phyllis Katz and Teresa Burton. According to
Austin, he was lured back into the fold after participating in a cold-
reading workshop that Austin held at his house to help actors hone
their audition skills for television and film jobs. "It was the first time
I had really ever seen an honest actor in Phil," Austin says of the session. "And by that I mean he dealt with the truth of the moment, but
there was no shtick and there were no broad characters. And he was
just terrific." Austin told him so and Phil was encouraged enough to
rejoin the group.

In late April 1979, the Groundlings finally opened its first show
on Melrose in an intimate 99-seat room the actors had personally
revamped and populated with secondhand folding chairs. The space
had previously housed an array of disparate establishments, including
a furniture showroom, a gay bar, and a massage parlor. By that point,

Phil had undergone nearly four years of training—and it showed. Plus, as he later explained, "certain people had dropped out of the company and now I was one of the stars of the show. I had what every actor needs to get a leg up: a showcase. Casting directors would come, as they would to the Comedy Store or the Improv, and I started to get some work. It slowly evolved from there."

"The Groundlings on Melrose in Hollywood are something else," wrote Gardner McKay, theater critic for the *Los Angeles Herald Examiner*. "Their feet may be planted firmly on the ground, but their eyes are planted firmly on social decay (moral, media and religious) and sometimes even on the stars." Others were equally upbeat. Among the two dozen sketches presented, McKay singled out Phil's "extraterrestrial sage" named "Lightman" as one to watch. Flaunting his shirtless, surfing-buff torso (the ever body-conscious Phil then dabbled in weightlifting as well), and wielding brightly beaming flashlights in both hands, he wore a headband, a white tennis visor, and a homemade cardboard mask with rectangular openings for the eyes that resembled something out of *Star Trek*. Tight black pants and a utility belt outfitted with several more upward-aiming flashlights completed the ensemble. His act: shining a beam of light on random audience members and answering questions they were merely *thinking*.

The character also paid a visit to the offices of Hartmann & Goodman, leaving behind a cryptic missive that read: "This Office is Laser Ionized for Extra Hipness. Lightman."

That same year Phil made what was very likely his first television appearance since *The Lloyd Thaxton Show* thirteen years earlier—on ABC's *The Dating Game*. Fellow Groundlings Jaye P. Morgan and Paul Reubens scored future spots on the program as well, Reubens several months later and Morgan in 1980. Phil's episode—hosted by Jim Lange and originating from the Chuck Barris Stages in Hollywood—presented him thusly: "Bachelor number three has actually designed the covers for over twenty-five bestselling record albums. He has appeared on over one hundred radio commercials. And they say he makes the best avocado sandwich in the world." Phil's competition for the potential affections of a singer-actor bachelorette from Texas—"the sensuous Gina Russell"—included a swinging dude in an orange shirt who made throat-clearing noises when asked what sound best described his love life. The other contestant, ring-a-ding-dinging in a black shirt accessorized with gold chains, made grunting noises to describe his appetite. When asked what sound best described his bank account, Phil responded, "Ooooooooh, baby." Incidentally, he wore a tasteful (for the time) ensemble that included an ecru Hawaiian shirt under a tan blazer and brown slacks with matching shoes. His neatly coiffed light brown hair was wavy and full.

Gina: What road sign should I heed while dating you and why?
Phil: Uh, slippery when wet. (Audience cheers lasciviously.) No, no, no. They've got the wrong idea. I like to swim, and sometimes I get slippery.
Gina: Are you real athletic?
Phil: Very athletic.
Gina: So you're real versatile.
Phil: Yes, and built something like a Greek god.

In the end, Gina chose "good ol' number three"—Phil—saying that they seemed to have some things in common. But the pairing wasn't to be. As Phil later revealed, Gina stood him up for their getaway to the Monterey Peninsula, "where the simplistic beauty of nature stands waiting, the ubiquitous vistas to awaken your romantic energy. . . ."

Regardless, it was good national exposure, and throughout Phil's Groundlings tenure he landed small parts in mostly forgettable television commercials, shows, and in films: as a frenetic customer in an ad for Ice Hockey by ActiVision; as himself in director Brian Trenchard-Smith's music-and-mayhem flick *Stunt Rock* ("a deathwish at 120 decibels!"); as various characters in Hanna-Barbera's *Scooby-Doo and Scrappy-Doo*; as "man at airport with gun" on Chuck Barris's *The Gong Show Movie*; in an unknown role on a short-lived sitcom called *The Six O'Clock Follies* (with Laurence Fishburne and Bill Paxton). Most prominently, Phil's Chick Hazard made his first billed onscreen debut in the July 1980 sequel *Cheech and Chong's Next Movie*. Voice-over work mounted as well, thanks in part to guidance from and associations with actor and Firesign Theatre co-founder Phil Proctor (the cover for his troupe's 1980 musical album, *Fighting Clowns*, bears Phil's handiwork) and popular radio personality Shadoe Stevens. One of Phil's commercial characters during his short but intense stint with Stevens was a man named "Mr. Bimble," whose voice Phil created by pulling his cheeks out while he spoke. "I'd never seen anybody do anything like that before," Stevens says. "He looked like Plastic Man." The late Kip King, a former Groundling and father of *SNL* alum Chris Kattan, reportedly was instrumental in getting Phil bit parts on Hanna-Barbera's cartoon *The Smurfs*, which in 1981 began its nearly decade-long reign on NBC.

More than any of his other ventures, however, the Groundlings provided a creative sanctuary where Phil could try out new characters and premises to see what worked and what tanked. His experiences there proved psychologically insightful too, bringing out emotions that Phil had long surpressed—particularly ones from his sometimes puzzling and neglect-filled childhood, which he began to regard less rosily than before. As he later revealed, this period was the worst of his life—mentally, financially, and otherwise. Thankfully there was improv, an integral component of which is self-examination. For many practitioners it's a form of public therapy. To some extent, Phil saw it that way, too. "I noticed in the beginning that a lot of my characters had a tremendous amount of rage," he told interviewer Stanley Moss in 1991. "I had never had any therapeutic experience, but it was all welling up and coming out of me because I was in an environment where it was OK to do that . . . There's something about rage: we all have it [but] too many of us don't have a healthful way to express it. Mr. Henderson suddenly murders a guy in a bar, and he was the last guy you would have expected to do that. I'm convinced, from my therapeutic experiences recently, that we need wholesome ways of expressing our rage, or we suffer the effects of disease that are incumbent upon repression."

Groundlings co-founder Tracy Newman—who went on to write for *Cheers* and *Ellen*, and co-create ABC's sitcom *According to Jim*—was especially taken with Phil's unwavering commitment to the work. He had those qualities right from the start, she says, even when his skills were raw. "I don't know if he understood it intellectually, but maybe he understood what he wanted to see, so he knew how to do it," she says. "There's nothing that makes an audience more comfortable than a committed performer, and he was the most extreme committed performer. It also made him really desirable in terms of being onstage with him . . . Because it didn't really matter what you did. He never said 'no' onstage and he always made you look good."

Although Phil was no genius in Newman's eyes, nor was he especially original in his approach or characters, his utter commitment begat brilliance. Groundlings cast member and teacher Phyllis Katz talks of Phil going "to his own planet" while performing, during the process of which there was "no room for monitoring himself." Onstage, she says, his normally reserved personality was turbo-charged. An uncanny ability to exist in the moment and an instinct for knowing when to remain still or underplay a part also helped Phil's sketches shine. Audiences quickly took note.

But offstage, some observed, Phil's magnetism diminished. "There was no there, there," Tracy Newman says, though not pejoratively, of Phil's search for his own identity. Moreover, he often seemed preoccupied and could come across as distant or disconnected. "The first time I saw him onstage it was obvious that he was a star. But as a person, no." Former Groundling John Paragon attributes some of that distance to the fact that Phil led a separate and in ways more grown-up life outside the theater. He had a full-time job doing important and nationally regarded work when most of his compatriots were laboring at temp gigs or waiting tables.

And Phil was always immersing himself in various books or practicing other disciplines—sailing, guitar playing, and whatever else piqued his interest. "He'd have a character, and he'd also have this wealth of technical knowledge [about that character]," Katz says. "Or, if he didn't know and was making it up, you couldn't be sure." When it came to his beloved sailing, however, Phil never had to fake it. "Sometimes on weekends he'd just go to the beach and rent a boat," Katz remembers. "It was cheap, and he said it brought him peace."

Because everyone at the Groundlings regularly participated in workshops, Phil learned from those who came before him such as Austin, (Tracy) Newman, Katz, and Maxwell. "They may be competitive but they're also very supportive," Paul Reubens (aka Pee-wee Herman) has said of his former troupe. "The opposite of that was the Comedy Store, where everyone's out for themselves. The Groundlings was a workshop with people who wanted everyone else to succeed." Impressively for Phil's lack of experience, characters and sketch ideas generally came easily though rarely performance-ready.

And no matter what scene he was in, you could always count on Phil to make it sing. Alan Cranis, who managed the box office, recalls Maxwell's quipping about Phil's indispensability. If he could put Phil in a concrete box to keep him safe from accidents or illness, Maxwell said, he would. That value as a utility player, someone who could be counted on in all scenarios, would eventually serve Phil well in other professional endeavors. "He really belonged in England, where even the butler character is worked out in detail," Tracy Newman says. "It didn't matter what role Phil was playing, he would get out there and do it to the best of his ability and with a great deal of depth."

One of the funniest pieces Dozier saw Phil perform had its debut during a so-called "scene night," when material was showcased for an invite-only audience. This was pre-1979, when the theater had yet to be approved for paid public consumption. As a result, attendees were asked to sign waivers releasing the group from any liability should they become injured while on the premises—by, say, a crazed sniper named Norman Garrison. Played by Phil as a sweaty, twitchy, sleep-deprived nutcase clutching a vintage World War II carbine and wearing authentic soldier's garb, the jarring and offbeat Garrison nearly caused hemorrhaging. "I remember laughing so hard I couldn't breathe," Dozier says. "It's the first time I saw people actually rolling in the aisles."

As Phil began to shine onstage, John Hartmann talked up his younger brother to contacts around town. "It was our mission to get Phil discovered," John's ex-wife Lexie Slavich says. "And so we would [meet with] every agent and producer that we could get our hands on, we'd wine and dine them, then we'd go to the Groundlings and watch the show. And afterwards, we'd take them to meet Phil."

In time, as its newness wore off, Phil increasingly saw the Groundlings as more than a mere escape or diversion; it became a stepping-stone. "We were young and we were creative and we were energetic and we thought we were all going to be stars," Katz says. "If you're creative, you burn to create. And here, we had the opportunity to do it." Phil never voiced that specific ambition, she says, but it was definitely there. You could see it and sense it in his devotion to the work.

At first, that work was deeply collaborative and the actors were more consistently supportive of each other's efforts. But as time wore on, Katz says, the dynamic began to change. Phil wasn't immune to the shift. "I thought he became less friendly and more competitive and more interested in his own work and less interested in the work of his group," she says. Which might have had something to do with the increasingly large shadow cast by *Saturday Night Live*. "At the Groundlings, the goal is to get on *Saturday Night Live*," alumnus and former *SNL* cast member Julia Sweeney has said. "That's what everybody wanted to do." Reubens has expressed similar sentiments. "*SNL* was always a big force at the Groundlings," he told the *Hollywood Reporter*. "Just something that we all kind of were like, 'If you're successful, this might be an option.'" And though *SNL* wasn't Phil's primary or even secondary goal, he certainly wanted to advance his career. "Phil wanted to break into show business any way he could," says friend Mark Pierson, who met Phil in the early seventies in Malibu and was among those who improvised with him during off-hours at the Malibu Cinema. "He was really pining for it. As successful as his life was doing graphic art, he wanted it so much."

As a Groundlings instructor, Phyllis Katz made a point of drawing her students out of their respective comfort zones to perform scenes and characters that did not come naturally. Phil always had the toughest time playing himself. "You really have to bare yourself to get out of a character and just play a scene as yourself," Katz says. "But Phil was not much of a personality. He was like a chameleon." Others, including Maxwell, noticed the same quality. "He was a person who loved inhabiting other personas," Maxwell says. "So he was very comfortable assuming characters and really committing to them and doing impressions. That's what he would gravitate to, even in life."

Even offstage, costumes were key. One year Phil would drive a pickup truck, dress in all black, and perm his hair so it resembled an Afro of sorts. Eighteen months later he'd get his hair straightened, wear Hawaiian shirts, and drive a sports car. "He once called me up and said, 'I think I should tell you something before the show opens tonight: I've shaved my head,'" Maxwell remembers. "He was kidding, but that would be something he could have done." During another sartorial phase, he wore an impeccably tailored British suit—in brick red. As one former colleague puts it, "Phil was very vain and consumed by his appearance."

Had he tried to be a stand-up comic instead of a sketch actor, Tracy Newman thinks, Phil might have struggled "because he didn't have a point of view as a human being." Not onstage, anyway. He was most comfortable and at his performing best when cloaked or otherwise obscured by a crazy wig, a different voice, or the rakishly cocked hat and drab trench coat of one Chick Hazard. The Raymond Chandler–esque private dick was born of a goofy greeting Phil left on his answering machine. After hearing it, Maxwell suggested he use it as the basis for a new character. Phil had also included a Chick Hazard bit on his 1978 comedy album, *Flat TV*. The early effort, lost for a quarter-century after its recording, includes fake news segments, *Tonight Show* spoofs, a sketch about football/masturbation, and commercial parodies. Among the latter is a spot for something called Nescocaine. "Why not enjoy a delicious cup of Nescocaine?" Phil asks as the hopped-up announcer. "Or a second? Or a third? Hell, why not snort it right out of the jar?!"

Hazard, though, was poised to be Phil's first breakout character, and at the Groundlings it became far more three-dimensional—literally and figuratively. Hazard's voice, look, and patter all were honed in workshops before the noirish P.I. debuted during the Groundlings' first show on Melrose in late April 1979. With advisement and encouragement from Maxwell and others, the witty dick perfected his act and soon became an all-around favorite. Phil loved to play him, cast members loved to play with him, and audiences invariably roared their approval. Hazard sketches were showstoppers from their inception, and not only because they capped performances. Quick-talking and tightly wound, the all-business Hazard rarely smiled and spoke hard-boiled staccato sentences in a rat-a-tat-tat cadence. ("I was a sucker for long legs. I wanted to shinny up one of hers like a native boy looking for coconuts.") Every Hazard bit—always launched with a Chick monologue that conveyed crucial exposition—was a largely improvised murder mystery, with recurring characters and on-the-spot role assignments chosen by Phil. Lynne Stewart played a suspect named Missy. "You're going down for this, Missy!" Chick would exclaim, whereupon Stewart dropped to her knees as if to fellate him. Chick (sotto voce and glancing around nervously): "Not now!"

"Phil would dictate the scenes as he went along," Paragon recalls. "And as he would walk in, he would label the names of all the people onstage and who they were." Since Phil was known to be virtually unflappable onstage, Paragon often tried to crack him up mid-scene. Once, as a be-tuxed and big-assed "forties hitman" type named Nick Camaro, Paragon used his outsized backside as a tray to serve Hazard a drink. ("Cocktail, Chick?") While attempting to suppress his laughter, Phil snatched up the libation, chugged it down, and then flung his glass to the ground.

Victoria Bell (then Carroll) also attempted to throw Phil off his game via anatomical distraction. As his voluptuous female foil, a sexy 1940s vixen named Carmen Pluto, she initially appeared onstage with an era-appropriate dress and gardenias in her hair—nothing too risqué. "Then I heard through the grapevine that he really liked sexy lingerie," the award-winning costume designer says of Phil, who was then single. "So I made myself a nude leotard with black lace over it—a black chiffon negligee. And I wore black hose with the garter belt. And Phil knew nothing about it. So he started to introduce my character: 'There she was, Carmen Pluto, the atomic blonde bombshell . . .'" When the lights came up, Phil swung around to see Bell standing there with one stocking-clad gam (like something he might shinny up in search of coconuts) propped on a chair. In a split second, Bell recalls, he turned to the audience and said, "One look at Carmen and my cock shot down my pant leg like a snake through a vacuum cleaner." So much for throwing Phil off his game.

"We thought of him as a big star, even though he wasn't known outside of that [world]," Groundlings alum and *Saturday Night Live* cast member Jon Lovitz, one of Phil's best friends, told an interviewer of Phil's years on Melrose. As he recalled much later, "We'd all be sitting on the floor laying out the scene: 'Okay, Phil, you're a shoe salesman.' The lights would go down and come up, and we were just waiting. We knew whatever he was going to say was nothing you could ever imagine or think of. Then he would say it, and our jaws would drop open. He could do any voice, play any character, make his face look different without makeup. He was the king of the Groundlings." Maybe so, but as Newman notes there were several others back then who displayed the same charisma and "brilliance" as Phil in their own ways. "It's confidence that makes a person charismatic most of the time," she says. "And the way confidence plays out is with commitment onstage. People are drawn like moths to the flame. They're drawn to the brightest light." By dint of his formidable skills and copious stage time, Phil was often that light.

More than a few former cohorts say he was artistically generous besides. "He wanted everybody to succeed," says friend and former Groundling Randy Bennett. "He didn't like to see people left behind." Phil proffered valuable advice, too, both as a teacher and a colleague. Case in point: Every year at Christmastime, starting in 1981, the nearby Crystal Cathedral hosted holiday blowouts featuring live animals, flying angels—the works. So Groundling Doug Cox wrote a parody of the extravaganza featuring facsimiles of Sandy Duncan as the Little Shepherd Boy and Eurythmics rocker Annie Lennox as the Virgin Mary. Phil was a Wise Man—as played by Frank Sinatra. For several years, Cox says, "it really killed." Emboldened by its success, he decided to mock the traditions of another Christian holi-day: Easter. "We were rehearsing it and we thought, 'Oh, this is gonna kill. They're gonna love this,'" Cox says. "And we did it once and it just totally, totally died." In retrospect, he thinks, promoting the availability of a Crucifixion-themed drink—the Rusty Nail—at the Groundlings bar was perhaps a bit much. Phil doing a Sinatra-esque Pontius Pilate probably didn't help. "The audience just hated it," Cox says, but he and his cohorts finished what they'd started. Afterward, seeing that Cox was in the dumps, Phil walked up to him and offered the following insight: "You can make fun of Christmas, Doug, but you can't fuck with the Resurrection." And they never did again.

Phil's magnetism, though far more understated offstage than on, proved effective on the dating front within the Groundlings ranks as well. Stewart has called him the group's "resident sex symbol," and oth-ers concur. Phil was "a jock" on the female front, Jaye P. Morgan says. "He loved women, but he was always in trouble." Newman employs a marine metaphor: "He was a big fish in a little pond right away," she says, "because he was really good-looking, very funny, and really, really gifted. And women flock to that." Even those with whom he wasn't romantically involved gave him wider social boundaries, allowing him to do and say things that would get other guys slapped or worse. "Hartman would go further than anybody," Stack says. "But nobody's getting away with that other than Phil Hartman." Groundlings co-star Edie McClurg laughingly recalls how Phil "loved to grab my tits." And because only the ladies' dressing room had a sink, Phil would "saunter in and start washing up. And you could always feel his eyes looking down the mirrors to see what state of dishabille we were in. He was a horny guy, but not in a dirty way. He really appreciated women."

Even onstage he retained a certain politesse, making himself the buffoonish target of sexual jokes. For instance, when the va-va-voom-y

Carmen Pluto commented on the .45 caliber pistol Chick Hazard appeared to be packing, he replied that it had previously been a .22. The hapless shtick was a ruse, though, as Phil was never hard up for companionship. For a long stretch, friend John Mayer says, he "had a lot of time to freelance. It was like the old Dean Martin saying, where Dean told a reporter, 'I've never chased women in my life. But the way I look, a lot of them chased me. And I have to confess, sometimes I didn't run fast enough.' Phil never said that, but I'm sure that was him." Which is to say, as Mayer puts it, Phil got "a lot of action." Not that he bragged about it like some dime-store lothario. "I think one of the things that made him charming to the women was that he was discreet," Mayer says. "He was not the kiss-and-tell sort."

Only in retrospect have some friends surmised that Phil's "infatuation with beauty," to re-deploy Lester Brown's description, and his predilection for attractive mates from whom he invariably drifted was more than the mere rakish folly of a man who loved women; it was his Achilles' heel.

Chapter 6

Phil as Kap'n Karl and Paul Reubens as Pee-wee Herman
at Roxy Theatre, West Hollywood, 1981.
(Photo © Abe Perlstein)

C hick Hazard was but one of several standout characters to stalk
the Groundlings stage during Phil's time with the troupe. A
petulant and somewhat effeminate man-child named Pee-
wee Herman—created in a workshop led by Phyllis Katz, developed
in an outside class led by Gary Austin, and skillfully embodied by
Paul Reubens starting in the late 1970s—got his share of spotlight,
too. He was based at least in part on a hack comic Austin had seen at
the Comedy Store stand-up club, located nearby on Sunset. "He
looked like Sirhan Sirhan," Austin says, and he was less funny.

"At first he was incredibly offensive," Austin says of Pee-wee, who
dressed in a slim-fitting light-gray suit, a red bow tie, white patent
leather shoes, his hair slicked like a squeaky-clean schoolboy's. "He was
like a thirteen-year-old spoiled kid. Very aggressive." Pee-wee even

pelted audience members with mini Tootsie Rolls before the character was softened a bit to make him more palatable, and soon he became one of the Groundlings' biggest draws.

"Paul Reubens had such enormous power as a performer that he
was instantly enamored by all the people who worked at the Groundlings," Phil later said, stumbling over syntax. "Pee-wee was just one of
several fully realized characters that Paul could do. His gift was beyond
anything I've ever seen." As both Phil and Reubens were drawn to talent, they soon became friends as well as artistic cohorts. In many ways
they were yin and yang. As easy as Phil was to work and get along with,
Reubens was more temperamental and could be off-putting. They complemented each other well—for a while, anyway. "Paul's concerns
were visceral and Phil was able to stand back," Tracy Newman says.
"He didn't have that visceral anger."

In late 1980, Groundling Cassandra Peterson (who would become
famous as Elvira, Mistress of the Dark) introduced Reubens to her
producer and writer friend Dawna Kaufmann. Kaufmann had showbiz contacts galore. When a late-night sketch-music concept she had
developed for CBS fell through, she envisioned staging "a big kiddie
comedy show for people of all ages." But she needed someone to host
it. After seeing Pee-wee in action on Melrose, where at first he performed short interstitial bits between set changes, she thought he was
the perfect man-child for the job. They met for dinner the next night
to talk further, and talk soon turned to action. In December 1980,
aided by what Kaufmann says was an $8,000 loan from Reubens's par-
ents (Reubens himself has confirmed *a* loan but not the amount), they
began the process of casting and work-shopping their new venture—
what Kaufmann described to *Inside Pee-wee's Playhouse* author Caseen
Gaines as a "live pilot" they hoped would catch the eyes of industry
muckety-mucks and become a weekly late-night series. Phil was the
first to come aboard, as salty dog sailor Kap'n Karl—named after
Kaufmann's father.

One night in Kaufmann's apartment he sang a ditty that became the gruff-but-lovable pirate's signature tune: "Oh, a sailor travels to many lands/Any place he pleases/And he always remembers to wash his hands/So's he don't get no diseases!" Then and there, she knew they had the beginnings of a hit. Of course, Kaufmann and Reubens needed more than just Phil to flesh out Pee-wee's maniacally magical world. "Paul knew he needed help onstage," says Kaufmann, now a true-crime journalist. "He couldn't do the whole thing by himself." Fortunately, their future cast was all in-house. Forsaking his trademark physicality for life in a box, John Paragon came aboard as Jambi the Genie. Additional players included Edie McClurg as Hermit Hattie, John Moody as Mailman Mike, and Lynne Stewart as Kap'n Karl's dream girl—"the most beautiful woman in Puppetland"—Miss Yvonne. Phil did double duty as the voice of Mike's puppet pal Monsieur LeCroq.

Offstage, Kaufmann says, she and Phil began seeing each other casually, and Kaufmann sometimes hung out at his home in Sherman Oaks. On one memorable occasion, Phil insisted on showing her his "gun collection," which then (according to records) included only one registered model: a Colt .45-caliber pistol purchased in August 1980. At first Kaufmann thought he was kidding, because Phil leaned left politically and guns seemed anathema to his liberal viewpoints. But he wasn't kidding at all, she says, and even suggested they visit a firing range together. "He was really delighted about it, bragging. If I was a gun nut, I probably would have said, 'Hey, cool. What does this one do?' But I just got so scared and weirded-out that I said, 'That's it, I'm never going to spend another night here.' And I never did." They stopped dating in short order.

Promoted via funky posters and flyers created by now renowned artist Gary Panter (who was also in charge of Pee-wee production design), midnight performances of *The Pee-wee Herman Show* began on

February 7, 1981, and continued on Fridays and Saturdays at the Groundlings Theater for several months. In those opening weeks especially, Kaufmann says, the room was often heavily papered. Which is to say tickets were given away, always strategically, to celebrities and anyone else in showbiz who might be in a position to help raise this unique (if unproven) venture to the next level. One night Martin Scorsese and Robert De Niro (then shooting *The King of Comedy*) were in the crowd, the next Penny Marshall and George Carlin. For many of the show's actors, including Phil, it was the greatest exposure of their careers.

"[T]here would be twenty or thirty people in the audience for the [Groundlings] late show, and during that show the lobby would fill up," Reubens later told the *Hollywood Reporter.* "'Cause my show was sold out. We had a waiting list of hundreds of people. It created a little bit of an awkward situation for me within the Groundlings because I had this extremely happening and successful show and we still weren't selling out the late show."

While Reubens and Kaufmann worked on a script with director Bill Steinkellner, Phil and his cohorts contributed ideas and honed their onstage personas. "Phil improvised his scene with Paul, Lynne improvised her scenes," Paragon says. "I improvised my scenes. And we helped write each other's parts. It was very collaborative. There was no jealousy or envy. There was no competition." In a 2004 story for *L.A. Magazine,* Reubens grew wistful when recalling that simpler time. "The thing I remember more than anything," he said, "was sitting in my ratty car—just me, Phil, and John Paragon, the three male stars of the show, on top of the world, talking and laughing and fantasizing and projecting about what would happen soon."

In the spring of 1981, when *The Pee-wee Herman Show* had outgrown its Melrose incubator, production shifted to L.A.'s famed Roxy Theatre on Sunset Boulevard, where the public was welcomed, actors were paid a handsome $25 per night, and the next several months saw plenty of packed houses. Now the stakes were getting real. As a result, some of the show's principal cast members say, the enterprise became more businesslike and Reubens along with it. But he never messed with Phil, whom Paragon says possessed "amazing strength" and was "probably the only person who ever stood up to Pee-wee." Others agree. Aside from having had a successful career in graphic design—one he could fall back on should this acting thing cave in—Phil quickly became a central player in Pee-wee's world. "He really was too important for Paul to mess with," says Kaufmann. And because Reubens "couldn't alienate him," Phil had more leverage. When Phil missed a show one evening and Edie McClurg's brother filled in, Kaufmann says, he knew all the lines "but you could just tell the energy, the humor, the twinkle wasn't there. And so it wasn't an easy role to assign to someone else." Gary Panter's now ex-wife Nicole—then a punk world denizen and budding impresario—sensed it as well. "Phil had other irons in the fire that looked like they were going to go somewhere. That's what I think gave him the backbone to not give a shit about what Paul thought." Hired as the show's unofficial "cool consultant," Nicole also played the part of Pee-wee's friend Susan. "Paul's leverage with people had to do with, 'This is the show that's going to make you,' and I don't think Phil ever believed that."

Although receipts from the Roxy extravaganza barely covered costs, Kaufmann says, the popular production kept on keeping on in hopes that a tipping point was near. And soon enough, it came. Reubens and his handlers at the Agency for the Performing Arts (APA) struck a deal with HBO to film closing night with multiple cameras for the still-nascent cable network's comedy series *On Location*. Marty Callner, a rising star in the music video and live comedy realms, was brought in to direct. Kaufmann was wary. "The whole idea was to run it for a long time and keep running it until we had an agreement as to where [on television] we were going to do it," she says of her vision for a late-night kids' program for adults. Not only did Reubens effectively quash that scenario with his HBO arrangement, Kaufmann and others contend, he served associates far smaller pieces of the Pee-wee pie than had originally been promised. Kaufmann says she was supposed to get 5 percent of the proceeds from anything Pee-wee-oriented that emanated from the Roxy show. Phil and other principals were to have a 3 percent stake. "For as much as I loved Phil, he would barely stand up for himself," Kaufmann says. "He did not stand up for *anyone* else. And anyone will tell you this. He never, ever, ever stood up for someone else. He just took the path of least resistance."

Only years later would Phil grouse publicly about his allegedly shabby treatment, and only in the sparest terms. "There was a lot of fucking disappointment among all those people that worked so hard and tirelessly and got credit taken away from them for their contribution to making Paul Reubens a star," says artist Richard Duardo, who did some artwork for the Roxy show with Gary Panter. "And Phil, for one, was hurt profoundly, deeply. So was Gary. Paul hurt the core group that really propelled him."

Not long before Pee-wee and his gang of adult adolescents stormed the Roxy, Phil had begun dating a fiery woman who'd soon spur him to give matrimony another try. Her name was Lisa Strain (now Strain-Jarvis), a vim-brimming, self-possessed free spirit of twenty-three. She then worked as the personal assistant to a real estate developer and was, by her own admission, a handful—though not, she thought, in a bad way. They first encountered each other at a restaurant and music venue called Madame Wong's in L.A.'s Chinatown district. "Can I dance with you?" Phil asked her, wiggling anxiously as she boogied solo. His manner was so genuine, his tone so eager that she couldn't say no. "Dance," she told him, and he did. When he'd had enough, Phil thanked her for the opportunity and returned to his friends. At closing time, while the band packed up its gear, Phil spied Lisa sitting at a table and again approached her. But when he asked if he could walk her to her car, Lisa declined. Having arrived with one of the musicians, she thought it only appropriate to leave with him, too. Phil, however, succeeded in procuring her phone number, which she spoke aloud for lack of a writing implement. Phil said he'd remember. She was sure he'd forget. To make certain that didn't happen, Phil chanted her digits all the way home and rang her the next day.

During their two-and-a-half-hour conversation, Phil asked Lisa out and she assented. He originally wanted her to accompany him to a wedding (Duardo's) that coming Saturday in Santa Barbara, which struck her as too strange for a first date, so they went for sushi instead on Friday. "I remember the minute my heart opened to him," she says. "We were driving up to this sushi place on Pacific Coast Highway and he got out of his car to pump gas and he left his wallet open on the seat. And he had his passport or some kind of picture of him as [a kid] when his family had emigrated from Canada. And I just fell in love with that little guy. When he got back in the car I said, 'When was this?' And he told me the story, and I said, 'Oh, my God, what a little baby you are, it's darling.' He was just so dear." After Phil dropped her off, he went home to Sherman Oaks and threw what he told Lisa was "the most amazing *I Ching*" called "The Marrying Maiden." Oddly, for something Phil characterized as "amazing," it symbolizes a younger woman under an older man's guidance who enters the relationship as the man's mistress or slave. As an Internet sage explains, "It is not the happiest period of your life. Circumstances dictate the terms. There is no freedom of action. No joy and satisfaction. You'll have to sacrifice your desires for the sake of duty, or simply follow someone else's will."

The next day, despite Lisa's initial misgivings, they headed for the wedding in Santa Barbara. Things moved fast from there. A couple of weeks later, Lisa lost the lease on her apartment and, at Phil's invitation, moved into his modest abode at 4656 Norwich Avenue in Sherman

Oaks, whose $265 monthly mortgage he paid with earnings from voice-over work and proceeds from his graphic design projects. More romance ensued. "Phil was glamourized by people," Lisa says, using Phil's term for what amounted to a state of bewitchment. And he was definitely, hopelessly glamourized by her. (Phil marveled about Lisa to his co-star Lynne Stewart: "She doesn't have an ounce of body fat!") And although Lisa's fierce independent streak sometimes left Phil wondering if she felt similarly, she was strongly attracted to him as well. "I was lovestruck," she says. "And I wanted to be in love." For his thirty-third birthday, in late September 1982, she surprised her beau with a helicopter trip to Catalina Island, where they stayed in "some dump" and had a swell time. Phil's enchantment with the destination continued to grow. As he marveled to one interviewer in the 1990s, "You just can't believe how beautiful it is."

In their bliss-filled courting months, though, Lisa was the object of his most intense affection (private and public) and he of hers. Nicole Panter recalls the lovey-dovey duo's rather aggressive canoodling at the wedding of a mutual friend in Palm Desert. "They were pretty overtly sexual with each other all over the place," says Nicole, who was accompanied by her then-husband Gary. "Lisa was in a Victorian-style dress that one is meant to wear slips and petticoats under. But she wore nothing under it—and it was a very sheer dress. And I remember Phil turning her around and saying to Gary, 'Look at that ass!' You could totally see her ass. I thought, 'If I were the bride, I would send someone out here and ask her to put on something'—because it was definitely going to deflect attention from the bride. But you could tell they were both in a sort of full-on happy exhibitionist mode, which was kind of amusing. I'm just glad it wasn't my wedding."

Phil and Lisa—whom he nicknamed "Royal" or "Royal Boom" or "Royal Boom the Electric Peach," after the name of a company (Royal Electric) that was emblazoned on a vintage bowling shirt he bought for her—expressed their mutual adoration in love letters, too. Sometimes Phil, whom Lisa nicknamed "Plaz," decorated his gushy missives with silly doodles—of hearts or little cartoon characters or a nude couple copulating after they'd lost weight and become sexy-buff. (Phil was always on the lookout for new ways to stay in shape.) In one, he called her his "electric peach." In another he penned a cosmic ode to her awesomeness.

Phil proposed to Lisa in late summer of 1982. He had asked her repeatedly, if informally, for months, but Lisa thought they weren't ready. Finally and suddenly, she changed her mind. "If you asked me to marry you, I wouldn't say no," she told him one day as they motored down L.A.'s 405 Freeway. Pumped, Phil tore off at the next exit, stopped the car, and asked for her hand. No ring, no fanfare. He then did a numerological evaluation to determine the best wedding date, which turned out to be December 18. It was set.

Letter from Lisa to Phil on his thirty-fourth birthday, September 24, 1982:

My darling my love,
This is the last birthday you'll spend as a single man. To link my arm in yours, my life with yours is a sublime joy, a summer holiday. I know our love will be as the wind on a lake like this.

Sometimes our sails will fill & we'll speed off on a brisk current. Or it will be balm: soothing cool & serene. Whatever we have, it will be good because we give our goodness to each other. I'm so happy with you. So happy. . . .

So, happy birthday my precious & may Jehovah give us thousands more together.

I'll love you forever,
Lisa

With Dozier as best man, Phil and Lisa dressed formally (Phil in a black tux with tails, Lisa in a form-flattering sleeveless white dress) and wed in a small backyard ceremony at the home of a friend on Chandler Boulevard in Sherman Oaks. Rock photographer Henry Diltz shot video of the nuptials, and a two-day honeymoon in Santa Barbara followed. Early the next year, on January 30, family and friends gathered again on Chandler for a larger reception—a "dancing brunch," as Phil and Lisa dubbed it in a one-page invitation that was adorned with tiny cartoon cupids and 1950s-style images of couples in love. "Flamboyant attire" was requested, and a recording of the newlyweds' vows was shown on a television for anyone who cared to watch.

Phil continued to perform with the Groundlings on weekends, which always improved his mood and energy level. After being onstage, Lisa says, "He was really high and really happy. And he'd have to go eat something really bad. Like, he'd have malts and cheese chili burgers at one o'clock in the morning." He also kept working on graphic design projects and did occasional radio and TV spots (the most significant being a local ad for Toyota wherein he played the well-coiffed scion of a rich old woman). Lisa, meanwhile, created neon installations and freestanding wood sculptures. They made quite the artsy pair. To earn a healthy bit of extra scratch ($2,500 a month, she says), four nights a week Lisa waited tables at the Hollywood hotspot Restaurant Muse on Beverly Boulevard. A scene that buzzed with showbiz somebodies, Muse was what one former employee described as "the quintessential Los Angeles restaurant of the '80s. All white inside with gray booths and banquets, gray industrial carpeting on the floor, polished concrete in the bar area, and an amazing tank of tropical fish over the bar. Windows up high on the street side so it had a fairly dark interior during the day. An immense metal sculpture by Jonathan Borofsky hung from the ceiling and dominated the dining room." Lisa's earnings helped pay the mortgage and resupply the bathroom with "bum wad," Phil's name for toilet paper, the frequent shortage of which caused him to whine. He forbade Lisa from using his special shampoo, too, because Phil was "horrifically cheap." "We never shared money," Lisa says. "We always had separate accounts. If you're keeping all that apart, you're not really committed to the person, you're not there for them hundred percent."

In the middle of a Muse shift one evening, Phil phoned Lisa at the restaurant. He'd soured on acting, he told her, and had decided to resume his previous career in graphic arts. (It wasn't the first time he'd talked of tossing in the towel and it wouldn't be the last.) Lisa couldn't believe it and eventually talked him off the ledge. "Over my dead body," she told him. She would pick up extra serving shifts, get a third job—whatever it took to keep him doing what he did best, what she was *sure* would make him a star. Her bolstering, she says, also took the form of constructive criticism that pulled no punches. He needed to take acting lessons, she advised, and learn how to bare his soul—to be *real*. Not only would it improve his psychological health, it would make him more professionally viable. At the Groundlings and elsewhere, Phil tended to play arch characters that often bordered on, and risked devolving into, caricature.

His support for her theatrical aspirations, Lisa says, was far less enthusiastic. When she expressed a desire to begin acting—maybe even join the Groundlings—Phil was firmly and vociferously against it. "He was very, very disturbed about my wanting to be anywhere in a world where there'd be young guys around me," she says. "Very possessive, but not in a jealous way."

Then again. . . .

"I really embraced the marriage and that partnership," Lisa claims. "And I was completely loyal to him. But he was jealous. He was really jealous. I remember him yelling at me in the car, just screaming at me on New Year's Eve a month after we got married, because I had been talking to a guy I'd gone to high school with. He wasn't even a boyfriend or anything. But when I saw him, it was fun, and so

I spent probably forty minutes talking to him at this really boring party. And when Phil and I got into the car [afterward], he just freaked out about how I'd embarrassed him and how I was with this guy all night and blah blah blah. I'm like, 'You are nuts. What's wrong with you?'"

Old-fashioned in many respects and, Lisa thinks, "a reluctant eighties guy," Phil also became flustered when she ordered for both of them at a restaurant, or strutted her stuff with such sizzle that heads swiveled. And though he could burn up a stage like nobody's business, Phil was otherwise subdued at home—the opposite of his spunky bride. "He was very boring to live with," Lisa says. "He was brilliantly funny, but he didn't want to do anything or go anywhere. His idea of a great night out was to go to Häagen-Dazs and get an ice cream and then drive up Ventura Boulevard and look at old cars in a lot. I was thrilled. *Thrilled*."

She gently needled, trying to coax Phil out of his shell: *Hello! Hey, mister, what'd you do with my husband? Hey, mister, is my husband in there somewhere?* Eventually sex all but ceased because, Lisa says, "I was just too demanding." A poor excuse, she was sure. "I mean, come on! I'm a bodybuilding firecracker, adorable, 112 pounds of solid muscle. And I'm a punk rocker. I'm wearing miniskirts and tights and handcuffs in my ears and stilettos and vintage clothing and spandex everything and rubber skirts. That was the scene then and I embraced it. Not in a way that looked trashy; I always looked cute. But I was definitely a little sexpot. And it freaked him out. Of course he wanted it, but when he got it, it freaked him out. I overwhelmed him."

Phil let that be known—to Lisa and others. One day, as he and fellow Groundling Tim Stack sat in a theater board meeting together, Phil began talking (apropos of nothing) about his carnal tribulations—but in such a way that his genuine concern came off as flip. "I don't know what to do," he announced in a Charlton Heston–like voice, bringing the session to an extended and welcome halt.

"Lisa wants to have sex eight, ten times a day! I need breaks. I like to watch television. I enjoy *The Jeffersons*."

The more Phil ignored her, the more Lisa sought solace in work.

"He had sublimated his sexuality into his career—period," she says. "He was a person without a high libido to begin with, and that's normal. A lot of people don't have a really powerful libido. Big deal." He was also, she adds, "kind of an obsessive eater. So if there was free food, he had to have it, no matter [if] he was hungry or not. And that came from being a hungry kid. He had kind of an insatiable quality [regarding] certain things. Certainly when he wanted sex, he wanted sex, but when he didn't you couldn't get him to."

Sexual incompatibility was only part of their problem. Lisa's need for constant engagement, Phil grumped, was getting on his nerves and distracting him from creating new material. "You just need to entertain yourself," Phil told her. "Stop bothering me. You need to have a life." But they were married, Lisa shot back. It was supposed to be *their* life. *Together*. Phil had sold her a vision of them as Katharine Hepburn and Spencer Tracy, Claudette Colbert and Clark Gable, William Powell and Myrna Loy. They were going to be a Hollywood power couple with "this snappy, jazzy life." But when would it start? Would it *ever* start? Phil's extreme distance felt "emotionally abusive." Lisa was "insatiable," he snapped. "A black hole." Nobody could make her happy, so why didn't she just stop bothering him? Lisa told him, "Be careful what you ask for. Don't push me too hard, because I *will* go."

Phil was sullen, told her she never really loved him anyway. But his refusal to argue or even to talk about issues drove Lisa crazy. He never wanted to make waves. *Ever*. Consequently, untended molehills became unscalable mountains. "One time we were arguing about a word and I was right, because I'm a word freak," Lisa says. "So I jumped out of bed naked, went into the living room, grabbed this giant dictionary, and came back into the bedroom. And I was standing there with this huge book in my arms, and I looked up the word and I read it to him and he goes, 'Yeah, so what.' And I was so mad that I threw this huge dictionary at him and hit him in the head. Because he was so *infuriating*! He would just make you go *grrrrr*. 'I can't be married to you anymore,' he'd say, and then he wouldn't talk to you. He'd just go into the bedroom and go to sleep.'"

In Lisa's mind the death knell of their marriage sounded only a year into it, on a trip in late 1983 to celebrate their first anniversary. Here they were, back in lovely Santa Barbara, with a gym-toned Lisa romp-ready in stockings, garters, bikini underwear, a push-up bra, and high heels. "I remember he was lying on the bed and I climbed up on it and stood over him," she recalls. "And he said, 'Could you just stop?' I said, 'Yeah, I can stop. I can stop altogether, actually.' And that was it, really. We lasted probably another six or seven months." That New Year's Eve, even as they smooched at midnight, she knew it was only a matter of time. Aptly enough, the final verse of that New Year's staple "Auld Lang Syne"—an ages-old tune by Irishman Robert Burns that Phil always said was his favorite—summed up their situation pretty well: "We two have run about the slopes/and picked the daisies fine/But we've wandered many a weary foot/since auld lang syne."

Chapter 7

Phil as Chick Hazard, Groundlings, early 1980s.
(Photo by John H. Mayer)

J ust as his marriage to Lisa was disintegrating, Phil's career was improving. In 1981, on the advice of Tracy Newman, he'd signed with the William Morris Agency—first as just a voice-over client—and soon began landing more commercial jobs as well as bit parts in films. Until late 1986, his screen credits alternated between Hartmann and Hartman. "We were living together and playing around with numerology," Lisa says, "and he had always been interested in possibly changing his name." For one, Phil thought Hartmann with two n's looked too Jewish and wanted to avoid any hiring bias or pigeonholing that might hurt his chances of getting work. He also told Lisa that he'd been shuffling letters in his name to manipulate its numerology value and thus affect his professional fate. By dropping the second N, he discovered, he'd go from a five to a three, which represented the pinnacle of creativity.

In late 1983, having shifted his focus to writing rather than acting, Phil began working with Michael Varhol and Reubens to dream up and script a future Pee-wee Herman movie. Reubens's first stab (with Gary Panter) had tanked at Paramount, but Warner Bros. showed interest and paid a healthy advance that was split three ways. Phil wrote in a short note to Lisa:

Our movie deal came in! 150K!! Front money right away!! I LOVE YOU! Ya Big Sweeter.

Converging at Reubens's home, a converted garage in L.A.'s Miracle Mile district furnished (as Varhol remembers it) mostly with cardboard packing boxes, the trio brainstormed by writing ideas on three-by-five index cards and tacking them to a wall: Pee-wee as an astronaut; Pee-wee as a magician's assistant. Early in 1984, the guys moved into offices rented for them by Reubens's manager Richard Abramson. Owing to his ongoing romantic travails—he and Lisa were legally separated in early February—Phil often found it hard to concentrate.

Letter from Lisa to Phil, early 1984:

Plaz—

I don't know what to suggest anymore but separation. You tell me you love me. You tell everyone else too, but I feel like a prize Dalmatian you leave out on the porch. You call me a "black hole" and I am too demanding when all I want, have ever wanted, is my husband to take pleasure in me who wants all the passion we can have and then too is sufficient without me. I need to be your true partner. I need to "dive in." You accuse me of ratcheting things up—I agree. I would rather ratchet to the top and fall than piss around in the middle going nowhere. Perhaps a pause is what we need, a stopper in the stream that will allow the water to fill up, father to flow over or push aside the obstruction we feel. Please think about what we need. Not what we want. If we return to the source as the "I Ching" always talks about, we can find fresh water, a new well.

We need simplicity and joy—it's all gotten so dark and muddy.

I know you resist this—Please don't for us.

If we can't find a way to enjoy our lives together, I don't want to continue. I feel as if I am letting go in a way. That breaks my heart, but it is happening. I am tired. I won't cease loving you. I will relegate it to the part of my soul where all my other disappointments live.

I will grieve but I will move on.

This is not a threat or an ultimatum. It is the painful reality I face.

I love you,

Me

Please talk to me ♥ *Bloonda.*

In Phil's letters to Lisa, which were shorter and in which he addressed her as "Bleentl" and "Bloonda," he expressed his desire to be with her and his concern for her happiness.

They were soon separated, Lisa had begun seeing another man, and Phil was crushed. As Varhol remembers it, he came in one day and, "in a very low-key way," announced his impending divorce. "It was very surprising to me," Varhol says, "and it affected Phil's concentration at that point in terms of the writing process." Phil never talked about it after that initial revelation.

"He was a beautiful soul," Lisa says. "That was the hardest thing of all: leaving all of that irreplaceable specialness because the frustration of getting it only in glimpses, like a sunny day in Scotland, was too much." She dropped ten pounds from her already "too-skinny" frame after they parted, and had plenty of crying jags inside the walk-in freezer at Muse during her shifts. Though Phil was equally upset over the failure of his second marriage, his private anguish was hidden in public.

At Pee-wee Central, however, his distractedness was becoming a distraction. "Paul would call me up during the writing [of *Big Adventure*] and complain about Phil a lot," Varhol says. "When the three of us were doing the rewrite, I was really into it and Paul was into it and Phil would sometimes be sort of tuned out, sort of daydreaming. And sometimes Paul would go, 'What do you think, Phil?' And Phil would be caught off-guard." Even so, his presence was far more advantageous than detrimental. Besides his creative contributions, Varhol says, Phil had a grounding effect on Reubens. When the mercurial performer flew off the handle or into the ether creatively, Phil calmed him down and tugged him back to earth. "I remember one time, Paul was talking about how he couldn't wait to get famous so he could start hanging out with Spielberg, and Phil and I were looking at each other and rolling our eyes," Varhol says. "When Paul got into this world domination phase—and he was deadly serious about this—Phil did a very funny Ed McMahon voice and routine. 'Right you are, Mr. Herman! You are correct, sir!' And he would break Paul's spell." Phil's Pee-wee impression, which Varhol deems "the world's worst . . . a mealymouthed Uriah Heep Pee-wee," was similarly effectual in leveling with laughter. Quietly, Phil's resentment of Reubens grew.

In early May, after settling on a Pee-wee movie story line that involved Herman moving in with his rich uncle and saving the town's swimming hole, Phil, Varhol, and Reubens pitched the concept to Warner Bros. head Robert Shapiro, who hated it. "He wanted to fire us on the spot," Varhol says. "As a matter of fact, after Paul did the pitch, Shapiro walked out of his office for, like, ten minutes. When he came back, he said, 'Paul, I want you to stay, and you guys can go'—

meaning Phil and I. So I walked out to the parking lot with Phil and said, 'What do you think just happened?' And he goes, 'I think we just got fired.'" Fortunately, that wasn't the case. Varhol says Reubens fought for the project and them in the process, winning his team another chance to produce something the boss wouldn't loathe. "Paul was very astute about certain showbiz things," Varhol says. "And I know that if Paul thought we were going to get fired and he would have to start from zero again, it wasn't really in *his* best interest, either."

So the tweaking and brainstorming continued, eventually yielding a premise that stuck: Pee-wee's super-fancy bike gets swiped and he sets off to recover it. Hilarity ensues. Varhol contends the idea was his. "Paul has described it as a eureka moment that *he* had, and it wasn't that way at all." And it was Phil, he says, who came up with the bike's memorable description: *It's a classic with fat whitewall tires, a sparkling two-tone paint job and options galore. Mud flaps, headlights, a personalized license plate hanging from a hand-tooled brown-leather seat.*

Their pitch green-lit, Phil and Varhol were tasked with penning an early draft of *Pee-wee's Big Adventure* while Reubens embarked on a countrywide twenty-two-city tour with Paragon. Phil, though, was more artistically deferential to Reubens than Varhol would have liked. "Every time I'd make a suggestion, Phil would say, 'Let's wait for Paul,' and I realized this wasn't going to work out," he says. "So we basically decided to hopscotch scenes, where Phil would write some and I would write some. We went through the outline and I said, 'OK, Phil, you write *these* scenes and I'll write *these* scenes.'" Before long, they produced a first draft of ninety-three pages. Upon Reubens's return in early July, he read the script with fresh eyes before the trio revamped it from start to finish.

Perhaps soothingly for the diversion it provided, his break-up with Lisa wasn't the only thing weighing on Phil's mind. Besides the Pee-wee film, he was in early planning stages for an hour-long Chick Hazard show at the Groundlings Theatre. Set at the 1932 Los Angeles Olympics, it was scheduled to run during L.A.'s prestigious Olympic Arts Festival, beginning in June 1984. The wide-ranging, ten-week celebration mostly preceded athletic competitions and featured, as per a *New York Times* account, "more than 400 performances by 145 theater, dance and music companies, representing every continent and 18 countries."

"A basic premise for the Festival is that art is not a form of propaganda but an instrument of truth, an opportunity to put aside differences and rejoice in being alive," festival director Robert Fitzpatrick wrote at the time. "The Festival seeks neither to preach nor to dictate a hierarchy of taste. Participating countries have agreed to this premise. Governments that might have preferred more traditional representatives of their cultures respected the artistic integrity of the Festival and provided substantial support for artists of untraditional bent."

Chick Hazard's road to the Olympics began with Lynne Stewart. Then a member of the Groundlings board, she encouraged Phil to submit a proposal to the festival committee, and the committee (to Phil's surprise) approved it. "We tried very hard to raise the bar," the show's producer, Craig Strong, says. "The production values were much higher than in a usual Groundlings presentation. The period costumes were accurate and funny, but not over the top, and the comedy references were accurate to the period."

It was Chick's, and Phil's, widest theatrical exposure yet, and patrons flocked to Melrose Avenue for an evening of improvised intrigue with a comic twist. More than a way to promote the Groundlings, the production as Phil saw it was a chance to shine individually. Although he drove a black Porsche Carrera convertible (purchased used) and earned a solid living—"Phil always had a little bit more money than everyone else did," Strong says—nearly a decade into his Groundlings tenure nothing momentous had happened in his career. Promoted in part on Phil-designed fliers that featured a be-hatted Chick rendered in black-and-white with a bright-yellow banana gun held near his head, *Olympic Trials: A Chick Hazard Mystery* opened in early June 1984 and ran through mid-August. It was a hit from day one. Directed by Maxwell and staged at the cost of $25,000, its cast of eight supporting players included Stewart, Katz, Mayer, and future *Simpsons* voice actress Tress MacNeille, among several others. "What was great about the *Olympic Trials* production is that it was much more grounded in reality than the [original] Chick Hazard sketches, which were a little more free-wheeling," says fellow Groundling Randy Bennett. "And Phil's research on L.A. in 1932 was so impressive that he could just spew out these facts . . . He knew all of that history." In the four or five weeks of rehearsal leading up to opening night, Strong remembers, drama abounded, mostly involving actor egos. HBO wanted to purchase the rights to their Chick production, and "there was a huge fight among company members because we had not created any contract. And so it was, 'Who owns this material?'" The sale was nearly stopped but finally approved, though not without plenty of contentiousness. Phil himself was "very shy, uncomfortable" during a long contract conversation with Strong at Phil's home in Sherman Oaks.

In addition to the sticky contract business, Bennett and Strong say, Phil had trouble asserting his authority. He was always the nice guy everyone loved—the fun and generous and joshing hail-fellow-well-met. But as the lead actor of and a financial partner in this high-profile Hazard show, there were times when he needed to lay down the law more than he did. "Things would spin out around him," Strong says, "and he didn't want to be the bad guy." As in other life scenarios, Phil dealt poorly with other people's emotions and nearly always shrank from confrontation. "He had the creative sense and he knew how to help get the best out of people onstage, but anything administrative was not his forte," Bennett says. "And sometimes he would [tell people] things that were not possible, so it put the producers and director in a very awkward position." Even before the Olympic festival began, Tracy Newman got the impression that Phil was uneasy about choosing who would and would not be in a scene on any given night. "People would get mad at him for that," she says, "and Phil couldn't have been nicer." Perhaps more significantly, owing to his imploding marriage with Lisa and his ping-ponging back and forth between Chick rehearsals and Pee-wee writing sessions, Phil's attentions were ever more divided and his anxiety high.

Ten days or so before opening night, he decided to take a short leave of absence. "There was nothing we could do without him in the room, obviously, because he was in every scene," Strong says. So they told him he was free to go—with one caveat: He'd check in by phone once a day. With that settled, Phil set off for a two-day writing retreat at Two Bunch Palms resort in Desert Hot Springs. Ensconced there in nature, he recharged his batteries, wrote what he had to write, and headed back to L.A. refreshed and ready. "He really pulled it all together and it all worked," Strong says. "It was really tense, but under pressure he could really perform."

The *Miami Herald*, for one, mostly praised the production:

Though its fluid improvisational nature results in flaws, Olympic Trials *does for '30s-style private eyes what* Little Shop of Horrors *did for monsters.*

The play has every requisite element: The private eye who talks and shoots fast and who drinks too much; the bleach-blond secretary in love with him; the Oriental opium den; decadent rich folks; the good-hearted ex-con. It's also got sensual, melancholy, trombone-dominated music.

The audience gets to supply the name of the victim, the site and method of his or her murder, his occupation, and important clues and

other details that change nightly. Some of the resulting improv is
rough, but some of it sounds as if the actors have rehearsed for ages.

Nonetheless, Phil was soon disappointed to discover, no one who could help him professionally seemed to care.

After the Olympics festival, in addition to his scriptwriting, Phil remained engaged at the Groundlings by way of teaching. Among his students was Julia Sweeney, then a Columbia Pictures accountant with acting aspirations. Her first improv instructor had suggested she repeat the introductory class, so she signed up for another session that happened to be helmed by Phil. "I was in love with him immediately," she says. He was charismatic, interesting, funny—an urbane gentleman like she'd never encountered. He was even friends with his *ex-wife*, Sweeney marveled of Phil's relationship with Lisa post-split. "He was sort of like Cary Grant to me," she says. "So my introduction to him was like this gateway into a world I'd only suspected existed."

Now and then, as rapt pupils hung on his every word, Phil told stories of his past life—including his stint designing album covers for rock legends. "But I have to say, it was not braggy," Sweeney says. "Of course, it *was* braggy. We thought he was really in the business. He was a working show business guy, and I had never been around anybody like that." He was a great teacher to boot, she says, explaining things simply and clearly, and regarded as something of a minor legend in his own time by male and female charges alike. "I think every girl was in love with him and every guy was in awe of him and wished that he was their friend," Sweeney says. "That class was really powerful and really exciting." During one of Phil's most memorable improv drills, students were asked to morph into hybrids of their favorite cartoon characters and close family members who bugged them. "And really funny things happened," Sweeney remembers. "I didn't know you could use formulas like that to come up with funny things. I didn't know there was logic behind it. And in some ways there isn't—it's really instinctive and impossible to explain, yet it's funny. But there are some things that are really tried and true, and he would tell you about those."

And all the while he yearned for something more.

Chapter 8

Phil on his sailboat, early 1980s.
(Photo by Lisa Strain-Jarvis)

In the fall of 1984, as he approached the age of thirty-six, Phil's disillusionment with his dearth of progress on the acting front hit an all-time high and his thespian ambitions were jettisoned altogether. Auditions were soul sucking, he decided, and from a skill standpoint he felt unequipped to compete. "[Y]ou can only go on so many hundred cattle call auditions, and suffer so much rejection, before it takes its toll," he once explained. Though it may have been exasperating at the time, he later seemed relieved not to have been selected as announcer for *The Price Is Right*: "'You win the chain-link fencing, and the meat by-products! Congratulations!' Can you imagine?" But if he could write or co-write a hit, Phil reasoned, doors would open that so far had remained closed.

He remained morose about his second failed marriage, too. Both

Lisa and Phil were "horrid" toward each other for many months after their separation, Lisa says, and they maintained a mutual disdain for several more months after Lisa signed (unwittingly, she now says) papers granting Phil an uncontested divorce that became official on May 23, 1985. But when the anger and resentment subsided, they began talking again. Talk led to sex led to an attempt at reconciliation. They should get back together and have babies, Phil told her. As with Gretchen, he still longed to have kids. That Lisa was now cheating on her current boyfriend with her ex-husband made the situation extra-sticky. "I was living with this other boyfriend and I wasn't happy," she says. "I really missed Phil. I was still really in love with him." With strong reservations, she left her newish suitor and moved back into Phil's house on Norwich. Disappointingly but not surprisingly, in a couple of weeks he reverted to his old ways—the emotional withdrawal, the antisocial tendencies—and all hope was lost.

Lisa wondered: Why was he letting this happen? Couldn't they see a therapist and work things out? She loved him, he loved her, but the situation was beyond horrible. And now they'd brought another person into it, one who treated Lisa well and whose heart she had broken in her naïve belief that Phil could and would change. In spite of their differences and the considerable friction between them, she adored him and Phil her. "We're soul mates. That's just the way it is," he remarked, a bit too nonchalantly for her taste. Not exactly, she replied. Not if they couldn't find a way to mend their shattered bond. So she moved out again and they lost touch for many years.

Sometime in late 1984 or early 1985, Phil hooked up with a movie producer named Victor Drai. It was through Drai—whose films include *The Woman in Red* and *Weekend at Bernie's*, and for whom Phil was writing a dark comedy titled *Mr. Fix-It* (destined for MGM, where Drai had a development deal)—that he met a statuesque blonde named

Brynn Omdahl at a party Drai threw at his Hollywood home. She'd been lamenting that there were "no nice guys in Hollywood," and wanted to find a winner. "She was such a sweetheart," Drai says. And though he knew she had done drugs in the past, "she was a totally straight girl" during that period.

Brynn's given name was Vicki Jo. She had also been Brindon Cahn and, during a short-lived first marriage back in her hometown of Thief River Falls, Minnesota, Vicki Jo Torfin. The daughter of an engineer-turned-father (Don) and a retail shop owner mother (Connie), she had dropped out of high school, done some modeling in Minneapolis, and lived in Arizona before heading out to L.A. (like so many other young and comely women before her) to make it in show business. Early on, she also modeled fashion swimsuits for Catalina Swimwear. ("Think California sunshine," reads promotional verbiage for the century-old company. "The glamour of Hollywood starlets. The smile of Miss America.") By the early 1980s, though, Brynn's career aspirations had stalled and her recreational use of alcohol and cocaine had escalated. A stay at the famed Hazelden addiction treatment and recovery center helped her get clean. One former acquaintance, Hanala Sagal, says she and Brynn began attending Alcoholics Anonymous meetings during that period, some of them at Beverly Hills Presbyterian Church on the corner of Rodeo Drive and Santa Monica Boulevard. The Rodeo meetings, Sagal says, were Brynn's favorite. "That's the kind of meeting she liked to go to. The kind where your eyes wander around to see if there's a famous alcoholic in the room." They also had beauty maintenance in common, Sagal recalls, driving each other to appointments for such minor cosmetic procedures as facial peels. "She was always doing things to herself, like I was, trying to look good and stay young."

When Phil met Brynn, he may well have been at his most vulnerable state in years. His marriage to Lisa had collapsed, his triumphant run during the Olympic Arts Festival had failed to boost his career, and acting jobs were scarce. In light of his anguish over personal and professional shortcomings, the attention from and affections of a statuesque blonde would have gone a long way toward bolstering Phil's deflated self-image. Whatever the reason, he was once again glamourized.

And once again, not everyone was comfortable with his choice of mates. Victoria Bell—Carmen Pluto from the Groundlings—had briefly met Lisa and some of Phil's other girlfriends, all of whom seemed "fun and silly and kind of kooky. So when Brynn came into the picture it was kind of like, 'Hmm, that's a dangerous woman for Phil.' She just didn't seem like the kind of woman that we had seen him attracted to over the years." He *was* attracted, though—and strongly. But their relationship was bumpy from the get-go. A friend of Phil's, actor Ed Begley Jr., remembers inviting Phil and Brynn to the home he shared with his then-wife in Ojai, California, about seventy miles from L.A. They would arrive around noon for lunch and then, that evening, all four of them would dine at a nice restaurant in town. But noon came and went with no sign of Begley's guests. There went lunch. When it got to be around seven P.M., he knew dinner was dead as well. At around nine P.M., Begley's phone rang. It was Phil. Here is Begley's re-enactment of their conversation:

"Ed, it's Phil. Ohhh, I'm so sorry. We were headed there and I couldn't call because it was just too bad. Brynn, this woman I'm dating—we got into a horrible fight on the way there. Horrible! We'd just split up and I had to take her back home. We are, of course, not coming out. I'm so sorry to do this to you, but you have no idea how contentious it was. That's why I could not call."

"Phil, Phil, take it easy. As long as you're OK. I was worried about you on the highway, on that windy road to Ojai, that's all. You're OK?"

"Well, I won't say I'm *OK*. We split up. I can't do this."

"I totally understand. Come on your own whenever you want, Phil. I'd love to see you."

Phil never made it to Ojai, but before long he and Brynn were back together. They weren't done fighting, though—or splitting up before making up and reuniting. As their relationship evolved, a pattern emerged.

Amid Phil's mounting frustration about his seemingly stagnant career, and in the way that only mothers with blind confidence in their progeny can do, Doris Hartmann encouraged her middle child to keep his chin up—everything would work out for the best. She told him other, less heartening things, too. A psychic Phil's sister Martha had visited confirmed it, predicting that Phil would be "very successful." Doris underlined "very." She told him other, less heartening things too, namely that life's clock was ticking and Rupert was "depressed" he didn't know his kids better. Doris, though, knew that neither he nor she could turn back time—that it was "too late to make amends for all the things we should have said and didn't—all the things we said and shouldn't have."

As Doris advised, Phil forged onward. He spoke with a casting boss at ABC, who told him (as Lisa had years earlier) that a return to acting school might be just the thing to help him transcend mere characterizations and find the funny in Phil Hartman. Tony Danza and Ted Danson were playing versions of themselves with great success on *Who's the Boss* and *Cheers*, respectively, and Phil would do well to follow their leads. But he wasn't buying it. Even before Katz had tried to coax him out at the Groundlings, being himself—or even a close facsimile thereof—had never been Phil's forte. As he told the *L.A. Times* in 1993, "I wasn't that secure with myself. I felt vulnerable trying to be anything close to myself on stage or in front of a camera. I felt more comfortable being buried in a person. The deeper the burial, the better." Meanwhile, he watched friends and former colleagues become famous.

Reubens, for one, was already nationally known and about to break big thanks to his tour and multiple appearances on NBC's *The Late Show with David Letterman*. Lovitz, too, was on the rise. In a development that surprised some, Phil's Groundlings mate and recent voice co-star in the Disney animated film *The Brave Little Toaster* was selected to join *Saturday Night Live* during its 1985–86 season. If there was jealousy on Phil's part, Julia Sweeney failed to sense it. More than a few people, though, were puzzled by Lorne Michaels's decision to hire Lovitz over Phil. "I remember one of the times Lorne was at the Groundlings, standing in the back watching a show, and I was standing next to him," Tracy Newman says. "And I said, 'Are you here for Phil?' Because I was watching the show and thinking, 'If I were him, I would [take] Phil.' But he was interested in Jon Lovitz. And I remember thinking, 'What a fool. What a fool.' Not that Lovitz isn't funny. I like Lovitz, too. But to stand back there and watch a guy like Phil Hartman and not see how valuable he would be. . . ." Randy Bennett was also bewildered. "The fact that Lovitz got on *Saturday Night Live* and Phil didn't was an enormous shock. I love Lovitz, don't get me wrong, but come on." Even Lovitz himself was surprised. The very idea of auditioning for *SNL* struck him as "ridiculous," he has said. But Michaels—who says Lovitz first came to his attention in the big-screen comedy *Last Resort*—was obviously impressed by what he saw. So were Al Franken and Tom Davis. As Lovitz later recounted, they came to the Groundlings in search of "a Tom Hanks–looking leading person." Franken even told Lovitz outright, "You were everything we weren't looking for in one person, but you were funny."

Robert Smigel, who began writing for *SNL* in 1985, recalls that when Michaels returned that year as executive producer after a five-year hiatus (in the process taking back control from executive producer Dick Ebersol, who had been charged with fixing the fractured show after a lame 1980–81 season), he was "looking for people who were outside the box. A guy who's going to pick Robert Downey and Randy Quaid and Anthony Michael Hall," Smigel says of the '85–'86 season's individually talented but creatively dysfunctional cast members, "is not really looking for Phil Hartman in that particular year. And he was taking a risk. I think maybe Lorne wanted to challenge himself."

Michaels, though, says Phil could have joined *SNL* if he wanted to. But he opted out. "He wasn't passed over. It was his decision." Not only was Phil still embroiled in his divorce from Lisa at the time, Michaels recalls, he simply didn't want to leave his comfortable life in L.A. for the bustle of New York.

As per Michaels's edict (after a thorough housecleaning and the threat of cancellation), starting the following season (1985–86) there would be more emphasis on ensemble work, and no actor would earn more than another. He also planned to revive the "live" component that he believed had diminished under Ebersol by way of more prerecorded material. "It became a television show," Michaels has said of *SNL* during his extended absence. "There's nothing wrong with it being a television show, but I think it was something more."

Back in Pee-wee land, Phil and his original Roxy cohorts—namely, Lynne Stewart, John Paragon, and John Moody—were relegated to minor on-camera roles in *Big Adventure* (Phil played a reporter, Paragon a movie lot actor, Stewart a Mother Superior, and Moody a bus clerk). But Phil's part in the movie's creation and subsequent box office success (it grossed $4.5 million on opening weekend—enough to cover the $4 million budget—and has to date earned ten times that amount) cannot be underestimated. True, by mid-August of 1985, when *Big Adventure* was showing on nearly 900 screens across America, Pee-wee's profile had risen considerably. And, true, budding director Tim

Burton (then little-known but mega-talented) and composer Danny Elfman (ditto) imparted their respective magic touches. But according to Varhol, *Big Adventure* "couldn't have happened without [Phil] for a number of reasons." His writing was chief among them.

As Phil told radio broadcaster Howard Stern in 1992, "I wrote a lot of the scenes." Of course, since *Big Adventure* was a team effort, it's nearly impossible to pinpoint which ones are Phil's alone. But Varhol remembers at least a few portions that bear his co-scribe's distinctive stamp. Besides the inspired description of Pee-wee's tricked-out bike, Varhol says some of Phil's other contributions include snappy action synopses (e.g., "Pee-wee stands pie-eyed and slack-jawed") and part of Pee-wee's now-famous "rebel" monologue through which he coolly informs his love interest, "There's a lotta things about me you don't know anything about, Dottie. Things you wouldn't understand. Things you couldn't understand. Things you shouldn't understand."

In late October 1985, Phil and Paragon accompanied Reubens to New York, where Pee-wee was slated to host *Saturday Night Live* on November 3. Reubens and his manager, Richard Abramson, had gotten the OK from Lorne Michaels for Phil and Paragon to serve as additional writers. The arrangement was and remains atypical. In contracts finalized afterwards, Paragon and Phil were each paid $1,750 for their contributions. "Pee-wee was really hot and we hadn't done the show yet," Abramson says. "When they said they wanted him to host, I told Lorne that it would be very difficult for other people to write for Pee-wee. It was a specific character; it wasn't like bringing Justin Timberlake on and you could write a few things and put him in different roles. Pee-wee had a specific voice."

On their first day at 30 Rockefeller Plaza, in a conference room that lacked enough chairs for all who were present, Michaels introduced Phil, Paragon, and Reubens to *SNL*'s writers. Being that many of them were Pee-wee Herman fans and the show was Thanksgiving-themed (easy to parody), smiles and laughter abounded. Paragon, for one, felt welcome despite his outsider status. Al Franken and Tom Davis were particularly laid-back and helpful, he says. And Michaels was extremely involved from day one. His TV baby had almost died during his time away, and public opinion was at an all-time low. Critics were especially unkind—one famous headline declared "Saturday Night Dead!"—and ratings reflected the show's shrinking viewership and diminished status. "Many of the cast members and writers seemed nervous," Paragon says, "like they had all been threatened before. I was told that Lorne had a way of punishing and rewarding. He would pull a sketch or replace an actor in a sketch, depending on whether or not they pleased him—like Captain Bligh. My experience was that he was totally hands on and a control freak. There was no doubt about whose show it was."

After seeing Phil in action—he was funny in writing meetings and easy to work with—Michaels expressed his admiration to Abramson. Abramson told him, in effect, "You ain't seen nothin' yet."

In preceding months, Phil's career had begun to gain some traction. Since signing with William Morris, he'd landed minor voice parts on a short-lived TV series titled *The Dukes,* Tom Selleck's hit show *Magnum P.I.*, and an instantly forgettable cartoon called *The 13 Ghosts of Scooby-Doo.* A few small movie roles also came his way, albeit in generally panned flicks such as *Last Resort* (with Charles Grodin), *Jumpin' Jack Flash* (with Whoopi Goldberg) and *Three Amigos!* (shot in Simi Valley, not far from Phil's home, with Steve Martin, Martin Short, Chevy Chase, and Lovitz). Phil's biggest score during that stretch was the animated television series *Dennis the Menace,* for which he voiced George Wilson (as an approximation of Paul Ford's Colonel John T. Hall from *The Phil Silvers Show,* aka *Sgt. Bilko*), Dennis's father Henry Mitchell, and his dog Ruff. He did sixty-five episodes in all. "It was one of those ironic things," Phil told CNN host Larry King in 1993, "where as soon as I quit acting I started getting every part I went up for . . . Because I was relaxed. A casting director and producer can smell the desperation of someone who really needs the job, and I started going on auditions and not caring if I got it. I was relaxed, natural."

Reluctantly, Phil also committed to reprising his Kap'n Karl role—renamed, less quirkily, Captain Carl—for a Saturday morning kids' series Reubens was doing for CBS called *Pee-wee's Playhouse*. The colorful and frenetic program's cast also included Stewart (back as Miss Yvonne), Paragon as the voice of Pterri and Jambi ("Mekka lekka hi mekka hiney ho!"), future big-screen luminary Laurence Fishburne as Cowboy Curtis, and future *Law & Order* veteran S. Epatha Merkerson as Reba the mail lady. The eye-catching set—populated by Chairry the talking chair, Globey the talking globe, Magic Screen, Mr. Kite, and a gaggle of wonderfully odd-looking puppets—was once again designed by Gary Panter (with assists from Wayne White, Ric Heitzman, and many others). Zippy original sound track music came courtesy of award-winning songsmiths Mark Mothersbaugh (of the techno-pop band Devo), Todd Rundgren, and Elfman, among others. Pop star Cyndi Lauper (credited as "Ellen Shaw") sang the *Playhouse* theme song.

"I really had to twist Phil's arm to get him to do the first season in New York," says Abramson, who produced *Playhouse* with Reubens. "He really didn't feel like doing it. I think he felt left out of [*Big Adventure*], but he did create this character [Captain Carl] and he did really well with it. So he came to New York and we all had a good time." In late July or early August, not long after Phil finished work on the Blake Edwards comedy *Blind Date*, he and Varhol flew east together and headed to the *Playhouse* set. When they arrived, tension and temperatures were high. "Both of us couldn't wait to get out of there," Varhol says. "It was hot as hell. And Paul was in a very bad mood. Rich Abramson was pretty nuts at the time, too." Over the next few months,

Phil also became increasingly perturbed—with Reubens in particular. "There clearly was resentment on both sides," Abramson says. "Phil was more of a B-type personality. But there came a point when he was like, 'Why isn't Paul treating me better?'"

The break that had come Phil's way a couple of months prior, in mid-1986, made everything else—the bit parts in movies, the cartoons, the commercials, *Big Adventure, Playhouse*—seem small by comparison: another chance to audition for *Saturday Night Live*. In a nearly eleven-minute set, he earned rare laughs in a typically laugh-less setting (Michaels, in particular, is known to be nearly mirthless when spectating) while showcasing an array of characters. Donning a jauntily cocked fedora and lighting a cigarette, he led off with Chick Hazard ("My life was rapidly going down the porcelain convenience. I could barely afford cigarettes, whiskey, and food. Looked like the food was gonna have to go.") Next came a fast-talking commercial pitchman followed by impersonations of Jack Benny, John Wayne, and Jack Nicholson—as done by "the funniest man in Germany, Gunter Johann." He then did a brief bit about marijuana use among teens before Phil slipped on his dark Nicholson shades and launched into a Jack-enhanced scene from *Hamlet*.

He also brought with him a list of sketch suggestions, such as *Playhouse 90*—"ninety-second dramas that are very intense. Like, 'Johnny! Johnny! The cops are here!' 'Shut up! Shut up, will ya! I'm tryin' to think!'" A "permutation" of the old radio-turned-television program *You Are There*, in which news anchor Walter Cronkite and others hosted from the sites of historical events, was another. He also wished to mock "obnoxious" *Lifestyles of the Rich and Famous* host Robin Leach. Among impressions Phil hoped to perform on *SNL* were Peter Graves, William Shatner, and Charlton Heston. "I can also do any dialect," he announced confidently. "Go ahead, call out a dialect." So someone yelled a request: "French." Phil: "I don't do that." But he did—over-the-top French and Greek. Then he and Lovitz swapped lines as Master Sgt. Ernest G. Bilko (Lovitz) and Col. John T. Hall (Phil). An old Groundlings sketch was resurrected as well, with Lovitz playing a movie mogul named Harry and Phil a washed-up actor named Johnny.

> **Harry:** You're through! Do you hear me? Through! You'll never work in this town again! Your life is finished!
>
> **Johnny:** What's the word on the street?

"I remember Lorne saying, 'He's been in the Groundlings eleven years. Don't you think there's a reason why?' Lovitz recalled in *The New York Times.* "I told Lorne, 'If you like me, you've got to like him. He's better than me. He's a genius.'" Laraine Newman offered high praise as well, telling Michaels that Phil had "the talent of Danny [Aykroyd] without the drama. You can't go wrong." It came as something of a shock to those who knew him, then—particularly in light of his career frustrations—that Phil was deeply ambivalent when *SNL* called with an offer. He was settled in L.A., writing screenplays, living quietly in Sherman Oaks. Being famous or merely better known would change his life drastically. Plus—and this was significant—he half-dreaded moving to New York and diving into *SNL*'s well-chronicled shark tank. "Phil was very laid-back," Lovitz once explained. "He wasn't competitive." Julia Sweeney, who joined *SNL* in 1990, has said that his reluctance may have stemmed in part from age concerns. Phil would be thirty-eight at the start of his first *SNL* season, from a few to a dozen or more years older than his fellow cast members and writers. "I think he struggled with that," Sweeney theorized, "feeling like maybe it was too late or something." But after speaking with the famously flamboyant and straight-shooting producer Joel Silver, who reportedly told Phil he was nuts to pass on this chance of a lifetime, Phil accepted the job. Studio 8H at 30 Rockefeller Center in Manhattan awaited his arrival. "I always thought he was coming," Michaels says, "so perhaps the agony of his decision was overplayed."

Chapter 9

Phil as Frankenstein with Jon Lovitz (Tonto) and
Kevin Nealon (Tarzan), *SNL*, December 16, 1989.
(Photo by NBCU Photo Bank)

S oon after Phil accepted the offer to join *SNL*, he called his
Groundlings mates Craig Strong and Randy Bennett to tell
them he could no longer spend time on a project they'd all been
working to mount in New York: an Off-Broadway play starring Chick
Hazard. The show—titled *The Greenwich Villains*—was to be set in the
late 1940s "Red Scare" era, and fund-raising efforts had already brought
in around $25,000 from family and friends. New initiatives, they
hoped, would raise substantially more. But now Phil had to focus on
the highest-profile gig of his career, which meant putting the kibosh
on Chick's debut off the Great White Way. Then again, it was never
a done deal—not even close. Financial problems stymied it from the
start. "We had given up hope," Bennett says. "No one could afford to
lose this money." Fortunately, Phil had a solution. As Bennett and

Strong remember it, when he sold the rights for a Chick Hazard film to Universal, Phil insisted that his play investors be reimbursed as part of the deal. "This was Phil being a real gentleman," Strong says of a bold move that could have scared off Universal. "He stood up and said, 'I owe it to these people. They've invested in me and I want them to get their money back.'" Adds Bennett, "That's unheard of in Hollywood. And we were so moved." Unfortunately, as Phil himself admitted, he lacked the industry clout to get his Chick film made, and so it sat and sits on the proverbial shelf.

Toward the end of September, NBC alerted the media: Phil Hartman was the next Groundling to join *SNL*. By then he had found a small apartment in Midtown Manhattan for (as Floyd Dozier recalls) around $3,000 a month. Brynn hadn't yet arrived; they had broken up when he left L.A. and Phil was still uncertain if they'd reunite. "He had a difficult decision," says Lorne Michaels, who remembers Phil's "agonizing over whether or not he was going to commit to Brynn. And he came down on the side of 'I love her.'" When Phil flew back to L.A. while *SNL* was on break in early 1987, he and Brynn reconciled and she returned to live with him in New York. At Phil's urging and despite the fact that he was earning the biggest salary of his career, Brynn got a receptionist or secretarial job to chip in for rent. She also signed up for acting lessons.

Besides the shelving of his Chick Hazard play, Phil's joining *SNL* also meant he could no longer play Captain Carl on *Pee-wee's Playhouse*. He was able to shoot only six episodes before leaving it behind for good, and insiders say Reubens was less than thrilled about losing one of his show's most popular characters. It's also worth noting that Reubens himself had tried and failed to get hired by *SNL* for the 1980–81 season; the job instead went to Gilbert Gottfried. "I knew I had to figure something out," Reubens told *L.A. Weekly* in 2010, "or I knew I'd spend the rest of my life being the guy that almost happened."

Years later, and with typical tact, Phil talked about their split. "We had kind of a falling-out way back when, and it's too bad," he said. "Because that part of my life [*Pee-wee's Playhouse*] was a real turning point. We were doing work that changed the look of Saturday morning."

Wistful though he often was in his public retrospection, on at least a couple of occasions Phil revealed his true feelings toward Reubens and the causes of their schism. Here is what he told NBC late-night host Bob Costas in mid-February of 1992, not long after Reubens ran afoul of the law and became tabloid fodder for allegedly masturbating in a Sarasota, Florida, adult movie theater—charges Reubens continues to deny:

He's a complex guy and, I think sadly, a seriously wounded individual, and not just because of his recent problems. But he's hiding some pain. And I guess I only say that so that people might show some compassion for him. But the greatest thing about him is that I think he's a true genius and I think he's a true artist . . . [S]o much of what you've seen of his work has been all him. And in a way, that's his downfall, because he has an artistic temperament, where he wants to be the one who does it all, and he's working in media like film and television that are highly collaborative and where you have to give up control to others—to art directors, to designers, to directors, to writers. And that didn't come easy to Paul, because he has a personality that is more suited to a painter or a sculptor or something.

When prodded by Howard Stern late that year, Phil was less magnanimous. During their exchange, however, he chose his words carefully—almost as if on the witness stand. Telling Stern of their estrangement ever since he began on *Saturday Night Live*, Phil admitted that part of their differences lay in the fact that he felt financially shorted after having been a key part of the Pee-wee Roxy show, out of which grew *Pee-wee's Big Adventure* and the Saturday morning CBS program.

"We had a contract," Phil explained, "that said that we get three percent of whatever happens with this show." Stern was stunned to hear that Phil hadn't made a stink about it in court. But that wasn't Phil.

"The truth is everybody was in love with Paul Reubens and his talent," he said, "and I still remain a great admirer of his.

The truth was also this: although it had sagged in the ratings for a while after Michaels took his five-year sabbatical in 1980 and again in 1985 after the departure of stars Eddie Murphy, Martin Short, Christopher Guest, and Billy Crystal, *SNL* remained a highly desirable destination for comedy types and a far better showcase for Phil's comedic talents. Rather than being stuck as a single character (Captain Carl) week in and week out, he (like Aykroyd before him) became one of the most versatile players Michaels had ever hired. And he was happy for the excellent exposure. "This is Rockefeller Center, New York City, live comedy television," he said in an interview that fall, shortly before his first season began. "There's nothing like it."

Phil's early focus, however, wasn't only on the work but where the work might take him. "There's a lot of heat on me as a writer, and we figured with the exposure I'll get on *SNL*, my acting will catch up with my writing in terms of saleability," he told the *L.A. Times* a couple of weeks before his *SNL* debut. In another baldly careerist statement, he admitted that *SNL* was merely a stepping-stone to create "box office credibility so I can write movies for myself." He was fully aware, though, that regaining popularity with viewers after the program's abysmal eleventh season and several years of prior tumult wouldn't be easy. When he'd visited *SNL* with Reubens and Paragon in late 1985, he said in the *L.A. Times*, "there was rather a feeling of mayhem. This year we feel like there's a better shot at it. But, of course, we're on the other side of being praised."

As evidenced in his voice-overs for commercial spoofs and his portrayal of slick talk show hosts, celebrities, and many other types of characters (frequently minor ones), Phil's knack for transforming himself to suit any context and his usual unwavering commitment to character—no matter how goofy or minor—proved invaluable. "So many people have a tendency to wink at the audience," says Jan Hooks, who was also hired in 1986. "Phil never did that. He played it for blood." A quality that surely helped set the boss's mind at ease. In the wake of a thorough housecleaning that saw the jettisoning of several writers and many members of the prior season's individually talented but creatively mismatched cast—Anthony Michael Hall, Joan Cusack, Randy Quaid, and Robert Downey Jr. among them—he was determined to get things back on track. "Everybody was coming in on eggshells, because word had gotten out that [the show] was very close to being cancelled," Hooks says. "And so Lorne was like, 'Don't you guys embarrass me.'"

Whereas someone like Jon Lovitz was a *type* with limited versatility in terms of the roles he could credibly play (Donald Trump, for instance, would have been a stretch), Phil was an Everyman ("Mr. Potato Head," as he liked to describe himself) who could become almost anyone. "When you are so average looking, when they put a wig on you and some glasses, if you alter your face and your voice in any way, you can look a lot different," he explained during the Costas interview. Lovitz, on the other hand, could "look like people who have his coloring and maybe similar ethnic qualities. But it's more difficult for him to do Phil Donahue than it would be for me. And I love that, because my favorite thing in the world is just doing a lot of different things."

In the late '80s, upon encountering Michaels at a party for *SNL* alum Gilda Radner, Tracy Newman asked him what it was like to have Phil on the show—all the while thinking to herself "I told you so." She says Michaels replied, "Tracy, I don't even have to go into work." The implication, of course, being that Phil was exceptionally self-sufficient and needed no babysitting. Since *SNL*'s inception in 1975—as fans of the 2002 oral history *Live from New York* and other backstage exposés of the program know—that hasn't always been the case. "It might have been a way of saying something nice about Phil," Michaels says of his remark to Newman. "But I said I really did still have to come in to work."

From his *SNL* debut, on October 11, 1986—one day after he popped up on movie screens in the Penny Marshall–directed *Jumpin' Jack Flash*—Phil maintained a remarkably regular on-camera presence and glided smoothly between disparate roles. (He eventually became such a ubiquitous presence that David Letterman half-joked, "I was watching your program one weekend and it was 90 percent you. You were in everything.") Although Phil's first episode was hosted by actress Sigourney Weaver—fresh off of her *Aliens* hit and promoting another flick with Michael Caine—and included music by the pompadoured pop sensation Buster Poindexter, Madonna opened it with an effacing nod to *SNL*'s dismal run of late.

"As you may remember, one year ago tonight I hosted the premiere episode of *Saturday Night Live*. Therefore, NBC has asked me to read the following statement concerning last year's entire season. Ready? 'It was all a dream, a horrible, horrible dream.' And now, to confuse you even further: Live, from New York, it's Saturday Night!"

The first sketch after Weaver's monologue, a mercifully brief relationship bit called "General Dynamics," features Phil in a voice-over role. Hooks and Dana Carvey, both of whom became close friends of Phil offstage, are in it, too. "We were all virgins," Carvey told then *Rolling Stone* contributor Bill Zehme. "Jan, Phil, and I had never done live television." Phil added, "We didn't know whether we were going to fall on our faces."

Next comes Lovitz, reprising his Groundlings character the Pathological Liar, before Phil, Carvey, and Hooks (as dim-witted contestant Lane Maxwell and his perky competitor Marge Keister) return for a game show called *Quiz Masters*. Phil, predictably, plays host Bill Franklin. Owing to his jaunty bearing and stentorian tone, authority figures—announcers, hosts, fathers, teachers—quickly became his stock-in-trade, as he knew they would be from the start. From the first sketch Phil, Carvey, and Hooks did together, Smigel says, he and his fellow writers felt a surge of confidence. The show had been faltering, but now they "knew that everything was going to be OK. The show just felt completely different in the hands of these three people." And overall, Michaels says, it was "a charmed cast." A seasoned one, too. "A lot of them were people who had banged around for a bit. It wasn't their first job. They'd all been out in the world and they knew how great an opportunity this was."

During his debut Phil also appears—in a flashy red suit (from his sartorially swell Groundlings days?)—alongside Weaver as one of two record executives for whom Carvey, as fictional (and freshly rehabbed) British popster Derek Stevens, showcases half-assed, spontaneously composed tunes. "There's a lady I know," he sings earnestly, haltingly over a mournful melody plunked out on an upright piano. "If I didn't know her/she'd be the lady [pause] I didn't know." Ultimately, you might recall, said lady winds up "choppin' broccoli . . . choppin' broccolehhhh." (Interesting side note: When Weaver greets Carvey she reminds him they'd met "at the Roxy in 1981"—the year of Pee-wee.) And while Chick Hazard wouldn't appear until November (in the first of two instances that were the only ones of Phil's *SNL* run) a parody ad has Phil portraying fictional New York Deputy Commissioner Craig W. Doyle. It opens with Phil/Doyle kneeling before a bloody corpse at the scene of a homicide. Its premise: Murder someone in New York City and get an automatic ten weeks in jail—"no ifs, ands, or buts." "So long, sucker," Phil says in his best Big Apple–ish accent (comprised of perhaps 30 percent Chick) as a perp is hauled off to the pokey. "See you sometime in . . . late January."

The next episode of Phil's inaugural season (*SNL*'s twelfth) marked the debut of his first celebrity impersonation: talk show host Phil Donahue. To prepare, he watched tapes of Donahue in action, made drawings of his various postures and gestures, and was heavily coached on the character by *SNL*'s resident writing overlord James Downey. When it came to comedy, both shared the sensibility that less was more.

Wearing a lustrous white wig, large spectacles, and a dark suit, the fake Donahue's play-to-the-cameras emotionality runs the short gamut from incredulous to exasperated as he questions women trapped in exploitive relationships—sometimes with one foot propped on a step, his face aimed downward and a microphone thrust out in front of him. Nora Dunn and Victoria Jackson lend a hand along with Hooks, Lovitz, and Nealon. "You women are exploited because you *want* to be exploited," fake Phil posits to jeers from the studio audience. "If *I* don't exploit you, you'll find someone else who will."

Another fellow Canadian, Rosie Shuster, helped write the Donahue sketch with Al Franken and Tom Davis. (These days, Franken is a U.S. senator; Davis died in 2012.) Even when he first started, she says, Hartman came off as "very smooth and silky, but not in an unctuous way." Neither did he "put a lot of ego into stuff." This confidence born of experience—not to mention the knowledge that he could always go back to drawing were his showbiz career to tank—made him something of a calming presence among excitable and emotional young pups. "You could sit in a room with some of those guys and they would just be completely randy, acting out weird shit," Shuster says. "And Phil would just observe more than being a wild participant. They would be like, 'OK, does this shock you? How about this?' Phil would not be that guy."

"All these guys were young and hungry and, boy, they just wanted to get out there and show what they could do," Hooks says. "Phil had that ambition, but he was a very stately man." Or, as Shuster describes him, "the grown-up in the room." Offstage and on.

In a spoof called "The Crosby Show," co-written by Phil and Smigel, Phil plays paternalistic crooner Bing Crosby opposite guest host Malcolm Jamal-Warner's Theo Huxtable. But instead of reasoning with his misbehaving children in the folksy style of Theo's TV dad Cliff (portrayed on NBC by Bill Cosby), Bing jauntily summons them to the family library for a beating with his belt. As Phil's brother Paul later noted, it was an instance of art imitating life—Bing's *and* Phil's—for to some degree Phil was channeling his father Rupert. "That was exactly how our household was," Paul told Canada's *National Post*. "If you screwed up, you were going to get the belt. And so, consequently, everyone toed a tight line." Phil, he added half-jokingly, was "working out his neuroses on TV."

In what is arguably the episode's best sketch, Phil and Lovitz reprise their Groundlings scene featuring the movie mogul and the washed-up star of shoot-'em-up war flicks—essentially the same scene that had garnered them laughs on Melrose Avenue back in L.A. and at Phil's *SNL* audition. This time around, though, it was polished to perfection. Set in 1947, it was also (as it had been at the Groundlings) an excellent showcase for Phil's throwback sensibilities.

Harry: You're *finished,* Johnny!

Johnny O'Connor: Don't mince words!

Harry: I think you stink!

Johnny O'Connor: Listen, Harry, if you're unhappy with my work, tell me now!

Harry: You're *through,* do you hear me, *through!* You'll never work in this town again!

Johnny O'Connor: Don't leave me hanging by a thread! Let me know where I stand!

Phil certainly had plenty of experience with showbiz rejection, having toiled mightily to gain notice until *SNL* came calling. He also played lame-brained brilliantly, often by melding ignorance with overconfidence to achieve his own breed of a comedic style he claimed to have borrowed from Bill Murray. "He's been a great influence on me—when he did that smarmy thing in *Ghostbusters*, then the same sort of thing in *Groundhog Day*," Phil said. "I tried to imitate it. I couldn't. I wasn't good enough. But I discovered an element of something else, so in a sick kind of way I made myself a career by doing a bad imitation of another comic." But most of all, he adored Old Hollywood—its characters, its rhythms, its look, and its lingo. He was, as second wife Lisa put it, "a reluctant '80s guy" who would have been thrilled to live and work three or four decades earlier during the heyday of John Wayne and author Mickey Spillane's tough-talking fictional detective Mike Hammer. "Phil had an affinity for old movie stars, or at least the perception of what he thought old movie stars were like," says comedy writer Jay Kogen, who saw Phil play many such characters at the Groundlings and worked with him later on *The Simpsons*. "Chick Hazard was like that. And there was a Groundlings improv [sketch] where Phil would come out as a sort of New York–Broadway 1950s bon vivant guy in glasses and a suit, and it felt like he was putting on this thing from the past but bringing it forward."

Above all, Phil relished the chance to do impressions. Not only were they fun to perform, they required full immersion. And, as at the Groundlings, he was never more content than when fully immersed. The experience, he once said, was "like a great natural high." After a sketch ended, he'd "sort of snap out of it, like I'm waking from a dream." Almost from the start of his *SNL* tenure, Phil had "this notion of myself as the man of a thousand faces, or a thousand voices." His approach to them was simple: To the extent possible, he embodied the actual person rather than an exaggerated version. From a physical standpoint, as with Donahue, he studied tapes to glean mannerisms, gait, and other outward details. In imitating voices, which ultimately numbered more than seventy, he paid close attention to the place from which they emanated in his throat. The only ones that eluded him were Regis Philbin's and Johnny Carson's. Both soon wound up in Carvey's expansive canon of caricatures, the latter complemented by Phil's obsequious and occasionally boozy Ed "Hi-yo!" McMahon. "One of the reasons that Dana and I became best friends is because our approaches to the work were so different that we weren't really competing with each other," Phil said. And both were masters of disguise.

Phil and Carvey were personally similar, too. Each grew up with many siblings (Dana four and Phil seven) and each had a tendency to compartmentalize and camouflage his pain or problems so as not to burden others. And despite their often offbeat on-camera personas and proclivity for performing, be it for a crowd of three or three hundred, each was reserved in person and exuded a seemingly natural regular guy–ness. ("In real life if I met you socially," Phil once said, "I think you would find me to be a regular guy and perhaps more modest than you might imagine. But believe me, it would make for a better time for you, because we could take turns being the star of that encounter.") Frugality was also a common trait, though each held different definitions of the term. While Carvey bought the least expensive house among those of his monied friends and lived below his means, Phil liked toys and researched potential acquisitions exhaustively before making a purchase. As his fortunes rose, his collection came to include boats, sports cars, a Harley-Davidson Fat Boy motorcycle, and even a plane. But such purchases required a level of financial solvency that was years off. And even then, John Hartmann says, Phil remained thrifty and "only spent money to avoid giving it to the tax man. Part of growing up poor, I suppose."

Throughout his inaugural season, Phil had little time for anything outside of *SNL*. Although he and Lovitz tried "feverishly" (as Phil put it) to finish a movie script for Lovitz's breakout character "The Liar," life inside the comedy crucible at 30 Rock was even more hectic than usual owing to Phil's contracted dual duties as a performer and writer. "The writers burn themselves out the first half of the week and the actors burn themselves out the second half," he explained years later. Doing both, particularly since he was in so many sketches, proved too exhausting to sustain for more than a few seasons. But his solo creations—the ones that made it on the air, anyway—were few (a handful of Peter Graves parodies and a sketch called "Egg Man" in which Phil stars as a fragile sage-in-a-shell opposite a volatile Kathleen Turner), so maybe it was just as well. According to James Downey, however, Phil wrote relatively little after season one—but kept getting a fatter writer-actor paycheck. It was a source of consternation among his fellow cast members. "It could be awkward, and there were some frayed feelings at the beginning," Downey says. "I think it eventually worked itself out, although maybe never during the time that people were actually at the show. But there was never any issue in terms of personal animosity. It was a sort of principled resentment of the situation and nothing to do with the way Phil acted."

As 1986 came to a close Phil once again appeared on movie screens from coast to coast, this time in the John Landis–directed and Lorne Michaels–produced/co-written comedy ¡Three Amigos! While the vast majority of screen time naturally goes to the Amigos themselves—Chevy Chase, Steve Martin, and Martin Short—Phil and Lovitz enjoy several spotlight moments as yes-men to cigar-chomping movie studio mogul Harry Flugleman (Joe Mantegna in full gruff tough mode). With his clipped dialogue and no-nonsense demeanor, Phil's portrayal of Harry's minion "Sam" is essentially a rehash of Chick Hazard, sans rakish hat and sporting a three-piece suit. Though it did well at the box office, Amigos was a critical flop. Roger Ebert awarded it a measly one star (out of four) and slammed the would-be farce for being, among other things, "too confident, too relaxed, too clever to be really funny."

Phil's part as the brother of Bruce Willis's character in Blake Edwards's comedy *Blind Date,* which marked Willis's big-screen debut, was already in the can and set for release in late March 1987. It, too, would garner more pans than praise. Additional voice-over opportunities arose as well, including a part in Disney's *DuckTales* cartoon series and Hyperion Pictures' animated adaptation of Thomas M. Disch's popular children's book *The Brave Little Toaster.*

At *SNL,* Phil was fast becoming the go-to guy and a utilitarian player extraordinaire even though test marketing sporadically implemented by network suits when ratings slumped consistently showed him in last place among audience favorites. Downey wasn't surprised, attributing Phil's low likeability scores to his dearth of a clearly drawn persona like that of frequent winner Victoria Jackson. That explanation carried little or no weight with the network honchos who paid Phil's salary. "If you like him you can keep him," Downey says was the general attitude from on high. The popular sentiment was equally tepid. "If it had been up to America who was voted off the island, it would have easily been Phil." Michaels, though, wasn't worried at all and says Phil "was fine. The only person who ever scored high, in the first five years, was Jane Curtin. It's not the value system we use here."

On the other hand, his creative cohorts were impressed and appreciative from the start. "He was the ultimate professional," says Jackson. Downey agrees, saying that Phil was especially disciplined among his driven and talented peers. He was always on time, with his lines and blocking memorized, and almost never had trouble with character impressions or finding just the right tone to help sell the hell out of a writer's piece at table reads. Considering that Phil regularly appeared in more sketches than anyone on the show, Downey was doubly impressed. "He would show up at read-through and he'd have a giant stack of scripts in front of him," Downey says. "And the cast members to his left and right would have two or three pieces. But life's not fair."

As season twelve wore on, Phil's value became increasingly apparent. "His skill was that he could kind of catch the rhythm of who he was working with," Michaels has said of his fellow Canadian and frequent companion at *SNL*'s fabled post-show parties around town. "If he was working with Dana, he was completely different than if he was working with Jan Hooks. He would submerge. He could dominate or he could blend in." Like Carvey and Dan Aykroyd, Michaels adds, Phil was "built for the show." According to fellow cast member Mike Myers, another native of the Great White North, Phil "never gave up on a sketch."

"We both kind of came from the same place, which is we loved doing character and came from ensembles," Myers, a former member of Second City in Toronto and Chicago, said in *Live from New York*. "I just worshipped Phil. I looked up to him. I think he's one of the best character-based comedians ever . . . He was extremely, extremely supportive, and hilarious."

Because of that, *SNL* cohort Kevin Nealon has said, he had a bonding effect and kept the whole from crumbling. Nealon's small office was located next to Phil's, which came equipped (like all the offices) with an IBM Selectric typewriter on which Phil often wrote screenplays during lulls in his *SNL* work. (In later years, Phil had one of the show's first personal computers.) Nearby were various implements of his wide-ranging hobbies: an easel for oil painting, an electric guitar and amp for teaching himself to play the blues. Later on, he learned to tie flies for fly-fishing. Brochures were common, too—for boats or whatever else he planned to buy.

Appearing with a slew of starry guests—Sam Kinison, Candice Bergen, Robin Williams, William Shatner, Bill Murray, John Lithgow, Gary Shandling, Dennis Hopper, and others—Phil was initially relegated to largely generic roles: a waiter, a game show host, an emcee, random dudes. He was so many characters, in fact, that special meetings were held with Phil, Downey, the makeup artists, and costume designers to figure out how best to fine-tune the show's rundown in light of Phil's many transformations.

More prominently, besides his early outing as Phil Donahue, Phil appeared as flamboyant Vegas showman Liberace and a cunning Ronald Reagan. The latter employs a doddering public persona to mask his razor-sharp intellect and evil genius. "The Red countries are the countries we sell arms to," he explains to his staff as they sit before a map of the world. "The green countries are the countries where we wash our money. The blue countries . . ." He is interrupted by an aide, played by Dennis Miller, who informs the president that his 11:30 photo op has arrived: a little girl who sold the most Girl Scout cookies. Reagan: "Damn! OK, let's get it over with. Everybody out! Move! Move!"

Assisted by Downey, Franken, and George Meyer, Smigel co-wrote the sketch, whose premise came to him after comic actor Robin Williams played Reagan while hosting *SNL* in late November 1986 (Phil was "Aide #2"). "It was funny, but it was very typical, down-the-middle 'Reagan is doddering,'" Smigel says. "It worked, but it just made me think, 'What would be an original way to do Reagan?'" Several others had tried on the role by then—Harry Shearer, Randy Quaid, and Joe Piscopo among them—with only modest success. Smigel's solution: take the opposite tack and make the Gipper a changeling who morphed from disingenuously folksy and good-hearted to whip-smart and deeply diabolical as circumstances dictated. Other *SNL* writers, including Al Franken and George Meyer, chipped in as well. Thereafter, Smigel says, the old doddering Reagan made a comeback. "I think we all felt like it was the shock of the new and to keep doing it would dilute the impact."

Some of Phil's best sketches were performed with Hooks, his work wife. Throughout five seasons together (Hooks left in 1991), their characters were often married or somehow romantically attached: Jim and

Tammy Faye Bakker; Donald and Ivana Trump; Donald Trump and Marla Maples; Bill and Hillary Clinton. "I loved Phil, even though it was only on-screen," Hooks says. "But that bleeds into real life, too. It was a very unique relationship. I knew what it was like to kiss him and hug him. And even though it was only make-believe, it was real to me for that moment."

It was real to Phil as well. As Hooks recalled in *Live from New York,* "We were doing 'Beauty and the Beast' with Demi Moore and Jon Lovitz, a sketch about the two beasts going out on a blind date. Phil and I were in the backseat of a car making out; he was the Beast, I was the Beauty . . . At the end of it, they cut to the commercial, and Phil had to rush off and be, you know, whoever. But first Phil said to me, 'You gave me a huge boner. Oh God. I've got to run!'"

Because of his steadying influence on *SNL* and his rock-like presence in sketches that helped her deal with bouts of near-crippling stage fright, Hooks nicknamed Phil "The Glue." Or simply, as some began referring to him, "Glue." As Hooks told writer David Bianculli of the New York *Daily News,* Phil's scene-bolstering presence also came from his ability to listen. "[H]e knew how to look you in the eye, and he knew the power of being able to lay back and let somebody else be funny." Perhaps just as important, she says, he was never greedy for screen time and no role was too small. That attitude, which initially worked to his advantage, would also become a detriment.

At one A.M. Eastern, on May 23, 1987, Phil's debut season of *SNL* came to a close and with it his longest stint by far on a non-animated national television show. Ratings were slowly increasing, reviews were more favorable, and the once-sinking ship was again seaworthy. In an Associated Press story headlined "Saturday Night is Alive and Well Again, Thanks to Lorne Michaels," writer Kathryn Baker noted the breakout successes of Carvey and Lovitz, both of whom had achieved acclaim with popular characters (the Church Lady and Tommy Flanagan the Pathological Liar, respectively) and oft-repeated catchphrases ("Well, isn't that special!" and "Yeah, that's the ticket!"). "Waiting to be discovered is Hartman, the mainstay of the show, doing everybody from Reagan to Liberace to Phil Donahue to Peter Graves."

Michaels realized it, too.

"I know the things that are more accessible or have a little more sugar in them that are instantly taken up by the public," he said, "and real brilliant work doesn't necessarily get appreciated until years later. That kind of ability to do five or six parts in a show where you're playing support or you're doing remarkable character work is different than doing [John Belushi's] the 'Samurai' all the time or well-known or more popular characters.

"Phil Hartman," Michaels added, "is the least appreciated—except [at *SNL*]."

Hooks always said that she and Phil were the show's Clydesdales. While "show ponies" like Carvey and Lovitz pranced in spotlight and basked in applause, the Clydesdales often performed less glamorous tasks that were nonetheless crucial to the enterprise as a whole. "I don't think I'm the guy that everybody just wants to fall in love with and cuddle up and take into their homes," Phil admitted. "There's something a little forbidding about me, a little unusual."

But deep down, in his "heart of hearts," he longed to stand out as "something unique in the overall scheme of things." And that day would come—if he had the patience to wait.

Chapter 10

On *SNL* set of "Love Is a Dream," Phil, Tom Schiller,
Jan Hooks, 1989. (Photo © Neal Marshad Productions,
www.marshad.com)

A couple of weeks after Phil's second season of *SNL* kicked off, during the days leading up to a Halloween episode featuring Phil's former Groundlings co-star Cassandra Peterson (as Elvira, Mistress of the Dark; Dabney Coleman hosted), Peterson dropped by Phil's office to chat. While she was there, he showed her a small jewelry box and opened it to reveal a diamond ring. The rock was for Brynn, Phil said. He was about to pop the question. In retrospect, Peterson says, her response to Phil's surprising revelation was impolitic and insensitive: "Oh, God, no!" But he had to be kidding, right? Why marriage? Couldn't they just live together for a while longer before taking the plunge? Phil, though, was deeply offended by Peterson's reaction. "He got up from his chair," she says, "and it's the first time—and, I think, last time—I ever saw him angry. He walked over to the door, opened it and said, 'I think you'd better leave now.'" Peterson's profusion of apologies had no effect; she was banished. "He was very, very unhappy," she says. They lost contact for years.

While Peterson quickly realized her diplomatic gaffe, she stood—and stands—by her sentiments. Brynn just wasn't right for Phil, who "seemed like he got into relationships really, really fast. It seemed like one day he was dating [someone] and the next day he was going to get married. He was head-over-heels and that was the only girl for him. I saw this happen several times. And [with Brynn], Phil had a lot to lose monetarily. I also didn't care for her that much personally. All I can think about when I think of Phil is the word 'authentic.' And my feelings toward Brynn were: 'phony.'"

Peterson sensed that Brynn was intensely jealous of anyone—especially females—she deemed a threat to her relationship with Phil. "But first of all," she says, "I was married. And even if I wasn't, Phil and I were really more like relatives, so she had nothing to worry about. But she was kind of weird and cold. I'd met Phil's other exes and liked them all. With this one, I was like, 'Oh, my God.'"

What Phil failed to tell Peterson, and what may have provoked his ire, was this: Brynn was two months pregnant. Perhaps just as important, as he'd told his Groundlings pal Tim Stack, Brynn was definitely the one for him. This time, it was for real. For good. In private as in public, he made no secret of his feelings for her. "I love you, Brynn. I'm in love with you," Phil gushed in an early romantic letter. "I've never had a relationship that had so much promise for success. I feel like the luckiest man alive that you've chosen me as a mate."

They wed on November 25, 1987, a day before Thanksgiving and during an extended *SNL* break, in a small New York ceremony. Phil wore a light-brown suit and dark tie, Brynn a white dress, white pearls, and a strand of white flowers in her hair. Afterward, a reception was held at an upscale restaurant in Manhattan, and a couple of weeks later Phil headed back to 30 Rock for three more weeks of

SNL before he was L.A.-bound on a month-long holiday break. Among his characters during that stretch were Reagan (giving a movie-themed limo tour of Washington, D.C., to Danny DeVito's puzzled Mikhail Gorbachev), the film critic Roger Ebert (reviewing holiday porno flicks with fellow balcony dweller Gene Siskel), Donahue, and Frankenstein. Throughout his *SNL* run, Frankenstein remained one of Phil's all-time favorites to play. And it was always a crowd-pleaser. In a late 1987 sketch, as part of a three-member panel that also includes Tonto (Lovitz) and Tarzan (Nealon), the nearly mute monster growls two-word answers such as "Fire bad!" and "Bread good!" in response to probing questions from a talk show host played by Nora Dunn. But just as the sketch nears its end, Phil pulls a quasi–Harvey Korman circa *The Carol Burnett Show* and breaks up on camera—a rarity. It's essentially a repeat of the Groundlings episode featuring Chick Hazard and Paragon's big-assed gangster Nick "Cocktail, Chick?" Camaro, only this time on a widely watched national broadcast. Frustrated by his inability to stop laughing, Frankenstein-Phil bolts from his chair, growls, "Fire bad! Fire *bad!*," and bursts through a flimsy backdrop. Moments later, he re-enters via the same jagged hole, still growling "Fire bad!" and lumbers toward the camera with arms outstretched. The outlandish premise is what got him first. He then began thinking about how ridiculous it must have looked from the audience's perspective to see Frankenstein laughing, which made him laugh even more. That never happened again. Not live, anyway. "When I watch the show and I see people do that, it bugs me," Hooks says. "'Cause if we had done that regularly, we would have been fired."

Not long after the 1987–88 season began, Lorne Michaels hired a couple of writers named Bob Odenkirk and Conan O'Brien. While staffers Bonnie and Terry Turner, Jack Handey, Al Franken, and Robert Smigel wrote much of Phil's material, Odenkirk and O'Brien contributed occasionally. In one of Odenkirk's favorite early sketches, initially written by Franken (possibly with an assist from Phil), Phil's character enters a subway car packed with people and tearfully introduces himself as a down-and-out Vietnam vet with two kids to support. Any help would be much appreciated, he says, and then doffs his hat to collect donations. After he traverses one car length, the cap filling with cash and change, his mood suddenly shifts from morose to upbeat. He's not *really* a hard-luck Vietnam vet, but a local actor doing promotion for a play about that very subject. Any donations to support the production would be much appreciated. Phil and his hat make another pass. Upon arriving where he'd begun, Phil undergoes yet another transformation—from friendly actor to a jittery "psychotic" who's having a tough time due to "government cutbacks." "I'm not violent," he assures freaked-out passengers while moving through for collection number three, "just a little crazy." Moments before the sketch ends, Phil morphs again. He's actually (no, *really*) a mugger, and this is a stickup. Hat out, money in, sketch done.

In the original version, as Odenkirk remembers it, a series of different people walked through the car with similar spiels in "pretty much the same order." It was Odenkirk's idea that Phil should do all of them instead—a joke turn that, in Phil's hands, made a good sketch great. The sometimes "very possessive" Franken knew it and gave Odenkirk full credit.

That same year, Phil and Hooks co-starred as a just-released ex-con named Mace (Phil, in a sleeveless white T and boxer shorts) and his motel room hooker (Hooks, in a nightgown and painfully bored expression), who are repeatedly interrupted by a Peeping Tom (Kevin Nealon, who also wrote the scene). Every time Mace tries to put the moves on his comically uninterested date, Nealon shows up outside their window, prompting Mace to loudly and repeatedly threaten him (but nothing more) with murder by gun. Like Odenkirk's subway sketch, it goes on for several minutes past today's typical three- or four-minute cutoff, which usually worked to Phil's advantage. Slow-building scenes allowed him to develop a character more fully, which better showcased his acting chops, which in turn enhanced the over-all comedic effect. "I think he would have done fine in any era of the show," Downey says, "but there were certain things that I'm really glad we were allowed to do—pieces that were long enough [in which] you got to see Phil's subtlety on display."

Across the board, colleagues agree, working with Phil was a breeze. But off-camera and off-stage, few of them could see past his hail-fellow-well-met veneer. "He was always kind of in character," O'Brien recalled not long ago. "The Phil I knew . . . would come in and I'd say, 'Hi, Phil,' and he'd be like [jaunty voice], 'Keep 'em fine, boys!'" Oden-kirk, who was struck by Phil's mature and calm demeanor in a roiling cauldron of twenty-something angst, regarded him as "a dad who was at peace with the world but also a little bit distant—a little bit Reagan-esque in his way. He didn't put his heart on his sleeve all the time for everybody to bat around."

As Downey tells it, O'Brien was also somewhat puzzled by Phil's apparent cluelessness about how the sausage was made. "Conan used to tell me that Phil would call him up and say, 'Hey, Conan, you wanna go skiing?'" Phil's plan: They could drive to Middlebury, Vermont (about five hours away), on Monday and be back in time for read-through on Wednesday. O'Brien then had to explain his job and its responsibilities. As a writer on the show, he told Phil, he was obliged to write sketches. That was how the actors had material come Wednesday. If he and his fellow scribes went *skiing* Monday through Wednesday, those sketches would not exist. Phil: "Oh, so you don't wanna go?"

"[Phil] didn't live to be onstage," Downey says. "That was what he did as a living, and he enjoyed it. But his life was about the whole package, which very much included leisure time."

————

Shortly after Brynn gave birth to a son, Sean Edward, in June 1988, Phil's second wife Lisa—with whom he'd reconnected and begun talking by phone every few months—sent Phil and Brynn a congratulatory card. On its cover was a baby in a high chair illuminated by the light of an open refrigerator. Inside, as Lisa recalls, her handwritten sentiments went something like this: *Dear baby, welcome to the world, you've chosen great parents. I hope you have a fantastic life and get lots of brothers and sisters and everything you ever wanted. And if you ever need anything, you've got an auntie in me.* "Just sweet, totally sweet," Lisa says.

The note Brynn sent to her in response was anything but.

"I got back four pages of the most vitriolic vituperation, threatening my life, telling me if I ever came near her child she'd kill me, calling me every name in the book, telling me I'd better keep my hands off her husband or she'd come and rip my eyes out," Lisa says. "Just insane. She never knew me. She never met me. She never knew anything about me." Alarmed, Lisa called Phil to alert him, but he already knew. Brynn was furious, he said, and he was partly at fault. When Brynn had asked Phil if she and he were soul mates, Phil had answered honestly—too honestly: "No." Instead, inexplicably, he told Brynn that he and *Lisa* were soul mates. When Lisa heard this, she was dumbfounded. Was he stupid? she wondered aloud. Moreover, why was Brynn's rage directed at Lisa if Phil's comment is what sparked it? "I said, 'Not only do you have your head up your ass, your wife is a scary creature,'" Lisa recalls. Phil, though, warned her not to contact him through "them" ever again. He also told her, "You should have seen the letter she *wanted* to write." That gave Lisa pause. Phil *knew* what Brynn wrote *and* he let her send it? Ugh. They deserved each other. Phil should have protected Lisa from that hideousness and didn't. She hung up. They didn't speak again for almost two years.

Phil was nearly forty when Sean was born, and the two formed an immediate bond. When friend and Cassandra Peterson's then-husband Mark Pierson spoke with Phil soon after Sean's birth, they had a "deep" conversation about parenthood and life in general. "He was going through that transition of getting over his hang-ups with his [own] father," Pierson says, "and on the high road with his son. You know, a new beginning." Nonetheless, Brynn was Sean's primary caretaker— and by all accounts a highly competent and doting one—from the start as work consumed more and more of Phil's time. Brynn was there to nurse Sean through his first cold, to feed him and change him and keep him safe in the big city. As Phil's star rose, so did her frustration and resentment.

Throughout his third season of *SNL*—during which, in March 1989, Phil appeared in Chevy Chase's widely panned sequel *Fletch Lives* (Ebert: "[O]ne more dispirited slog through the rummage sale of movie clichés . . .")—he played mostly generic roles (businessman, waiter, soldier, a guy named Dan), including one that paired him with guest star John Larroquette as the co-host of a call-in show titled the *Gay Communist Gun Club*. Phil was tapped to play a Kennedy for the first time, too—Senator Ted—in the sketch "Dukakis After Dark." A parody of Hugh Hefner's ultrahip 1960s program *Playboy After Dark*, it features Lovitz as photo op–challenged presidential hopeful Michael Dukakis in rarely seen Cool Mode as Phil's beer-chugging Kennedy drunkenly hits on Dukakis's wife Kitty (Hooks). Once again, Hooks says, Phil nearly came unraveled. There was also "A Trump Christmas," with Phil and Hooks as Donald and Ivana Trump. Phil played the Donald by knitting his brows and spouting a ceaseless stream of words in a cockamamie New Yorkish accent.

The two shifted gears from comedic to semi-dramatic for a tonally unique short film by Tom Schiller called *Love Is a Dream*. Its title comes from a song that Bing Crosby recorded for Billy Wilder's 1948 film *The Emperor Waltz*. "Not putting them down, but we were around all of those stand-up comics [at *SNL*] who wanted a quick, cheap laugh," says Hooks, who did theater in Atlanta before moving to New York. "And Phil and I were kind of different animals in a way. We were comic actors instead of comics." Drama-tinged roles, therefore, weren't much of a stretch. Featuring top-notch cinematography by Neal Marshad, *Love* was shot on film in a small studio in downtown Manhattan and unfolds like this: After an older security guard (Phil, his face initially unrevealed) lets an elderly woman (Hooks) into a bank vault (located in TriBeCa), she pulls out a safety deposit box and opens it on a nearby table to inspect the contents: a bejeweled tiara and necklace carefully wrapped in velvet. Setting the tiara on her head, she is transported back in time to her younger days, where she encounters an equally spry Phil in an old-time soldier's uniform. Adorned with a red sash across the chest and epaulets on the shoulders, the getup causes him to resemble a toy soldier in *The Nutcracker*. By using only primary hues, Schiller and Marshad are able to approximate a Technicolor effect à la *The Wizard of Oz*. As Phil and Hooks dance to an orchestrated melody in three-quarter time (a small string ensemble plays nearby), both lip-sync to a prerecorded track. Since the original tune features only Crosby's singing, Schiller found a female vocalist to perform Hooks's portion. Channeling Crosby once again, this time in tone and not temperament, Phil begins:

Love is a dream, yet it's so real
Hard to explain, just how you feel

"I always liked to take the comedians from that show and put them into sort of bittersweet roles," says Schiller, to whom Phil touted his lip-syncing abilities before shooting began. During Schiller's first stint on the show, in early 1978, he wrote and directed the now-iconic short film (a "Schiller's Reel") *Don't Look Back in Anger*, wherein an elderly-looking John Belushi takes viewers on a guided tour of his cast mates' graves and describes how they died. The sole survivor, he dances among their tombstones. "So it's not exactly jokey, or a laugh-a-minute," Schiller says of his style, "but it shows another side of their acting ability that I perceived in [Phil]. I thought he had a lot of depth and sweetness." And Hooks, Schiller adds, was a perfect counterpart. "Phil was a gentleman and she was a gentle lady. They weren't crass. They weren't showbiz types, climbing to the top. That's why they had fun on the shoot, because it was away from Studio 8H, they got their own costuming, they were the stars. There was no one else telling them what to do. And it wasn't just laughs every two lines."

Some years later, Schiller wrote and directed Phil in another lesser-known short called *Laura*. It stars cast member Melanie Hutsell as a restaurant hatcheck girl and Phil as the singing driver of a horse-drawn carriage. When Hutsell steps outside the restaurant in a female patron's fancy fur-collared cape, Phil's carriage rolls by and splashes her borrowed garment. The two then embark on a romantic buggy ride through Central Park. As with *Love Is a Dream*, some point to it as evidence that Phil could have become a solid dramatic actor in the vein of *Breaking Bad*'s Bryan Cranston or any number of comedic types who've made the leap.

Besides traditional sketches and Schiller's wonderfully surreal *Love Is a Dream* production, Phil's third season saw him star in the first of several *SNL* commercial parodies directed by Jim Signorelli, who had previously guided Phil and other Groundlings in an Elvira production with Cassandra Peterson. Phil's debut Signorelli spot—with Hooks, Carvey, and several others—was a spoof called "Compulsion." A send-up of Calvin Klein's uber-sultry ads for its perfume Obsession, the parody stars Hooks as a neat freak who compulsively scrubs her house (even during fancy soirees) with "the world's most indulgent disinfectant" from Calvin Kleen. Phil plays the tuxedoed and vaguely French narrator, melodramatically wondering aloud, "What was the greater transgression: loving her, or abiding her immaculate madness?"

During time off, Phil's *SNL* exposure proved lucrative on the commercial front. He had long done local radio spots on the side, but now the exposure was getting broader and the money bigger. Starting in the late eighties and continuing for the remainder of his career, there were national on-camera ads and voice-overs for (in no particular order) TGI Friday's, Bell Atlantic Yellow Pages, Cheetos, M&Ms, Pot Noodle Soup (UK only), CDi, 1-800-Collect, Slice (in which he peddled soft drinks to schoolkids), McDonalds, and Coke, among many others. The latter, in particular, earned him big bucks for little work: a reported $1.2 million for McDonald's (he was a vegetarian at the time and throughout much of his life, especially when he grew thick around the middle) and $600,000 for Coke, which never aired a spot that featured (as Phil's William Morris agent Betty McCann remembers it) Phil as a flamboyantly gay dog groomer with pink hair and a canine to match. "They were nervous about that one," McCann says.

Reviews were mixed at the start of *SNL*'s 1989–90 season—Phil's fourth, and his first as a performer only. "The current cast is as good as *SNL* has seen since the originals," declared a review in the *St. Petersburg Times*. *Time* magazine wasn't so sure. "Laughs are still coming," read the subhead on one story, "but the old gleam is gone." Phil, though, was shining more than ever. Just prior to the season's start, on September 17, 1989, he'd shared an Emmy for outstanding writing in a variety or music program. (Despite nominations for writing and individual performance in 1987 and 1998, respectively, it would be the only one of his career.) Jack Handey was present in the writers' room afterward when Phil—holding a glossy of him clutching his infant son with one hand and his Emmy trophy with the other—turned to Lovitz and cracked, "Hey, Jon. Check it out: Here's two things *you'll* never have!"

Neither would Lovitz own a sprawling and rustic home like the one Phil had purchased for $1.4 million only a month earlier. Located at 5065 Encino Avenue in the celebrity-dotted town of Encino, about a dozen miles from Hollywood in the San Fernando Valley, it was for him a welcome refuge from the glitz and glam without being too isolated. "Someone will inevitably ask where you live, and I say 'Encino,'" Phil told the *L.A. Daily News* in 1997. "Then you get that Beverly Hills glaze," he added, affecting a robot-like monotone. "'Pariah. Must escape. Don't want loser dust on my Armani.'" But he liked the conveniences there and the family-friendly vibe.

Coincidentally or not, Phil's fellow Brantfordian Wayne Gretzky also took up residency in Encino. Kirstie Alley and David Crosby lived in the vicinity as well, and Dana Carvey's house was only a short walk away. Among the area's natural attractions are the Sepulveda Dam and Recreation Area—which an article in the *L.A. Times* described as "a green haven for wildlife and outdoor enthusiasts" (Phil!)—and the Los Encinos State Historic Park.

Phil put $420,000 down on his 4,019-square-foot English cottage–style home, located less than a thousand feet from bustling Ventura Boulevard. Situated on a corner lot, the low-slung ranch-style dwelling boasted chestnut-colored wood siding, hand-hewn Ponderosa Pine ceiling beams, solid pine doors, a large brick kitchen island with built-in burners, and a library with floor-to-ceiling shelves. Its master bedroom (one of four) was bigger than Phil's entire pad in Sherman Oaks (which he sold for $250,000 four months later), and the yard— handsomely landscaped and tropically lush—was shaded from searing California sun by a host of sycamores, oaks, redwoods, and Chinese elms. "I'm really having buyer's remorse about this," he confessed to his friend Chad Stuart. "Did I spend too much money?" Inspired by his *SNL* boss Michaels, who became a close friend and sometime vacation companion, Phil even took up gardening. "Really, it's a wonderful thing, just as an allegorical representation of life," he told writer David Rensin in 1991. "How, if you put something in the proper soil, it does so much better." To Phil, good gardening was "a metaphor for proper planning and doing things right. Paying attention to detail." "I think he saw that that was, for me, a sort of counterpoint to a life of stimulation and stress," Michaels says. "That there was something that balanced things."

Phil dubbed his new haven the Ponderosa (after the Cartwright family's ranch on TV's *Bonanza*), and he gradually adorned it with ornately framed paintings (many of them purchased at estate sales) of urban and pastoral landscapes: the ocean crashing against rocks; a dark forest; a river running through a canyon; a cow grazing in the stream of a grassy wooded area; an old-time village; a quaint city scene; a churning ocean lapping a rocky beach beneath an overcast sky. Except for summers, when Phil returned to L.A. for movie and voice work and to chill out by or in his beloved Pacific, the home was often vacant for the next four years.

Victoria Jackson, who visited Phil's Encino spread a couple of times in the '90s, was struck both by how handsome the place was and how oddly close it sat to such a buzzing intersection. "I thought, 'If I was a millionaire, I would have a more remote, hidden, gated estate that was a little bit farther away from the riffraff,'" she says. "I remember coming through the open [back] gate, and I said to Phil, 'Man, you leave your gate open?' And he said something like, 'Oh, yeah. We're just down-to-earth folk.' Here he was a block away from Ventura, where there's homeless people, and he had an open gate. And I thought that was kind of sweet."

To create and recreate in solitude, Phil fashioned a writer's den for himself above the garage in a 700-square-foot nook that had previously been maid's quarters. Over the years, he packed the space with guitars (one acoustic and two electric models—a Stratocaster and a Gibson), artwork, and a computer on which he played Flight Simulator. He sometimes smoked cigars up there, too, though he preferred to do his stogie puffing (mainly on weekends) near the ocean with some sort of libation—a beer, a scotch, or a glass of wine—in hand while he watched the waves roll in. More than a few joints were fired up in his Ponderosa retreat as well, much to Brynn's chagrin. "She hated it," says John Hartmann, who now and then shared a doobie with Phil. Dozier, too, recalls being put off by Phil's penchant for pot, but not because he had anything against marijuana. "I'd talk to him on the phone, and he'd say, 'I'm not doing anything. Let's hang out,'" Dozier says. "So I would go over to his house and he'd be smoking pot and was kind of spaced out. And I'd get on his case. I remember one time in particular, I said [sarcastically], 'Thank you so much for your presence, Phil.'"

Although Phil was now more valuable than ever at *SNL*, his preponderance of utility roles—president of the United States, senator, policeman, Garth's convenience store-owner dad in a "Wayne's World" sketch—did little to boost his profile. That changed slightly when he appeared as Gene, the Anal Retentive Chef—a fey and persnickety man who owns a homemade tape dispenser cozy and disposes of refuse only after properly packaging it in paper towel, tinfoil, and a stapled brown-paper bag so "it won't leak onto the other garbage." Created by Terry and Bonnie Turner, it was Phil's first original character that really stood out. Despite future Anal Retentive iterations, however, it failed to catch fire like Carvey's Church Lady ("Isn't that special?") or Myers's Wayne Campbell ("Schwing!"). Perhaps a memorable catchphrase would have helped—not to mention a more competitive edge. But when it came to comedy, Phil was more manatee than shark. At *SNL*, that was a blessing and a curse.

He was never "light" in shows, as the TV parlance goes, but neither was he a defining presence. "He wasn't clamoring to be the star," Schiller says, noting that Phil's ego "seemed more subdued" than those of his cast mates, "but naturally so—not on purpose. Because he was a good guy and had a good soul." As Phil would later remark,

"All of us know performers who feel it's their destiny to become big stars. I feel it's my destiny to do good work."

Schiller also sensed that Phil "wasn't clinging to [*SNL*] as his only vehicle for success," which in turn imbued his performances with a rare confidence. "He was good and he knew it," Handey says. And except for one instance, when Phil asked not to appear shirtless (he refused to be shirtless) in a scene with Sharon Stone, "He didn't seem needy like some actors are. He was never, like, sweaty. He was Mr. Unruffled." Then again, Handey says, "Maybe his versatility came back to bite him. Maybe it was a curse in disguise."

Toward the start of season fifteen, in late 1989, Signorelli directed Phil in another commercial parody—this time for a comically high-fiber breakfast cereal called Colon Blow. Thought up by Al Franken, it stars Phil as an initially skeptical consumer whose colon is about to be obliterated. Featuring the voice-over work of John Henry Kurtz, the spot employs camera trickery (namely, a "front surface mirror") to achieve its desired effect. After Phil fails to guess how many bowls of his favorite oat bran cereal it would take to equal the fiber content of just one bowl of Colon Blow, Kurtz tells him: more than 30,000. At which point a pyramid-shaped mountain of bowls erupts from below and carries a screaming Phil skyward. "Wow! I think I get the picture!" he exclaims. "Colon Blow must be the highest-fiber cereal on the market!" Um, wrong. That would be Super Colon Blow. Cue second eruption.

Budgetary constraints necessitated the eschewing of pricey special effects, including an exploding floor and walls. Optical illusion, therefore, was key. "I showed Phil the rig and he said, 'Sure,' and he climbed up on top of a ten-foot-high tower of real bowls, which was reinforced," Signorelli says. "He was strapped into a chair that was kind of catawampus. And he actually had a little safety rope around him, which would have not saved his life had he fallen. Thank God he didn't. And we then, on cue, pumped fifty-five gallons of oil into an oil drum to counterbalance him, and he kind of crept to the ceiling. I matched that to a tiny image that was sitting alongside of him at the other end of the studio. So the bottom of that [pile] isn't really there and he's not really on top of it."

"He was always game," Signorelli adds. "That was the best thing about Phil. It was a real Harold Lloyd kind of approach to the physicality."

On January 5, 1990, while Phil was in California during holiday break, he drove to 300 Los Angeles Street in downtown L.A. and demonstrated his ability to speak, read, and write in English during the multipart naturalization exam required to become a U.S. citizen.

Back in New York, throughout the remaining four months of *SNL*'s sixteenth season, Phil's glue had its usual bonding effect as he continued to yearn for a standout role. Carvey already had Garth, George H. W. Bush, Church Lady, and musclehead Hans. Myers had Wayne Campbell and the bizarre TV host Dieter on "Sprockets." But Phil's time would come. Meanwhile, he found a new outlet for his comedy skills and vocal talents: an animated show about a dysfunctional yellow family and their fellow yellow townsfolk in a soon-to-be-famous place called Springfield. At first Phil regarded his gig on Fox's animated comedy *The Simpsons* as just a lark. Before long, it became much more.

Chapter 11

Phil as voice of Troy McClure, 1990, *The Simpsons*.

On June 29, 1990, the year he became a client of the powerful Brillstein-Grey management agency, Phil pulled into the lot of Twentieth Century Fox Studios on West Pico Boulevard in Los Angeles and headed for the Darryl F. Zanuck ADR (Automated Dialogue Replacement) stage—a rather shabby subterranean space where the burgeoning cast of characters on *The Simpsons* was given voice. Created by cartoonist and animator Matt Groening, and developed for television with Sam Simon and James L. Brooks, the smart, topically relevant (especially given the long lead times for animation) and edgy-for-its-time program was launched as a series of shorts on *The Tracey Ullman Show* in 1987. It wasn't until mid-December 1989 that a then-fledgling Fox Network began broadcasting half-hour episodes to a mix of cheers and jeers. The former soon drowned out the latter.

Phil's first day of *Simpsons* duty, then, was barely six months into the show's inaugural year and in service of an episode—"Bart Gets Hit by a Car"—that was set to air around the halfway point of season two, on January 10, when *The Simpsons* had yet to become anything resembling the pop-culture institution or economic juggernaut it has long since been. Nancy Cartwright, who voices the brash and bold young trouble-maker Bart Simpson, was among the first to encounter Phil when he reported for duty to play lame-brained shyster attorney Lionel Hutz.

Lisa Simpson: You're a latter day Clarence Darrow!
Lionel Hutz: Uh, was he the black guy on *The Mod Squad*?

Aside from their shared gig, both he and Cartwright were parents to young children, and as they got to know each other better Phil some-times displayed photos of then-two-year-old Sean. "It was very easy to talk to him about his family," Cartwright says. And when *she* talked, Phil listened. "He was interested in the person who was sitting beside him, rather than trying to be the showman." Though he "didn't mind sharing his personal life," Cartwright never knew or asked if there was more to it than he divulged. "I never felt it was really my business to delve too far," she says.

On the subject of fatherhood, however, Phil was unbridled. "He was just gushing [about] how much he loved that time," Cartwright says. "And I got a sense that when he wasn't working, he could sort of take off that entertainer hat and just be a dad." She sensed correctly, though as more work came his way—not to mention the temptation of more expensive and intensive hobbies—Phil spent fewer and fewer days at home, much to Brynn's mounting dismay.

Simpsons writer and former Groundlings student Jay Kogen says he suggested Phil for the Hutz role because of his "great, strong voice." Phil's growing popularity on *SNL*—where he'd soon begin playing another slippery and much hairier counselor who only *pretended* at stupidity—was a plus as well. A couple of other *Simpsons* writers, Al Jean (who went on to be a *Simpsons* showrunner) and Mike Reiss, certainly thought so. Both were fans of the Hartman-Lovitz *SNL* cast and both told then-showrunner Simon that Phil could easily fit the bill. "At that time, there was sort of an internal debate on the show about whether to use well-known voices, or have everybody be a lesser-known voice actor," Jean says. "Especially in terms of guest stars. And so this was kind of an exception to that, but we pushed for Phil, and later for Jon [Lovitz]. We said, 'Look, these guys are funny. We should get them on the show.'" But when Phil agreed to guest star, Jean heard secondhand, it was with one caveat: he'd only do it once. Perhaps due to his long run on *Dennis the Menace*, Phil's interest in being an animated voice had apparently waned. In any case, Jean says, "We didn't take him at his word."

A bit later that summer, Phil returned to Fox for another session in the Zanuck studio (on the heels of Lovitz, who'd just been in to voice bitter geek tycoon Artie Ziff) and another portrayal of another hilarious boob. Only this time he was charged with playing a washed-up film (and possibly soft-porn) actor named Troy McClure for an episode called "Homer vs. Lisa and the 8th Commandment" that was set to air February 7, 1991. (He also voiced four minor characters.) McClure—whose handle was derived from the first name of one real-life B-movie actor and the surname of another (Troy Donahue and Doug McClure)—is a vain and clueless dunderhead in love with the sound of his own voice. His first appearance is brief but memorable.

Troy [in a radio announcer-type voice]: Hello, I'm Troy McClure. You may remember me from such movies as *Cry Yuma* and *Here Comes the Coast Guard*. But today I'd like to tell you about a pleasant-tasting candy that actually cleans and *straightens* your teeth.

Phil spent the next eight years as McClure, usually in short scenes but in one case as the focal point of an entire episode ("A Fish Called Selma"), and he quickly came to adore his animated alter ego more than any other character in his arsenal. "I would love nothing more than to play Troy McClure in a live-action film," he said well into his *Simpsons* tenure. "I've suggested it to the show's producers. If they don't want to do it, I may even buy the rights and do it myself." (For the record, McClure in his thirty-two appearances between 1991 and 1998 said "You *may* remember me" another nine times, "You *might* remember me" ten, and "You *probably* remember me" just once. There, that's settled.) The long and comically undistinguished list of his film, documentary, and telethon work came to include *Driving Mr. T, Smoke Yourself Thin, Suddenly Last Supper, Let's Save Tony Orlando's House!,* and *The Erotic Adventures of Hercules.*

As he had at the Groundlings with Phil's Chick Hazard and his "bon vivant guy in a glasses and suit," Jay Kogen saw Phil's affinity for Old Hollywood—or at least his perception of it—used as creative fodder, this time in animated form. Once again, Phil was borrowing a sensibility from decades past and bringing it into the modern day. "He had a real star quality," Kogen says. "But I felt it was an old-timey star quality. He was a sharp dresser. Even offstage, he always sort of resembled some sort of weird combination of a 1950s intellectual and Jack Benny."

The comedic effect of McClure was due in large part to the fact that Phil, as ever, played it utterly straight while imbuing the role with what came to be his trademark hybrid of obliviousness, arrogance, and earnest insincerity. "It's kind of a generic, authoritarian, theater-trained voice that we all grew up hearing connected to commercials or in performance," says Hank Azaria, whose *Simpsons* roles include gruff bartender Moe Szyslak and the chipper convenience store owner Apu Nahasapeemapetilon. Writer and former showrunner Mike Scully describes Lionel Hutz as "this combination of overconfidence and incompetence. He never doubted his ability in the courtroom for some reason, even though he had no idea what was going on."

In one instance, Hutz and McClure appeared in the same episode. Reiss was directing. "Suddenly it became a little embarrassing for Phil," he says. "He was changing one of the voices. Lionel Hutz didn't sound like Lionel Hutz anymore, because he was trying to differentiate these two characters." For Azaria, the tonal sameness spoke to an unfussy approach that works to the characters' advantage. "In all my voices, I try to think of something weird, a hook, a strange way they'll sound. For Phil it was like, 'Nope. It's just going to be as down-the-middle as possible.' But that made it genius."

For Matt Groening, Phil's golden pipes and acting chops were only part of his allure. "In Phil's voice, in his body language, in the twinkle in his eye, you could sense a performer fully enjoying himself," Groening wrote in 1998. "Phil was digging the acting process while he was in the middle of it, and the fact that many of Phil's characters were so blatantly consumed by a hilariously smarmy insincerity just added to the audience's enjoyment. You could always tell Phil was having a blast performing, and that he enjoyed his fellow actors' performances as well."

While *The Simpsons* became an increasingly significant part of Phil's life, the job was also a relative cinch. No long days on a set, no memorizing lines, no waiting for scenes to be lit. Sometimes, he recorded portions from multiple scripts during the same session. "He was just a machine," Reiss remembers. "He would embarrass you as a director, because he would come in and nail everything on the first take." There were times when they'd allot two hours for Phil's work on three different episodes, Reiss adds, and he'd "be in and out in fifteen minutes."

Moreover, when Phil came to recording sessions ("records," in show-biz speak) "it didn't feel like he was a special guest star," Kogen says. "He fit in with our cast in a way that was different than if Penny Marshall or Danny DeVito came in to do a voice. With Phil, it was much more friendly. He quickly began feeling like a regular, even though he wasn't." And though Phil only occasionally showed up for table reads, he invariably killed. "He really was the acid test of humor," Reiss says. "If Phil wasn't getting a laugh with it, it just wasn't good."

Life got hectic again after Phil jetted back to New York in early fall for the start of his fifth season on *SNL*. Beforehand, under the direction of Jim Signorelli, he shot a new opening sequence with his cast mates. In Phil's portion, he's sitting at the table of a swanky and dimly lit restaurant or club. His chair is red and so is the phone beside him. Phil wears a black suit jacket, a white dress shirt, and a tie. Facing him, but never the camera, is a mystery woman with long blond hair: Brynn. Though she is still, the earring dangling from her right lobe incongruously swings back and forth. Hanala Stadner Sagal, Brynn's friend from rehab, says the only time she spoke with Brynn during the *SNL* years was shortly after that opening aired. "Check out how my earring is swinging," Sagal says Brynn told her, explaining that she kept trying to face the camera but was directed to face Phil instead. As *SNL* makeup artist Norman Bryn writes in his memoir, *Makeup & Misery: Adventures in the Soap Factory*, the same story was "told widely around *SNL*." Signorelli, though, has a different take: "Having been the man in charge there, I don't think we ever had to go over and put a hand on her shoulder and say, 'Brynn, it's not about you.' I think it was just that she thought it was a couple at a table. I don't think anybody ever said, 'Lean out.'"

Three years into motherhood and six into Phil's *SNL* stint, Brynn was still searching for herself. "She was kind of struggling with her identity, from what I could gather," Hooks says. "It was, 'I'm a model. No, I'm an actress. No, I'm a mother with children and a wife. No, I'm a writer.' And those are the kinds of things that are perfectly natural and normal when you're in your twenties." Born in 1958, Brynn was no longer in her twenties. "Like so many people in L.A., her appearance was very important to her," Hooks says. "And not in a bitchy way. She was very sweet. But you could tell she wanted to look pretty and wanted pretty things. There was always a kind of deer-in-the-headlights quality about it."

Julia Sweeney had met Brynn back in California, and the two became friends after Sweeney moved to New York for *SNL*. "And it was funny," Sweeney says of the pairing, "because the way she looked is not who I would normally be friends with. She had this kind of high-end call girl look about her that was really almost cartoonish, frankly. It's such a cliché to say, but she had a heart of gold. She was a complex person and I found her fascinating—her story in life." When Brynn dropped by *SNL*, Sweeney remembers, "It was like an Amazon woman walked in—in the best possible way. She was so tall and beautiful. Sometimes I would just start laughing, because we knew each other. Like, 'Oh, my God, Brynn, people aren't even going to watch the show because you happen to be standing here.' And I think that was really important to Phil."

"He needed to be with a knockout," she says. "That was something I was so naïve about. I didn't understand that part of Hollywood, where it is as important as getting on *Saturday Night Live* or being a known name to have somebody that everyone turns their head [to see] when they walk into the room."

Sometime that summer Phil and Lisa happened to cross paths on the set of an L.A. commercial production where both of them had business. Burying the hatchet over Brynn's venomous letter, they had lunch and talked for a few hours at Lisa's apartment. "He apologized," Lisa says. Before long, she says, "I started being his crying towel—the person he would complain to about Brynn."

Mostly, though, he was discouraged about *SNL*, from which he began planning his May 1991 exit in order to pursue other opportunities—whatever those may be. "I think he was frustrated at times," Odenkirk says. "He would often write these sketches that played very well at read-through, and maybe didn't play as well in front of the live audience." Mike Myers sat next to Phil at many of those read-throughs. As he recalled in *Live from New York*, Phil was uncommonly committed and "would never tank your piece. Afterwards you would just hear 'Glue, Glue, Glue' from people around the read-through table. And then someone would always have to tell Phil, 'They're not saying *boo*, they're saying *glue*.'"

In his 1991 interview with Stanley Moss of *Bomb Magazine*, Phil admitted to sometimes feeling "cheated" while performing for the audience that occupied Studio 8H. Most often it was comprised largely of invited "elitist friends of the staff who sit and observe the show rather than getting involved." They should instead get "real people" to watch, Phil concluded. He told Moss that he felt well utilized at *SNL* and loved being a professional "clown" who provided a diversion from the grind. "People need to take a few moments and let go and escape from the burden of their day-to-day lives. It's important for everybody to get light about life because you can worry yourself into terminal illness."

But Phil admitted, too, that he felt like a mere "cog in the machine" and needed to "take that next step." His feeling of lagging behind was partly exacerbated by the exit of Myers, who in February 1992 made his first big box office splash in *Wayne's World*. Co-starring Carvey and spun-off from their recurring hit *SNL* segment, it was number one for five weeks in a row and took in nearly $120 million domestically on a $20 million budget. "From the start, really, I've been overshadowed by others on the show," Phil told another interviewer, "and so it's something that I had to get used to."

Phil reveled in his versatility but also longed to have a signature character—one that would catapult him to the next level. "I don't think it caused him a lot of angst, because he was the cool guy and so stable," says Julia Sweeney, who went on to have a breakout character of her own in the sexually amorphous "Pat." "If anything did come out about his frustration, that was it." As Phil's dissatisfaction grew during their time together in New York, Sweeney says, "It wasn't like it sullied his attitude at all. It was just there."

Even so, there were plenty of shining moments to come. Jack Handey's inspired creation Cirroc, the "Unfrozen Caveman Lawyer," provided several. Its wonderfully bizarre premise: *"One hundred thousand years ago, a caveman was out hunting on the frozen wastes when he slipped and fell into a crevasse. In 1988, he was discovered by some scientists and thawed out. He then went to law school and became . . . Unfrozen Caveman Lawyer."* There was even talk of a "Caveman Lawyer" movie spin-off. "He really wanted [it] to be big," Sweeney says.

Cirroc's courtroom spiel is equal parts faux humility and cynical maneuvering. "Ladies and gentlemen of the jury, I'm just a caveman . . . Your world frightens and confuses me . . . When I'm courtside at a Knicks game, I wonder if the ball is some sort of food they're fighting over."

"Phil had a total bullshit thing going," Handey says admiringly. "Lorne Michaels said it reminded him of Bill Murray—that fake, unctuous sincerity. He knew how to play an oily guy."

Tonight Show spoofs with Carvey went over well, too. After Bonnie and Terry Turner penned the first one, Johnny Carson fan Robert Smigel took over and made the characters edgier, their dialogue darker. "I had a really strong take on what I wanted to do with Johnny, and Dana had some great observations," Smigel says. But, he adds, the bits never would have worked as well without Phil's over-the-top McMahon. "Dana would do all these subtle, observant riffs on Carson, and the audience would not really laugh. They would laugh at Ed validating them. 'Yes! You are correct, sir!'"

McMahon was always a good sport about the parodies. So was

Carson, mostly, even when things got a little weird, a little wild. He was fine, for instance, with a sketch that aired in May of 1991—"The Carsenio Show"—that portrayed him as a hopelessly square Arsenio Hall knockoff (complete with spiky hairdo, double-breasted suit, and slang wholly unsuited to an older white man) while simultaneously mocking Hall's hipper-than-thou persona. Until then, however, *SNL* had reportedly been temporarily blacklisted by Carson after airing a fall 1990 *Tonight Show* send-up in which Carson (Carvey) comes off not only as unhip but somewhat doddering while talking with his guests Susan Dey (Jan Hooks) and Hall (Chris Rock). "Lorne liked the idea of Johnny mixing up *The Partridge Family* with *The Brady Bunch*," Smigel says of Hooks's role as Dey, the former *Partridge Family* star. "And it was funny, but Johnny took it as [us] saying that he was senile. It had the effect of making him take the sketch more personally, even, than had it just been Arsenio."

In May 1992, only days before Carson himself bid a final adieu after three decades on the air, Phil and Carvey shot a cold opening in which Carson and McMahon celebrate their long run by saying whatever is on their minds.

> **Johnny:** Boy, I gotta tell you, this feels good—just to say what you wanna. It feels good, doesn't it, Ed?
>
> **Ed:** Yes.
>
> **Johnny:** Now, is there anything you wanna say? Just get off your chest? Go right ahead.
>
> **Ed:** [looks at Johnny, his expression growing serious] You're the one who had the drinking problem. [Smiles and laughs.]

Hiyoooooooo!

As Phil's sidekick days wound down, he began polishing an impersonation that would, at long last, earn him the notice that had so far been elusive. When Phil first appeared as then-Arkansas governor

William Jefferson Clinton in a March 1992 sketch called "Star Trek Democrats"—with Carvey as former California governor Jerry Brown and Franken as U.S. senator Paul Tsongas—the audience went nuts even before he opened his mouth. "He kind of captured that self-satisfied charmer who knows he's going to charm you," Smigel says. "It must have been a huge rush, because he never got to enjoy a lot of that." In the end, Phil's Clinton furiously destroys his podium after a Trekker in the crowd (Chris Farley) informs him that Leonard Nimoy (Mr. Spock) has endorsed Tsongas. Though the real Clinton was known to have a temper, Phil never again played him angry in seventeen appearances that followed. Come-hither sexy, yes, but never angry. It was a portrayal to which Clinton himself took only a partial shine. Phil claimed not to mind.

Meanwhile, on May 22, 1992, Carson abdicated his *Tonight Show* throne. When he'd announced his plans during a broadcast the previous spring, a storied behind-the-scenes battle to fill his seat commenced. Ultimately and famously, comic and *Tonight*'s longtime permanent guest host Jay Leno won. At some point thereafter, Phil was invited to play a more regular role on the program. There is disagreement, however, on what exactly that role was. "I remember him calling me up and telling me he'd been offered the gig as Jay Leno's sidekick on the new *Tonight Show*," John Paragon says. Ecstatic, Paragon urged his pal to take the job. Not only would it entail far fewer hours than Phil was logging at *SNL*, it would finally enable him to resettle in California and do whatever else he wished to do on the side, be it acting or sailing. Nonetheless, Paragon says, "He was really on the fence about it." Phil's reluctance, he thinks, stemmed partly from his ambivalence about being a second banana.

Leno, though, says no such offer was made. "We never asked Phil to be a sidekick. That never even came up, so I'm not sure where that came from." There were talks with *SNL* about having Phil on *Tonight* now and then to play Clinton, Leno says, but that didn't sit particularly well with Michaels or Downey, the latter of whom thought Leno's crew was being overly aggressive about borrowing ideas from *SNL*. He was also irked when the show inquired about using Phil on a semi-regular basis as Jay's comedic foil. If Phil did his Clinton shtick on *The Tonight Show* and on *SNL*, its impact would inevitably be diminished. Even worse, the lack of context (Phil as Clinton in a random appearance alongside Leno, say, as opposed to in a political sketch) and the use of writers who were unfamiliar with the nuances and rhythms of *SNL* characters would surely be calamitous as well.

"Phil was not necessarily the person you wanted ad-libbing out there," Downey says. "He was not like a Bill Murray type who was great on his feet. He was a great performer, but [not] when he had to improvise if there was a technical problem or we lost cue cards or something. I remembered seeing him doing an impression on *Donahue* one time and sort of cringing. He had written it himself. I used to write those things and he hadn't consulted with me and given me any heads-up . . . The impression was good. I just didn't think his material was very good. And when Lorne told me that Phil wanted to do Leno as a regular thing, where he would be doing characters like he'd done on [*SNL*], we were kind of concerned."

When Downey and Michaels expressed their concern to Leno, who understood completely, Phil remained puzzled. He was "kind of thick in certain ways," Downey says, and "kind of bewildered as to how there could be any objection."

But if Phil was supposedly never offered a permanent *Tonight Show* post, Michaels (who today says the Leno job was never a serious proposition) seemed to indicate otherwise during a late-summer interview with *Playboy*. "Now, I would hate it if Phil Hartman left [*SNL*]," he told writer David Rensin. "Phil has done more work that's touched greatness than probably anybody else who's ever been there. Would he be paid more if he were Jay Leno's sidekick? Of course. There are probably thirty or forty other jobs that would pay me more. I'm not trying to make us sound heroic, I'm merely trying to say that I think we both know this is what we do best."

The NBC brass must have known it, too, for they signed Phil to an exclusive three-year contract that included the network's commitment to a pilot plus several more episodes (six or seven—accounts vary) of his own prime-time program. "I'm sure it was something I encouraged the network to do," Michaels says, "because I wanted him to stay at NBC."

The Phil Show (its working title) would be what Phil described as a "completely unpredictable," film-noirish, half-hour variety extravaganza. Shot on film with no live audience, it would "totally shake up the whole idea of what it is to do a TV show."

"I want to be able to come on as Trump or Sinatra or Saddam Hussein if I want," he said in the 1991 interview with Moss. "I think technically and artistically, it's gonna be fun, but nobody will ever accuse it of being the same old crap." But like many shows in development, it went nowhere fast. On the up side, a revised version of the *Mr. Fix-It* script Phil had originally written for Victor Drai in 1984 looked like it might finally get made—if director Robert Zemeckis could find backing for the black comedy. No easy task, that. The studios were skittish, and for good reason: Phil's screenplay was (as per his own description) "sort of a merger of horror and comedy, like *Beetlejuice* and *Throw Momma from the Train*. It's an American nightmare about a family torn asunder. They live next to a toxic dump site, their water supply is poisoned, the mother and son go insane and try to murder each other, the father's face is torn off in a terrible disfiguring accident in the first act. It's heavy stuff, but it's got a good message and a positive, upbeat ending."

Screenwriting, of course, didn't butter Phil's bread. *SNL* did. And with a presidential election looming, incumbent George H. W. Bush and his chief challenger Clinton became bigger targets than ever for Carvey, Phil, and the *SNL* writers. If Clinton won, Carvey told his friend, it would "put you on the map." There were many months to go before that *might* happen, however, and so Phil bided his time and spread his glue liberally. Increasingly, he reveled in his "Glue" status and was acutely aware of how colleagues on the show perceived him. Hooks, who left in the spring of 1991 to join the cast of CBS's *Designing Women,* is one of them. "He didn't flaunt it," she says of Phil's Glueness, "but oh, yeah, he knew." Newer players, like Sweeney, Chris Farley, Chris Rock, David Spade, and Adam Sandler all looked up to him as a sage of sorts and an avuncular figure—a guy who'd been around the block. "Phil was a mentor," Rock told *Playboy.* "He was the most prepared guy at *Saturday Night Live.* He could also show you about the good life. Sometimes he'd call me into his office and say, 'Hey, look at this picture of my new boat. Hey, here's the house I'm buying. You work hard, you can get this, too.'" Jay Mohr, who joined the cast in 1993, "never heard any gossip about him, positive or negative. Ever. From anyone. He was easy like Sunday mornin'. He just came in and got it done and left. He was like a closer in baseball."

To the sweet and eager-to-please Farley, Phil was a big brother and father figure combined. "How'm I doin', Glue?" Farley would ask as he plopped down in the makeup chair next to Phil's. "He kept an eagle eye on Chris, which was good," Farley's mother Mary Anne says. "And Chris listened to him, which was even better." Older brother Tom Farley Jr., who spent time with Chris and Phil at *SNL,* thinks the two got along so well in part because of their down-to-earth personalities. They palled around a bit off the clock, too, making treks to the ponds of Central Park, where Phil loved to watch and operate toy sailboats. They also went skiing in Stowe, Vermont. Concerned that his oversize co-star wouldn't be able to keep up, Phil was initially reluctant to invite him along. When they arrived in Stowe, however, the Wisconsin-bred Farley—whose boyhood winters were filled with skiing and hockey—tore up the slopes to Phil's great surprise. On another occasion, Phil squired a gaggle of Farleys—Tom, his then-wife, their very young daughter, Chris, and mother Mary Anne—to the Metropolitan Museum of Art, where he proceeded to act as docent. "I was blown away by the guy's intelligence," Tom says of Phil's off-the-cuff tour. "He was teaching us: 'Everybody knows about Rembrandt, but this guy here was a contemporary, and look what he did that was different than Rembrandt.' And I'm like, *What*?"

Back in the cauldron of 30 Rock, Phil was always a source of strength and confidence for Farley and others. "David Spade told me once that you had to work with the writers to make sure that you were in the sketch," Tom Farley says. "And Phil didn't have to do that." Meanwhile, though, young bucks like Spade, Adam Sandler, Rob Schneider, and Chris Rock were doing whatever they could to be seen. As ever, Phil stayed out of the fray.

"The worst things happened behind the scenes: the competitiveness, the heartbreak of working very hard on something and then having it cut, and not knowing if somebody had sabotaged it or not," he once said. "There was a lot of intrigue. It was a very politically charged arena, and anyone who's been willing to discuss it truthfully talks about the dark side. But I tend to focus on the good part."

In retrospect, Downey says, observers might have regarded Phil's buoyant demeanor somewhat warily, figuring it was easy for him to be Mr. Happy-Go-Lucky by dint of his consistent screen time and lighter workload. "He never had to lobby, to struggle, to make demands, to complain because he had absolutely nothing to complain about."

As *SNL* makeup artist Norman Bryn wrote in his memoir, Phil went "to great lengths to foster" his nice-guy status. But, Bryn adds, he didn't always treat the crew as he did his fellow actors. Now and then, under pressure from within and without, Phil's cracks showed. "I'll never forget my first meeting with him," says Bryn, who transformed Phil into Clinton, McMahon, Frankenstein, and others. "I met him for a pre-tape one afternoon and I started to put some straight makeup on him, and I'm trying to chat him up and get some idea of his personality.

And he snaps, 'Broad strokes! We use broad strokes here!' Because I'm not putting on the makeup quickly enough for him.

"He was quite fussy about his makeup," Bryn says. "He didn't want the makeup to be a joke. He wanted it to be part of the character, but he didn't want that to get the laugh. He wanted film-quality makeup, and that was difficult in a live television situation."

Bryn also claims that Phil could be jarringly bellicose before going onstage. "He could really shout and yell. I heard him scream at people to get out of the way when he made his way through the *SNL* stage doors. 'Clear that doorway! Clear that doorway!'" And they always did.

When Bryn groused to his boss, makeup supervisor Jennifer Aspinall, that Phil was "cocky and rude," she told him not to be offended. When she had extended her hand to shake Phil's, he'd spat on it. If it was his idea of a joke, she didn't get it. Although Aspinall was stunned by Phil's reaction, soon enough the two of them made up and began chatting over coffee. Phil told her about his gun collection and even when he'd banked his first million dollars. "That was a big deal," she says of the latter. "I remember him feeling like that was a big turning point."

In the cramped makeup room, where he typically shared space with Carvey, Nealon, Schneider, and sometimes Myers, Phil was always more comfortable with a male makeup artist. "We're in a very intimate space, and there are people who are more comfortable hanging out with a guy than hanging out with a girl," Aspinall says. "Touching someone to the degree that makeup people touch their actors, especially on a show like [*SNL*] where you're doing so many quick changes, is just a very intimate experience. Phil preferred guy-guys." The one who'd been assigned to Phil before Aspinall took over had been just that—and, as such, a Phil favorite. When he left, Phil was deeply dismayed. And so, after a few weeks of dealing with him herself, Aspinall sensed Phil's preference and assigned him to Bryn.

His high-stakes job at a major network that depended on ratings for advertising revenue was certainly one source of mood-altering stress, but some of Phil's darker moments at *SNL* also stemmed from troubles with wife Brynn—not that he often allowed his personal and professional worlds to collide. Most of the time, he compartmentalized his on- and off-camera lives to such a degree that few people knew more than basic and typically sunny details about his family, his cars, his hobbies.

On Saturday, February 8, 1992, Phil became a father for the second time—to a blond-haired daughter named Birgen Anika, whose birth was announced on the air that night by *SNL* guest host Susan Dey. Phil left 30 Rock to attend the birth, Lorne Michaels says, and was back before the show ended. As Dey locked her arm in Phil's during the show's closing moments and proclaimed the good news for all to hear, he tried and failed to stifle tears. He choked up, too, when he called Lynne Stewart to tell her how hopelessly smitten he was with his little girl. "I didn't fully experience my capacity to love until I had children," Phil later said. "And then I sensed this complete unconditional love in myself."

Not long after that joyous occasion, however, Phil's mood again turned grim. Early one Saturday night, he dropped into Bryn's makeup chair at *SNL* and vented. "Well, Norm, looks like the wife is gonna *divorce* me!" he said in a voice that sounded more like one of Phil's smarmy characters than Phil himself. At first, Bryn thought he was kidding; Phil's pale complexion convinced him otherwise. According to Bryn, Phil and "the wife" had just finished arguing by phone, which sometimes happened before eight P.M. dress rehearsals, and Phil was in no condition to perform. Uncharacteristically, he even flubbed some lines during the pre-show taping. "She would push his buttons," Bryn says. "Sometimes it was major, sometimes it was minor." Bryn thought it best not to further agitate Phil in his already agitated state.

Fortunately, only simple makeup was required for an "Anal Retentive Chef" sketch—which Bryn says Phil uncharacteristically botched during dress rehearsal. The reason strolled in around ten P.M., ninety minutes before air time, wearing a sexy black cocktail dress: Brynn. She and Phil argued in front of the eighth-floor elevators, and then Phil returned to the makeup chair for a pre-broadcast touch-up. "Looks like I staved it off *this* time, Norm," a disheveled Phil blurted.

Whether Phil's workaholic ways played any part in Phil and Brynn's tiff that evening is anyone's guest, but it was always a bone of contention between them. Brynn wanted him home more often. There were two kids now, and she had help from a nanny—after Birgen was born, Brynn hired a succession of them, all female and all plump (Hartmann men, Phil's niece Ohara Hartmann says, aren't attracted to plump women)— but Phil's long hours at work caused resentment and friction. "Phil had a weird marriage," Chris Rock has said. "He was always going through some shit with it, and I never liked to spend time with them as a couple. Every now and then, he'd talk about it. I remember him saying, 'OK, if I lose half my shit, I'll have to be on [*SNL*] another three years.'"

Brynn craved more communication as well as more paternal involvement from Phil, and she let him know it—not always at convenient moments. When Paula Grey (formerly Johnston) visited New York with her now ex-husband, Phil hooked them up with tickets to *SNL*. "We were going to meet up with him afterwards and go to the staff party," she says. "And he called me after the show and he said, 'I'm really sorry. I can't meet you for the party because I'm having problems with Brynn and this is the one time we can find where we can get together and talk about things.'"

During an *SNL* sketch in which Phil had to wear a bald cap that required twenty or so minutes to properly fit and secure, Norman Bryn went looking for him after Phil failed to show up at the makeup room. As Bryn approached Phil's dressing room door, he could hear him talking on the phone. Bryn knocked anyway. When Phil answered, he seemed to be in a flustered state. Bryn reminded him about the bald cap. Phil told him he'd be along shortly. The door shut. "They were having one of their tiffs," Bryn says, claiming he could hear Phil's end of an "animated discussion" with Mrs. Hartman from the outside. "She'd nailed him before dress rehearsal and he came to the chair in a very bad mood—and more annoyed that I had come to get him."

There were breezier makeup room chats, too—about classic movies or Phil's fear that parodying certain powerful show business figures— Walt Disney chief Michael Eisner and *Tonight Show* sidekick McMahon, to name a couple—could adversely affect his career. "He was afraid of Michael Eisner," Bryn says. "And he was afraid that playing him adversely, playing him like an idiot on a sketch we did, would affect his career. He was afraid that Eisner, who was very powerful, could make a phone call and ruin your career." As with Aspinall, Phil and Bryn also talked about guns. According to Bryn, Phil described his Walther PPK .38-caliber semiautomatic pistol (often toted by European police and easily concealed) and "joked" about his wife's pistol, which Phil said she'd brought to L.A. from Minnesota. As a public figure prone to kidnapping threats and "Manson-style home invasions," Bryn says, Phil confided that he felt safer having firearms around the house.

Shortly before Mother's Day in early May 1992, another Hartman— make that *Hartmann*—joined the cast of *SNL*, if only for one night: Phil's seventy-two-year-old mom Doris. Having been flown in with Rupert from San Diego (avid golfers, they were then living on the course at Shadowridge Country Club in the San Diego suburb of Chula Vista) to New York's JFK airport a week or so early, they were put up at the Omni Berkshire and ferried via limo ("at our beck and call all week," she later bragged) to 30 Rockefeller Center, where Doris rehearsed and was made ready for her close-up. Gathering with the mothers of hosts and cast members past and present—including Billie Carvey, Marlene

Jackson, Bunny Myers, Jeri Sweeney, Kathleen Nealon, Rose Rock, and Mary Anne Farley, the latter of whom became a close friend and pen pal—she taped a tribute called "All the Best for Mother's Day," which aired on May 10. Doris's paycheck, minus taxes and other deductions, came to $691.50, which she planned to spend on "something really special." "It was a really good group of ladies," Mary Anne Farley says, "and Doris was like the mother hen of us all. She took care of us. And she was sort of a pro. We'd say, 'Oh, we're so nervous, we just can't do this,' and she'd calm us all down. She was just a great, great lady."

During their stay in New York, Phil introduced his parents to Phil Donahue (at Donahue's insistence) and showed them some sights, including the Statue of Liberty. Doris and Rupert also attended *The Will Rogers Follies* and spent time with their grandchildren, three-year-old Sean and ten-week-old Birgen. "It's been the thrill of a lifetime," Doris said afterward. "Philip kept saying, 'Mother, I'm going to bring you to New York.' And he did." In a short, typed thank-you note, Michaels told her, "You'll always be welcome at Saturday Night Live. P.S. Now we know who the real talent is in the family." Doris and her fellow comedy matrons returned the following May for a repeat performance.

That summer, Phil was appointed honorary sheriff of Encino—a post previously held by John Wayne and other area luminaries. He also continued his work on *The Simpsons*, contributed to a few other animated projects, and played small roles in two movies: *CB4* (with Chris Rock and Khandi Alexander) and *So I Married an Axe Murderer* (with Mike Myers). A bit part in *Coneheads* (with Dan Aykroyd and Jane Curtin) was forthcoming. "My name is John Johnson. But everyone here calls me Vicky," Phil announces as a humorless and possibly psychotic Alcatraz park ranger in *So I Married an Ax Murderer*. While leading a tour group through the infamous prison, he stops to tell a story about the convict Machine Gun Kelly, who in a "jealous rage" cut out the eyes of his "bitch" with a makeshift knife, "or *shiv*." Vicky's history lesson continues: "And as if this wasn't enough retribution for Kelly, the next day he and four other inmates took turns pissing into the bitch's ocular cavities. [Beat, tone brightens.] This way to the cafeteria!"

Come September, Phil was back in New York for *SNL's* eighteenth season. Thanks in part to Carvey's departure midway through, Phil shone more than ever before. Another character of his had caught on, too. During the latter half of season seventeen, he'd achieved some measure of breakout success playing a mean Frank Sinatra. Literally— the guy was an asshole. And very funny in the way that assholes who don't care they're assholes can sometimes be. Unlike erstwhile cast member Joe Piscopo's more respectful and far less belligerent portrayal of the Chairman of the Board, Phil's Frank was all venom and swagger. "The Sinatra family was not happy with the impression Phil was doing at all," Piscopo claimed in *Live from New York*.

Phil's Sinatra debut, in a sketch written by Bonnie and Terry Turner, was inspired by a letter from Ol' Blue Eyes to then-reluctant pop star George Michael that was published in the *L.A. Times* (Sample excerpt: *"And no more of that talk about 'the tragedy of fame.' The tragedy of fame is when no one shows up and you're singing to the cleaning lady in some empty joint that hasn't seen a paying customer since Saint Swithin's day."*). In it, Carvey played a self-infatuated Michael ("Look at my butt!") opposite Phil's Frank. In a few other Sinatra outings, Phil ring-a-ding-dinged with Hooks alongside her cloyingly earnest (and, thus, quite hilarious) Sinead O'Connor with Tim Meadows's Sammy Davis and again as the secret lover of First Lady Nancy Reagan. (Phil played Ronald Reagan as well.)

Most notably, he scored big as the be-tuxed host of a cockamamie talk show called "The Sinatra Group." Dreamed up by Robert Smigel and based on PBS's *The McLaughlin Group*, it stars a bald and morose Hooks as O'Connor (whom Sinatra refers to as "Sinbad" and "Uncle Fester"), guest star Sting as a surly and scowling Billy Idol, Chris Rock as marble-mouthed rapper Luther Campbell, and Mike Myers and Victoria Jackson as grinning Sinatra sycophants Steve Lawrence and Eydie Gorme.

> **Billy Idol:** I think you're a bloody, stupid old fart!
> **Frank Sinatra:** You're all talk, blondie! You want a piece of me? I'm right here!
> **Billy Idol:** Don't provoke me, old man.
> **Frank Sinatra:** You don't scare me. I've got *chunks* of guys like you in my *stool*!

When Ol' Blue Eyes himself caught wind of the sketches, he picked up the phone and called his youngest daughter, Tina, for her take. She told him it was cool to be parodied on *SNL* and then phoned Lorne Michaels's office to request videos of Phil's Sinatra bits for her dad. When Phil ran into Tina on a couple of occasions, he was thrilled to hear that Frank got a kick out of his work.

But even Phil's Sinatra did relatively little to goose his *SNL*, and thus his overall showbiz, profile. An impression as opposed to an original invention, it was no Church Lady and it was no Wayne Campbell. Rising to that level, or anywhere close, would require someone even more powerful than the Chairman of the Board.

Chapter 12

Phil as Bill Clinton on *SNL*, 1992. (Credit: Makeup by
Norman Bryn, www.makeup-artist.com, photo copyright
Norman Bryn, all rights reserved)

On October 12, 1992, during the second episode of season eighteen and shortly after Phil filed paperwork in L.A. to legally change his last name from Hartmann to Hartman, controversial Irish pop star Sinead O'Connor appeared as *SNL*'s musical guest and sang Bob Marley's protest song "War" a capella. "We have confidence in the victory of good over evil," she intoned, staring directly into the camera with an I-mean-business expression. As she uttered the word "evil," O'Connor held up a photo of Pope John Paul II and tore it two, four, then eight pieces before tossing the shreds toward a stunned audience and proclaiming, "Fight the real enemy." On orders from the show's director, Dave Wilson, the applause sign remained dark and silence enveloped Studio 8H. Along with many others, Phil thought O'Connor's actions were uncalled for and distasteful. Not only did she disrespect the Catholic faith and its adherents, she cast a pall on whatever comedy came after—including a sketch called "Sweet Jimmy, the World's Nicest Pimp."

At dress rehearsal, O'Connor had used the picture of a child, thus setting up her live shot. Then, on air, she whipped out the Pope glossy to audience gasping. Phil was standing in the wings with the next week's guest star, Joe Pesci, watching it all unfold on a monitor. "Fuckin-A!" he exclaimed when the Pope shredding commenced. Pesci was equally floored, hissing, "What the fuck is the matter with that bitch!" Smigel was in the wings as well and remembers everybody "just avoiding her" afterward. Besides inappropriately flaunting her religious and political views, he says, O'Connor broke one of live television's unofficial rules: Don't surprise the producers. "If that happens too many times, then there won't be a live show. That's how we looked at it and I think that's how Lorne looked at it. It's something that's precious and rare, allowing something to go on totally live and to live with the kinks and the flaws. And I think Lorne was really afraid that it was going to inspire copycats in musical acts—that kind of thing."

When the show ended and everyone gathered onstage during the closing credits, as per *SNL* custom, Phil stayed back in the shadows. At the time, he wasn't quite sure why. In retrospect, it became clearer. "I realize that in her country it is very repressive in regards to women's rights, and I understood her motivation," he told journalist Bill Zehme a year afterward, in an unpublished 1993 interview. "But I do think it was just ill placed. The Church, for better or for worse, represents a moral absolute. It's a moral touchstone, and I don't think you should attack that."

Appearing on the Letterman show that same month, Phil's thoughts on O'Connor's desecration began on a serious note and devolved into shtick: Proclaiming he had been "hurt and offended" by her pushing a political agenda, he nonetheless allowed that her feelings on this "volatile issue . . . the whole idea of women's rights"—(she was actually protesting the sexual abuse of children)—were justifiable. "We were taught from childhood: You do not tear up a picture of the Pontiff," he said, beginning to crack wise. "If you have a choice between doing it and not doing it, what you do is *not*. And in school, similarly, the nuns taught us with the Catechism: You do not put Hitler mustaches on the twelve Apostles." He was so "angry" after O'Connor's stunt, Phil went on, that he now felt "an urge for vengeance." His plan, if O'Connor ever had "the guts" to perform in New York again, was to leap onstage while she sang and "tear up a photo of Uncle Fester. I'll see how *she* feels."

Downey recalls that religion was also to blame the only time Phil argued against speaking lines with which he disagreed. "Phil came to me and he was really upset," Downey says, and not because the October 1988 presidential debate sketch in question—in which Phil plays an extremely jaded version of news anchor David Brinkley and guest star Tom Hanks is ABC News anchor Peter Jennings—was unfunny.

"You're offending people," Phil told Downey. But what was so offensive? Downey wondered. There were no dirty words, no attacks on specific groups. "It was the strangest thing. And we sort of had to tone it down. But even then, it was one of the few times he was not very good on the show."

Jennings: Well, David, throughout your career, you've been known for your cynicism, but certainly you haven't lost that much faith in the presidency.

Brinkley: Well, Peter, as I get older, I find I've lost faith in a good many things—country, family, religion, the love of a man for a woman. I've reached a point where it's struggle to get up in the morning, to continue to plow through a dreary, nasty, brutal life . . . of terrible desperation . . . at the end of which we're all just food for maggots.

Usually, though, Phil was chilled out and unflappable; it took a lot to get him worked up. Lovitz, for one, would try—and always fail. Sometimes Phil even played along, as in this phone bit they did offstage.

Lovitz: *Hello, is Brynn there?*
Phil: Who is this?
Lovitz: *It's her lover, Bob.*
Phil: Oh, hello, Bob. Hold on.
Lovitz: *No, Phil, it's me, Jon!*
Phil: Oh! Jon. Thank God! I didn't recognize your voice.
Lovitz: *That's because this is Bob.*
Phil: *What?! Why I oughta . . .*

According to Phil's former Pee-wee cohort Dawna Kaufmann, who was hired as an *SNL* writer for the '92–'93 season, Phil also appeared the model of calm when Brynn stopped by one day to visit and mingle. Kaufmann liked Brynn, but thought her kind of odd—especially on this occasion. "The first time she showed up at the office, we were all in the big conference room, and she comes in and starts sitting on all the guys' laps and kissing them and putting her tongue in their ears," Kaufmann says. "And everyone thought, 'Oh, isn't that funny?' And I thought, 'How could she do this to Phil? This is so humiliating to him.' And he's laughing like he didn't care. How could you not care?"

As the 1992 election drew nearer Phil's Clinton impersonations became more frequent as more political sketches got airtime. On Sunday, November 1, Phil and Carvey hosted a politically themed clip show titled "Presidential Bash." Besides Clinton, Phil also portrayed the vice presidential debate-bungling Admiral James "Who am I? Why am I here?" Stockdale, out on a joyride with Ross Perot (Carvey). It had originally aired a week before, and afterward calls had flooded into *SNL* from military vets who thought the sketch disrespectful. Smigel says Phil never seemed reluctant to play the part, but that he later expressed some guilt about mocking the former Vietnam prisoner of war and subsequent Congressional Medal of Honor recipient.

Two days later, on November 3, when the silver-tongued Democrat from Arkansas—already nicknamed "Slick Willie"—beat out Republican incumbent George H. W. Bush for the most powerful post on Earth, Carvey's prediction came true: Phil won, too. "Phil was incredibly excited that he was going to get to be the president," Smigel says. "In a way that you wouldn't expect, because he was so laid-back. He'd seen Dana be George Bush and how important that was to Dana's career." Phil even wrote a personal letter to President-elect Clinton, Smigel says, "trying to be very serious and thoughtful" about his new responsibility. "In the overall scheme of his life," Phil said, "we're either a thorn in his side or a finger tickling his ribs." In the overall scheme of Phil's life, Clinton's installation as leader of the free world was a game changer.

"I don't think we'll be particularly vicious at first," Phil told *The Boston Globe* in late November, a few weeks after Clinton's election, of the "choice gig" that was now his for at least the next four years. "When Bush took office, we gave him one hundred days to establish a persona. Dana Carvey's take on Bush evolved from Bush's quirky traits—'It's bad! It's baad' and the manic hand gestures. So far Bill hasn't given me any broad hook."

Eleven days after America voted the real guy into office, a torch of sorts was passed in a so-called "cold open" (prior to *SNL*'s opening credits) that featured Carvey as a vanquished George Bush calling up campaign contributors to apologize for letting them down.

Bush's assistant, Marybeth: Sir, I almost forgot: it's 11:30, and President-elect Clinton is about to go on CNN.

Bush: Well, thank you, Marybeth. [Bush picks up remote control and turns on television. The U.S. presidential seal appears onscreen.]

Announcer: Ladies and gentlemen: the President-elect of the United States. [Shot dissolves to a grinning Clinton]

Clinton: Live, from New York, it's Saturday Night! [The audience cheers; Bush shakes his head glumly and slumps in his chair.]

Bush: I—I—I used to say that!

Then came December 5, 1992. Until then, Phil's most successful Clinton portrayal to date had been pre-election, when he played the then-governor bragging about Arkansas' dismally low literacy rate. This was not that—by a long shot.

Scene: President-Elect Bill Clinton [Phil] and two Secret Service agents [Kevin Nealon and Tim Meadows] jog into a Washington, D.C., McDonald's.

Clinton: All right, boys, let's stop here for a second. I'm a little parched from the jog.

Secret Service Agent #1: Sir, we've only been jogging for three blocks. Besides, Mrs. Clinton asked us not to let you in any more fast food places.

Clinton: I just want to mingle with the American people, talk with some real folks. And maybe get a Diet Coke—or something.

Secret Service Agent #1: Fine. But please don't tell Mrs. Clinton.

Clinton: Jim, let me tell you something. There's gonna be a lot of things we don't tell Mrs. Clinton about. Fast food is the least of our worries.

So begins the most memorable Clinton sketch of Phil's *SNL* tenure and arguably the show's history. Stopping by a McDonald's to chat with real people about real issues, Phil's cartoonishly bubble-assed president-elect—wearing a University of Arkansas sweatshirt, a Georgetown baseball cap, and his usual sex-you-up expression—snarfs down portions of an Egg McMuffin, a McLean sandwich, a McDLT, a Chicken McNugget, french fries, a Filet 'O Fish, a hot apple pie, a soda, a milk shake, and a young boy's discarded pickles while discussing loans for small businesses and college students and holding forth on the nefarious doings of Somali warlords. In the process, he nearly chokes and is saved by a sip of soda from sketch participant Rob Schneider.

"Phil Hartman was another one of the go-to guys," Schneider has said. "He was such a good character actor that he would get lost in something and didn't really pop as hard in movies as, like, Adam Sandler or some of the other guys or Eddie Murphy because he was just great as characters. People just saw him as that character. But he was a guy you could depend on to do anything. And . . . he never fluffed. You never saw him stumble his words or not be able to get it out or not go for it." Even on the verge of real-life choking in a make-believe scenario, Phil "never cracked."

Largely as a result of Phil's utter commitment, the sketch killed. Not only that, after six years of mostly blending in, he finally stood out—in a big way. "I became a recognizable face and somewhat of a household name," he said in explaining the Clinton Effect, "and the whole nature of show business changed. I didn't have to go out and look for work anymore. Work came to me."

Carvey to Phil, 1993: You *are* Clinton. That's why when people
go, "Are you going to try and do Clinton?" I go, "Well, the
guy already is Clinton." He does him perfectly, so what is
the point?
Phil: We're close in age. We're close in weight. Bulbous noses,
big jaws. Kind of bigheaded stocky guys.
Carvey: He's considered a stud.

Clinton had been difficult to nail at first, Phil admitted to *The Washing-ton Post*, "because he really fits the mold of the polished pol—he's very studied." So, too, was Phil—watching tapes of Clinton's debates and other appearances, making "little drawings of his hand gestures" and perfecting his subject's unique speech patterns until they felt right in the throat. "I'm loath to take credit for it," he told the *Toronto Star,* referring to his voice-manipulating abilities, "because I don't even know what it is. It's some kind of intellectual facility that just allows you to hear something and realize what muscles in your throat to tweak, where you have to pitch it." In Clinton's case, Phil seized on his allergies, which caused post-nasal drip and gave his voice a slight scratchiness.

Costume-wise, owing to his self-described "Mr. Potato Head" quality and the fact that he and Clinton shared similar facial features, Phil took a minimalistic approach that required little more than a suit, a lush silvery wig, and some basic makeup that highlighted the tip of his nose and lightened his eyebrows. Clinton's hand gestures were essential, too. "Clinton has beautiful hands [and] long fingers," Phil said in explaining his Clinton approach for the umpteenth time. "He uses the old stock political gesture, what I call the ATM card in the ATM machine. It's less intimidating than a fist or a finger point. It's almost like he's handing you something . . . . When all these ele-ments coalesce, you can create the illusion of this personality." While his pal Carvey did caricatures, and did them well, Phil was more concerned with realism—getting so close, he once said, "that it allows the audience to suspend disbelief."

Norman Bryn, whose makeup handiwork helped Phil become Bill for a couple of seasons at *SNL,* calls Phil "an ideal Clinton. He was getting a wig made for himself and he was going to pick up a lot of what he called 'quick extra money' doing what Dana was doing [with Bush]." At the time, Carvey commanded a healthy fee in the tens of thousands to perform his Bush shtick. Phil hoped to clean up, too, earning extra dough at Clinton's expense.

But while his portrayal of Clinton was often less than flattering, Phil insisted he wasn't out to get the guy. On the contrary, Phil liked him and felt they were in some ways kindred spirits. "He opposed the Vietnam War like I did," Phil told *USA Today.* "He tried marijuana. He didn't inhale. I did." The kindred thing wasn't exactly mutual. During Phil's 1993 appearance on CNN's *Larry King Live,* he once said, the show's producers tried and failed to have Clinton call in. Instead, Bubba sent over a signed photo with the inscription, "To Phil Hartman—You're not the president, but you play one on TV and you're OK—mostly." The word "mostly" was underscored with a squiggly line, which Phil interpreted to mean, *You're all right, but I definitely have my eye on you, because you cross the line.* Later on, in fact, Phil claimed he was shut out of White House events and other functions as a direct result of his Clinton skewering.

After meeting Clinton at a New York fund-raiser, Phil told David Letterman, "I found out the hard way that he really doesn't like what I do." The overseas crowd apparently was skittish, too. After being invited to perform for Queen Elizabeth, Prince Philip, and other fancy-pants figures at the annual Royal Variety Performance in London, Phil claimed the prime minister's office "got concerned" due to [here, Phil affected a stodgy accent] " *'a longstanding relationship with the United States. We certainly don't want to jeopardize our relationship.'* And so they called the White House and [the White House] went,

'No! Not Hartman! No! No!' So they put the kibosh on it and it was very disappointing."

Curiously, Phil told another interviewer that the president had proclaimed to "get a kick out of what we did on *SNL*." He also revealed that Clinton and his staffers had supposedly watched tapes of Phil's impersonations during the 1992 presidential campaign. Then again, the most pointed barbs flew only *after* Clinton took office. In any case, it wasn't Phil's job "to be the president's best friend," he confided to NBC host Bob Costas—though he still felt "a twinge of guilt" about doing his impression. He also told Costas this, half-jokingly or not, of his comedic targets: "I think deep down you want to kill the person, at least in my case."

But at least Clinton let Phil know where he stood. Other celebrities Phil played weren't so forthcoming, and it bothered him to know they might be offended. Whenever Carvey channeled radio personality Casey Kasem, Phil said by way of example, Kasem sent a thank-you gift. Phil got squat from the folks he lampooned. More disturbingly, he also received some "really scary militia kind of stuff" from dismayed viewers. As Phil was well aware, his Clinton jabbing tended to be more personal than political owing to Phil's own liberal leanings. Instead of mocking Clinton's stances on education or taxation, for example, Phil focused on his overeating or his lady killing.

By 1993 the money on *SNL* was, as Phil put it, "starting to get real"— possibly as much as $30,000 a week. It was still short of prime-time star pay, but combined with his growing revenues from national television ads and earnings from *The Simpsons*, it was enough to keep Phil in swell duds and random toys and nice cars. Over the years his ever-growing mini-fleet of automobiles came to include a white Mercedes S-Class coupe, a Porsche Carrera 4, a 1961 Bentley, and a white Ferrari 355—all except the Mercedes purchased used but in sparkling condition. Phil was even more enamored of his boats, from which he loved to fish and in which he made increasingly frequent trips to Catalina Island with a friend or two in tow when his schedule allowed. During summer hiatus work lulls, he made jaunts about once a week. "You just can't believe how beautiful it is," he marveled. The one and only time he brought Brynn and the kids there, friend Steve Small says, large swells on the open sea made their journey over quite unpleasant. "I'm sure it wasn't planned, but it was as though he arranged it so that he could go whenever he wanted to," Small says with a laugh.

Phil initially made the Catalina trip on a twenty-five-foot Egg Harbor boat, christened *Anika* after daughter Birgen's middle name, which means grace, gracious, or favor in several languages. He then switched to a thirty-six-foot Boston Whaler that topped out at 50 knots in calm water, 20 in choppy. (Later, Phil also bought a used seventeen-footer that he kept at Catalina.) On at least one occasion a pod of dolphins surfaced and began leaping alongside the boat. Often, he floated at a remote spot called Lover's Cove, at the island's more developed east end, and fed spray cheese to swarms of calico bass in a protected portion of Avalon Harbor. Just off shores where pirates, Spaniards, and Chumash Indians had dwelled in the 1700s, Phil also liked to moor his boat, kick back and chill out while blasting Neil Young's 1992 album *Harvest Moon* from the boat's speakers. Or he'd buy a can of spray cheese and feed it to swarms of Calico bass in a protected portion of Avalon harbor. In video footage of one excursion Phil does a 360-degree pan with his camera, catching glimpses of the clear greenish water, recreational boaters, and Indian Rock. "I think I'm gonna like it here in Emerald Bay," he says jauntily to no one in particular. "It's a happy place."

Phil was also an avid snorkeler (especially at the island's Long Point, his favorite snorkeling spot) and scuba diver, with all the latest gear and a philosophical appreciation for the sport. "It's so transcendental," he once explained. "It's like going to another dimension."

Mark Pierson accompanied him to Catalina on a few occasions, and

Small made the journey six or seven times, but Britt Marin was his most consistent companion on less crowded summer weekdays and during the off-season. They hiked for miles, marveling at the island's glittering steatite rock formations and unsullied wilderness. They scuba-dived and snorkeled. They dined at the venerable (and now shuttered) Armstrong's Seafood Restaurant and Fish Market, overlooking the marina and bay in Avalon. They smoked pot at the Wrigley Memorial & Botanic Garden.

Since 1990, Chicago's Wrigley family—the chewing gum magnates—has ruled Catalina, which hosted spring training from 1921 through 1952 for their Chicago Cubs baseball team. By the time Phil began regularly visiting again, the Wrigley's Santa Catalina Island Conservancy controlled 86 percent of the property. Phil wanted to re-tire on Catalina, he often said, maybe get a condo in the upscale section of Hamilton Cove. That was the life. The quiet life.

As extroverted as he was onstage, on-camera, and in the public eye, in private Phil would often shut down and seem largely absent in his presence. "I wouldn't say Phil was depressive," Dozier says, "but I think he suffered a little bit of depression at times." When Dozier dropped by Phil's Encino home to hang out and watch old movies, there were long stretches of silence between the two, punctuated mostly by Phil's remarks about actors, directors, awards, and the like. "I would begin to think, 'He's not talking or anything. Maybe he wants to be left alone,'" Dozier says. "And I'd say, 'Well, I guess I'll go,' and he'd look at me and say, 'Oh, no, don't go!'"

They had a similar dynamic on the open water. One afternoon, as they were cruising slowly downwind with their shirts off and the sun beaming brightly, Phil tugged his hat over his eyes and said, "You know what I like about you, Floyd? You don't talk too much." Phil's tone was joshing, but Dozier knew he was serious. Some things, Dozier replied, were just better left unsaid. Ohara Hartmann, the daughter of Phil's older brother John and at one point a part-time caretaker to the

Hartman kids in Encino, also noticed Phil's penchant for quietude. "He had a way of being what you would expect, kind of the *Saturday Night Live* guy," she says. "But the real Phil to me was kind of quiet, the shy middle child. During some of my best times with him, we just sat there, not really talking about much of anything."

Phil resumed his duties as honorary sheriff of Encino that summer, 1993, and spent most of August shooting *Greedy*. The big-screen comedy—written by the *Happy Days* team of Lowell Ganz and Babaloo Mandel—co-stars Ed Begley Jr., Michael J. Fox, and the legendary Kirk Douglas, and was Phil's meatiest movie role to date. As a nasty schemer named Frank, he plays one of several conniving relatives who attempt to scam their rich Uncle Joe (Douglas) out of his $20 million fortune. "I love to play weasels," Phil once said. "I just want to be funny, and villains tend to be funny because their foibles are all there to see."

During *Greedy*'s filming, Begley recalls, Phil agreed to bring Brynn along for a dinner outing. It would be just the three of them, as Begley was newly divorced. But about halfway through shooting, Phil rang Begley at his home in Studio City. He wasn't calling about their dinner plans. Here, once again, is Begley's reenactment of the exchange—almost a decade after the Ojai incident:

"Ed, can I talk to you?"

"Of course. You're OK?"

"Um, well, no, I'm not OK. Do I remember right—you have a guest room above your garage?"

"Do you have a friend?"

"No, it's for me. Brynn and I—it's bad, it's very bad. We've split up and I can't stay there in the house."

"Come over, buddy. We'll go there right when we're done with work. I'll give you a key."

But Phil never came, Begley says, though he doesn't know why and didn't ask. Perhaps Phil and Brynn kissed and made up. Perhaps not. Whatever the case, "He never stayed one night in that room."

Although Phil was spared most of their vitriol and even complimented in some cases, reviewers were again unkind and *Greedy* died a quick death upon release in early March 1994.

While Begley was privy to brief flashes of Phil's travails with Brynn, Phil increasingly gave his ex-wife Lisa an earful—about Brynn's object-throwing temper tantrums, her cosmetic surgeries (which included facial and breast), and what Phil perceived as Brynn's controlling nature. She was even furious when he got fan mail, Phil claimed. As if he could help that. He disliked it, too, when Brynn stood in his shadow. He disliked it when anyone stood in his shadow, even pals, though it wasn't an easy shadow to slip. "He wanted to be connected to people who were his peers," says Floyd Dozier, then a software development manager to whom Phil gave grief for blending into the background at movie premieres and other public events. "He wanted me to relate to him—and [other] people—as equals. In fact, I think I did most of the time, but we weren't operating in the same arenas. The more famous he got, the more I felt like an outsider, and the more awkward I felt at his social events when someone asked, 'So Floyd, what do you do?'" Brynn may have felt likewise. "She always wanted to be an actress, and I think she was kind of jealous that he was," Ohara Hartmann says. "But she was also a very talented artist. She'd sit down to color with the kids and I'd say, 'Oh, my gosh, Brynn, that's amazing. You should take classes.' And she went, 'Well, I'll never be like Phil.' She was just someone who wasn't fulfilled."

Much to Lorne Michaels's dismay—or so claimed a gossip item in the New York *Daily News* that Phil subsequently shot down—Phil announced that the 1993–94 season of *SNL* (his eighth) would be his last. The younger guard, though respectful of his status, was increasingly crowding him out. More important, he wanted to work on new projects, including a revival of *The Phil Show.* And so he bided his time and gave it his all, playing Clinton and Larry King, Michael Eisner and Frank Sinatra, creepy U.S. senator Bob Packwood, and (to his great delight) Jesus Christ while newer cast mates like Farley, Sandler, Tim Meadows, and David Spade soaked up ever more of the spotlight.

As the season wore on, Phil was indeed featured in fewer and fewer sketches—sometimes only one or two per show, and nothing especially memorable except for his old standby characters, or maybe his Ned Land (a role made famous by Kirk Douglas) opposite Kelsey Grammer's Captain Nemo in a parody of *20,000 Leagues Under the Sea.* His work, as always, was never less than solid, but it seemed subtle and almost quaint in contrast to Sandler's be-caped and clowning Opera Man or Farley's hilariously spastic motivational speaker Matt Foley, who lived "in a van down by the river!" "It wasn't just what was going on on-camera; I think he felt like he didn't have peers off camera," says Smigel, who left *SNL* in 1993 to become head writer at NBC's then fledgling *Late Night with Conan O'Brien.* "I think he probably felt more like an island." Carvey and Lovitz weren't there anymore, either. And Jan Hooks was merely in and out for guest shots. Of Phil's original writing crew, Downey and Franken remained, but Zander, Handey, and the Turners exited around the same time as Smigel. There was also this: *SNL* is a pressure cooker, even for the coolest of cats.

New cast member Sarah Silverman felt it, too, and was delighted when Phil approached her about writing a sketch for them to do together. "This moment of paternal encouragement randomly collided in my brain with an odd bit of trivia I'd recently picked up: that flies live for only twenty-four hours," she recalled in her 2010 memoir *The Bedwetter.* So she wrote a piece in which she and Phil were flies— one older, one younger—on a wall. At the end, as fly-Phil lies dying, the shot cuts to video of a dog shitting. "Go get it," fly-Phil tells his young charge. "It's beautiful." And though the sketch didn't survive past dress rehearsal, Silverman says, Phil "gave it his all. A lot of cast members would just bail on things they didn't want to go through. But he was very sweet about it."

Jay Mohr was also among those who regarded Phil as an avuncular figure and something of a living legend among the veterans who remained. "He certainly stood out from the pack," Mohr says. "He didn't put on airs. He wasn't a snob or anything. But you could just tell. It would be like if you're on a football team, and the star quarterback walks in. He just carries himself differently. Phil wasn't sittin' around with Farley and Tim Meadows and Sandler, making fart jokes and trying to curry favor with the writers. You had to write for Phil. If Phil was in your sketch, it had a much better chance of getting on the air because there really wasn't anything he couldn't do."

Phil later admitted he was "emotionally stressed" throughout his entire *SNL* run. "The rejection and backstabbing could be painful, but the hardest thing was competing against your friends for airtime." And from a purely creative standpoint, the shows were getting less sophisticated. "There's less political satire. The younger audience loves Adam Sandler," Phil told *Entertainment Weekly* in early 1994. "He appeals less to the intellect and more to that stand-up sensibility of 'Let's go out there and be insane.' I like Adam Sandler, but that's not my kind of comedy, so, yeah, in a way it makes me feel like, 'Well, it's time for me to go.'" Months afterward, much to Michaels's displeasure, he likened his departure to getting off the *Titanic* before it sank.

Despite his disappointment with Phil for being so publicly impolitic, Michaels understood what was going on. Leaving *SNL* was "very emotional for Phil," he says. "I honestly never took it [as] a real insult or anything. Saying good-bye to the show was really hard for him. I think he underestimated how attached he was." The firmer the attachment, Michaels says, the more forceful the detachment. "It's how people break up. They pick a fight." Not long after, Phil "apologized profusely" to everyone he'd insulted.

During his *Later* appearance with Greg Kinnear, he was equally sanguine about the prospect of leaving his professional home of many years. Asked if it "bothered" him that he'd depart without a big-time breakout character to his credit, Phil affected a deeply hurt look and replied in a high-strung tone, "You mean does it bother me that I'm a loser? Is that what you're saying? No, no," he went on, chuckling nervously, "I enjoy that. I enjoy the obscurity that I've had. Why should I be concerned that twenty-year-olds are running off and making two-hundred-million-dollar movies?" Then he dropped the act. After watching Dana Carvey launch a film career with the extremely successful *Wayne's World*, and Lovitz land a role in the enormously successful *A League of Their Own*, Phil admitted his confidence took a hit. But once he stopped comparing his career with anyone else's, those feelings of insecurity went away. "In truth, I am very happy with the kind of career I've had on *Saturday Night Live*," he said. "I haven't had that breakout character that went to the stratosphere and ended up on a T-shirt or a coffee mug or something. But I've done a lot of work that I'm very proud of, and I get fan mail from people who say I'm still their favorite person on the show. Not that that's the requirement.

"Look, this is comedy. I'm having the time of my life. I got this job when I was in my mid-thirties [actually, he was thirty-eight]. I had decided to quit acting and suddenly this dropped in my lap. So I see it all as a gift, and I think that's the way we should look at this life."

He wasn't taking any chances with his post-*SNL* career, though. So before making his escape, Phil began formulating an exit plan.

Sometime in the fall of 1993, in his *SNL* office (#1719) at 30 Rock, Phil received a packet of comedy-writing samples from two Greenville, Rhode Island–based brothers named Brian and Kevin Mulhern. They'd seen him talking about *The Phil Show* (then targeted as a mid-season replacement for the spring of 1994) on a Letterman appearance and were eager to contribute material. *The Phil Show*, as Phil described it some months later, would "reinvent the variety form the way David Letterman reinvented the talk show" via "a hybrid, very fast-paced, high energy" format "with sketches, impersonations, pet acts, and performers showcasing their talents." He also envisioned having "an interracial cast of at least two or three males and females."

However, since both Mulherns were then only in their early twenties and short on experience (Kevin was still in college; Brian worked as a pharmacy technician and radio station intern), they figured nothing would come of it. "We had made so many submissions [elsewhere] and gotten no response, so we were basically just wasting a lot of postage," Kevin says. Then Phil called and left a message. Their mother retrieved it, not knowing who this Phil Hartman guy was, and passed it along. They phoned him back the next day. Phil dug their samples, he told them, and wanted to meet them in person to further discuss possible writing roles on his show. Thrilled, the siblings soon headed to New York and 30 Rock, where they hooked up with Phil and pitched him ideas in his *SNL* dressing room. "When Brian and I walked out, we're like, 'What the hell does he need us for?' Kevin says. "'He *doesn't* need us! I hope he hasn't realized that.'"

During their brief meeting with Phil in New York, Brian remembers, Phil was eager to make Brynn a central part of his new venture. "There was a lot of talk about her and her role," Brian says of discussions then and thereafter. "He was hell-bent on making that happen and making her a cast member and trying to get her career off the ground. That was the one thing that kind of had a nepotism feel to it." Brynn, Phil gushed, was a beautiful, statuesque, talented actress with whom he had "great chemistry" that would "translate well over the airwaves." Although the brothers pushed for Jan Hooks to star alongside Phil, Hooks wanted to stay in New York rather than relocate to L.A., where *The Phil Show* would shoot. "He definitely had [Brynn's] best interests at heart," Brian says, "and he was hopeful for her that this would work."

While Phil finished out his final season on *SNL,* he and the Mulherns worked on sketch ideas. Most of them played to Phil's proven strength as the Man of a Thousand Voices—or at least a hundred:

Frank's Place: Phil plays the Chairman hosting a talk show from his home in Palm Springs.

Hollywood Babylon: Phil plays a gossipy Tony Curtis.

Happening L.A.: Phil plays "Bobby Vaneare," a showbiz cheeseball who wears metal-tipped cowboy boots and a leather jacket with fringe.

Collage: Phil plays an approximation of PBS talk show host Charlie Rose refereeing a bunch of loudmouths.

Inside the Third Reich: Phil plays Hitler's "personal architect" Albert Speer, who somehow abides his evil bosses' bad behavior in the name of career advancement.

Hollywood Tribute: Phil plays "a Beverly Hills matron" who interviews people famous and obscure and not at a charity event—just because.

Rescue 911: Phil, as William Shatner, hosts a parody of the reality television show.

Bosun Bob's Kartoon Korner: Phil plays Bob, a 1950s throwback, who doodles, plays with puppets, and raises weighty political issues.

Edge of Love: A soap opera parody with well-coiffed stars.

Hell's Kitchen: Phil plays New York–based PI Chick Hazard solving ridiculous cases involving monsters, aliens, and mummies.

Ed McMahon's World of Weirdness: Phil plays the former *Tonight Show* sidekick as the host of a bizarre interview program.

Action Figure Theater: Exactly that—action figures doing theater.

Lightman: Phil reprises his light-wearing, mind-reading Groundlings character.

Phil's feedback on the Mulherns' contributions was always upbeat and constructive. Often, he left critiques and updates on their answering machine. "Way to go, guys," he praised in one. "It makes me feel great to know that I've got buddies who can deliver, and it bodes well for your future, I might add."

Early in 1994, Phil added Joel Gallen (with whom he shared a talent manager in Brillstein-Grey's Sandy Wernick) to the *Phil Show*'s team as executive producer. His old Groundlings pal Tom Maxwell and Maxwell's writing partner Don Woodard were in talks to be the show's head writers. "It looks like we're making some incremental progress," Phil said in another message to the Mulherns. Once Maxwell, Woodard, and Gallen were "in place," they could "work out an overall strategy and start staffing up for the pilot." Things looked more promising by the day.

"He really felt like this was going to be his big solo break," says Gallen, who thought likewise. "It had so much potential to be a really groundbreaking, unique sketch comedy show from a different point of view."

As Phil's days on *SNL* waned, his presence on the storied stage of Studio 8H remained greatly diminished. "He was upset by it," Michaels says. "It was a time of turmoil. He had grown comfortable, and so had I. And at the same time, the network was being critical of us, so we were fighting on all sides." Even on May 15, during his record-setting 153rd and final appearance as a regular cast member, he was unusually light—industry lingo for short on stage time. Except for a cold open with guest host Heather Locklear (Phil played her first of several sex partners) and his part as a besuited emcee in the show's last sketch, a spoof of the Rodgers and Hammerstein song "So Long, Farewell" from *The Sound of Music*, he had little to do and there was no fanfare to trumpet his exit after eight exceptional seasons. But his final appearance was indeed memorable.

"So long, farewell . . . Hey, what am I chopped liver?" Chris Farley yawningly warbles in the guise of plaid-jacketed motivational guru Matt Foley. As he wearily plops down on the stage's apron and sings, "I need . . . to sleep . . . in a van down by the river," Phil emerges from the wings and sits beside him. Except for a spotlight shining on the two of them, Studio 8H is dark. Draping an arm over the slumbering man-boy as Farley rests his head on Phil's chest, Phil addresses the small audience before him and the millions of viewers in TV land: "You know, I can't imagine a more dignified way to end my eight years on this program." Smiling, he then sings, in a faltering head voice, "Good-bye . . . good-bye. Good-byyyyyyyyyye." The spotlight remains on Phil and Farley. Phil waves as the audience applauds. The camera zooms out as the spotlight shrinks. *Fin.*

Afterward, Phil's fellow cast members and others gathered backstage to present him with a special keepsake—a token of deep appreciation for his outstanding service. Phil had previously won an Emmy and an American Comedy Award, but the bottle of clear wood glue secured to a small pedestal that was bestowed by his peers that night immediately became his most cherished honor of all. As he had when daughter Birgen's birth was announced on the show two years earlier, Phil tried and failed to stave off tears. "It meant as much as an Academy Award, because it symbolized how they felt about him," says Norman Bryn, who was there. "And you could see that he was genuinely moved. There was a totally open, vulnerable human being there. Other than his falling apart during the night when Brynn really got to him, that was Phil as [emotionally] naked as I'd ever seen him."

Michaels was unsurprised by Phil's reserved but deeply genuine reaction. For eight years *SNL* had been "his life," after all. "He loved it. And it's the best work he ever did. He was not unaware of that."

Chapter 13

Phil as Bill McNeal on the set of *NewsRadio*, 1995.
(Photo © Alan Levenson/NBC/NBCU Photo Bank)

I n the summer of 1994, Phil left an answering machine message for Brian and Kevin Mulhern regarding progress on *The Phil Show*. There were no new developments yet, he told them, because NBC was "preoccupied with the problems of the new season," replacement shows were low-priority, and Phil himself had been busy with other work. Ideally, Phil said, he and a few other writers would begin outlining and scripting the program sometime in early October, after which the Mulherns could fly out to L.A. and join them. Nothing, however, was written in stone.

A couple of weeks after Phil bugged out of *SNL,* he spent a month or so shooting the comedy *Houseguest* in and around Pittsburgh with comedian Sinbad. Phil's character, a well-off but somewhat dense lawyer and father of three, marked his first co-starring role in films. Director Randall Miller told the *Pittsburgh Post-Gazette* that *Houseguest* was for Phil "a way to move into being a mainstream leading man," just as the *The Jerk* had been for Steve Martin. And, in fact, Phil was then in talks to play the lead in a movie called *Secret Agent Man*, but that project ultimately fizzled.

When *Houseguest* wrapped in late June, Phil was able to devote more time to shepherding *The Phil Show* into existence. Frustratingly, as he made clear in his message to the Mulherns, NBC suits kept dragging their feet. "I think they were just worried," Gallen says. "For some reason, they just never really felt like they had a shot to make it." It couldn't have helped that another *SNL* alum, Chevy Chase, was fresh off a disastrous stint on Fox's *The Chevy Chase Show*, which lasted just five weeks and cost the network millions. Chatfests featuring Martin Short, Robert Townsend, and Paula Poundstone had flopped, too. Over at NBC, newish 12:30 A.M. host and David Letterman successor Conan O'Brien's quirky program garnered consistently low ratings, tepid-to-poor reviews, and teetered on the brink of cancellation. Granted, those folks were all late-night personalities, but if they couldn't cut it during bedtime hours, how would the nontraditional *Phil Show* fare during prime time?

As Phil toiled to bring his vision to fruition, Brynn had a tiny career breakthrough of sorts when friend and director Rob Reiner hired her for his film *North*, which opened July 22, 1994. Appearing in only one brief scene as a diner waitress, she speaks a single line while serving beverages: "One Coca-Cola right here. And one Sex on the Beach." Her close-up, such as it is, lasts approximately five seconds. In retrospect, though, she was probably fortunate; the $40 million comedy—written by Alan Zweibel and based on his novella of the same name—crashed big and earned what Zweibel later described as "a veritable avalanche" of scathing reviews. Roger Ebert's was especially crushing. "I hated this movie," he famously wrote-stabbed. "Hated, hated, hated, hated, hated this movie. Hated it. Hated every simpering stupid vacant audience-insulting moment of it. Hated the sensibility that thought anyone would like it. Hated the implied insult to the audience by its belief that anyone would be entertained by it."

Phil spent a fair amount of time high above sea level that summer on his way to earning enough in-flight hours to get his pilot's license during Thanksgiving vacation late the following fall. Boats were fun but slow; he wished to master a mode of transportation that would allow him to travel to Catalina Island and back in far less time than it took to motor twenty-six miles across the sea. And seeing as Brynn often told him and close friends of hers that Phil spent too much time away from home, this was a perfect remedy—not to mention another toy with which to tinker. By October 1994, after many months of typically exhaustive research—and more than a year before he was certified to fly on his own upon completing at least forty flight hours, half of them solo—he spent high five to low six figures on a French-made TB200 Tobago XL GT by Socata. With its white top, gray bottom, and dark-orange body stripes, the handsome single-prop model—tail number N3057D—had a 200-horsepower Lycoming 10-360AIB6 piston engine, fixed tricycle landing gear, and room for four in its spacious cabin. As Phil gushed in an endorsement letter to the manufacturer a few years post-purchase, "This airplane is simply a delight. I appreciate it for its docile handling characteristics and its outstanding performance. And I'm especially pleased with its overall design. This is an aircraft that is very pleasing to the eye. It's a modern, fresh design. I appreciate the gull-wing doors and the well-designed cockpit."

Phil's college and surfing pal Clif Potts owned a Cessna 182 Skylane at the time and shared Phil's burgeoning enthusiasm for flying. "You're aware of something greater than yourself, a power," Potts says. "You're driving this ball of energy. The same thing with surfing—there's a place in the wave that's like the power point and you can move into it and ahead of it and back behind it, but you are connected to it in order to be able to do what you're doing." On a more surface level, Phil thought it "a superb diversion that gives one a sense of competence and skill" as well as "a way to get away from it all, because it's completely absorbing."

As Phil explained when he guested on Conan O'Brien's show, his attraction to airplanes sprang partly from his love of John Wayne's World War II movies, such as 1942's *Flying Tigers*. "The hardest part of flying isn't the flying," Phil noted. "It's the radio communications." He then affected the deep voice and nonsensical but official-sounding lingo of a pilot: "Learjet 3057 Delta inbound Sepulveda Pass with information Joliet. Roger 3057 Delta, make right traffic before 1-6 right before five Delta. . . . Spark 555 roger, sparking double nickel double nickel . . ."

When he wasn't bound for Catalina's tiny Airport in the Sky, where he kept a white Volkswagon Golf (used) not far from the runway, Phil loved to read up on his new hobby and practice his landings ("touch-and-go's"). He most often used the Tobago for Catalina trips, though, and as usual Britt Marin was his most frequent co-pilot to Avalan and Two Harbors. Together they made numerous trips from the mainland, always with a stash of primo weed on board for toking in-flight and upon landing.

Tearing through the wild blue yonder was an entirely different and far more intense experience than Phil had ever known. "He liked coming and going from the Airport in the Sky," Marin remembers. "Because it's kind of a tricky approach and takeoff. If you came in short you'd slam into a cliff, and if you didn't take off in time you'd fly off of one." An "excellent pilot" in Marin's estimation, Phil loved to fly between the Van Nuys airport (where he stored his plane in a hangar with his sports cars) and Catalina, purposely putting his nimble craft into stalls along the way. Every time he did so, its nose dipped and an alarm sounded. Still, Marin trusted him completely. "He was very methodical in applying the rules of flying," Marin says. "He'd put the manual in his lap to go through procedures. And he'd also say, 'Hey, Britt, pay attention here and you'll learn how to fly,' so I did. I never got a license or anything, but I know how to fly a plane."

Lovitz later remarked that after Phil had been flying only a short time, he already seemed like "a veteran pilot of twenty years for United Airlines." Tracy Newman was similarly struck with his proficiency and commitment to safety, qualities that helped to temper mounting terror when she took to the skies for her one and only flight with Phil at the helm. "We could have been going down, dying," she says, "and I still would have had confidence in him."

As Phil eased into his post-*SNL* life, there was also more time to be a dad—though he was never around nearly as much as Brynn would have liked. Dozier observed that Phil's tendency to disengage physically and emotionally at home "kind of applied to the kids, too. I think he adored his kids. Most parents do. I've heard from other people and seen video of him playing with the kids, which I know he did a lot. But usually when I came over, Phil and I would just disappear into his office." John Hartmann spoke of Phil the dad during his 2004 CNN interview with Larry King. "I'm sure that the kids would [have wanted] to have more time [with him] and I'm sure Phil would have wanted to work out more time for them. But he loved them and they loved him and they probably would have appreciated more attention."

When they were together, clowning was common. "We play a lot of silly games and we're kind of a silly family," Phil said. "We like to have a lot of laughter, but I don't think I'm special to them because

I'm a comedian. I just like to feel that I'm a participant in their lives, not so much the center of it." As such, he devised improv games, assisted with puppet shows, splashed around in the backyard pool and went on family outings. Sean ("Seany") was the more serious and introspective of Phil's children. He was also one hell of an artist, Phil liked to brag—better than Phil ever was at the same age. Father and son often played "squiggles," the drawing game Phil had invented with Sparkie Holloway decades back, and stored their completed pictures in a folder. Phil's wackier side came out in the sunny and extroverted Birgen ("Birgey"). One of their favorite daddy-daughter activities was theatrical in nature. "Do your happy face," he'd tell her. She beamed. "Now do your sad face." She moped. "Now do your angry face." She glowered. But her "handsome face" was the one that always made him laugh hardest.

As ever, though, it was Brynn who did most of the parenting. From infancy on she spent the most time feeding and diapering and nursing the kids through sickness. She volunteered at their school library and shopped for their clothes and planned their birthday parties. She recorded milestones of their childhoods—first cold, first laugh—in a journal. A nanny was often on hand, as was a housekeeper, but Phil's escalating absenteeism continued to provoke Brynn's ire. If there was one complaint she voiced (to family, to friends), that was it. "I thought she was a fantastic mom," Sweeney says. "But she was such a contradiction because [of how] she looked. I knew [her and Phil] when they first met, and then she was having a baby and I was thinking, 'Oh, God, should women like this really have kids? They shouldn't,'" Sweeney jokes. "They should really just be *this look*. This look takes a hundred percent of someone's time. There's no kid that should come into this when you have a mom who looks like that.'"

Despite her insecurities, Brynn struck Sweeney and a friend of theirs, now-former *SNL* writer Christine Zander, as a great mother in every way. She was patient, caring, engaged. "And it didn't seem fake, like, 'Now I'm in public, so I'm going to show you what a good mom I am,'" Sweeney says. "It seemed real. Every interaction I saw, which was a lot—I spent whole days at their house—was admirable."

As a friend, Zander says, Brynn was "a very sweet and goofy woman" who was exceedingly generous and always had an ear for someone else's problems. "She wanted all of her friends to be happy"—a state that Brynn herself found increasingly elusive. At one point she became so fed up with Phil's disappearing act, Sweeney says, that she began talking about filing for divorce. But an attorney friend had said to wait until her marriage hit the ten-year mark, Brynn confided. A solid decade together, combined with the fact that she and Phil had two kids, would assure Brynn of a generous settlement. Sweeney couldn't be sure, but she thought Brynn might have just been blowing off steam. "She *totally* loved him," Sweeney says. "I think she *really* loved him." But as far as Brynn could tell, her less emotionally demonstrative and often passive husband was growing less and less interested—in her, in them. He was no longer glamourized. No longer bursting with joy.

"Brynn needed to have somebody look at her like that. Not just the world, but a guy," Sweeney says. "And I think eventually Phil didn't care as much; he wasn't looking at her like that anymore. It happens in any marriage. You're not going, 'Oh, my God!' anymore. And along with other things, that was a really painful thing for her. He wasn't as excited to be with her as he had been. And I just felt so sad. Also, I thought, 'God, Phil doesn't even see that Brynn is also one of those girls who's also pretty interesting.' You'd think 'he's got a gold mine,' because he married her for her looks—and not even so much for her looks, but for how the world looked at him when he was with her. And then that wears off, because it wears off. If it were me, I'd go, 'Oh, my God, and I accidentally *also* married an interesting person.' But I don't think he could see that."

Besides the Mulherns, Woodard, Maxwell, and Gallen, Dawna Kaufmann says Phil also approached her about writing for *The Phil Show*. Kaufmann's original notion, which she claims Phil liked, was a Jack Benny–type program with Phil as the Benny-esque ringmaster and Brynn as herself. "Brynn loved me, because no one else was saying, 'I'm going to write for you both,'" Kaufmann says. After Phil promised to bring Kaufmann's ideas and sketches (written on spec) to his managers at Brillstein-Grey, weeks went by with no feedback. Kaufmann called him and asked what was happening. Phil told her she'd sit in on a meeting very soon. "And then," Kaufmann says, "I couldn't get him on the phone. I couldn't get his attention." Kaufmann contacted Brynn for insight; Brynn had none. That Phil was also having conversations with others, including the Mulherns, was unknown to Kaufmann. "It was my idea and we were working together," she says. "But that was Phil. It wouldn't have surprised me if he was making little deals on the side with [other] people. That's not a good thing about him."

With *SNL* behind him and *The Phil Show* in what seemed like eternal limbo, Phil began to feel adrift. He still did commercial work and episodes of *The Simpsons* (besides McClure and Hutz, his voices on the show had grown to include Moses, Johnny Tightlips, a Mexican wrestling announcer, Smooth Jimmy Apollo, Charlton Heston, and a host of others). He even did some bit parts for *The Ren & Stimpy Show*. But the absence of a regular gig made him anxious. When Martin Short's NBC sitcom tanked (in the fall of 1994, after only three episodes), Phil told David Letterman, "I got scared. I shouldn't say got scared. Well, for several weeks I shivered in the corner naked with the lights out. That's not fear. It could have been the flu bug." Seriously, though, the process of launching his own program had proved to be more Sisyphean than Phil had anticipated. And so it came as something of a relief when NBC passed on *The Phil Show* while at the same time offering its would-be star an opportunity to return to ensemble acting and his former network in an NBC sitcom pilot called *NewsRadio*.

Created by former Letterman and *The Larry Sanders Show* writer Paul Simms, a Harvard graduate then only in his late twenties, the pilot script (shot in the late fall of 1994) struck Phil as a cut above typical fare when he initially perused it in the offices of Brillstein-Grey. It apparently mattered not that his character, arrogant broadcaster Bill McNeal, had maybe a dozen lines in the entire episode. And while he was then being courted for the lead role in another sitcom on which he would play the father of two kids, Simms's craftsmanship and the fact that he'd created McNeal (an intelligent but insufferable schmuck) specifically for Phil ultimately won out. "One thing I've learned from my tenure at *Saturday Night Live* is that good writing is what it's all about," Phil said. "And this one just punched through." From a more career-oriented perspective, if the show got picked up, Phil could return to doing what he did best: being a comedic actor-for-hire. Spurred by encouragement from Dana Carvey, he took the job.

Before long, *NewsRadio* was green-lighted and Phil was back in the NBC fold at a healthy salary of $50,000 per episode. That totaled out at $350,000 for the truncated first season—which began airing on Tuesday nights in March 1995 and consisted of just seven episodes—and more than $1 million when NBC re-upped for an additional twenty-one episodes that began airing when season two picked up that September. Not bad for an ensemble player on an unproven show in 1995, though in ensuing years Phil's grumbling that he should earn more reportedly fell on deaf ears. That two of his managers, Brad Grey and Bernie Brillstein, also produced the show probably didn't help matters.

Scene from *NewsRadio:* Dave Nelson and Bill McNeal talk in the offices of WNYX-AM:

Dave: In the first place, why would you ask for a raise so big that it would cripple the station?
Bill: Greed.
Dave: And what has that greed gotten you?
Bill: Money.
Dave: And what can that money ultimately buy?
Bill: Happiness. But stop trying to cheer me up.

But Phil was no Bill. He was truly happy to be back—and not only for the paycheck, though it was bigger than he could believe. Just being free again to do his thing, unfettered by network red tape, thrilled him. "I don't feel like it has as much risk as a show with my name on it," he told *Entertainment Weekly.* "If it tanks, they usually put the blame on the label." With *The Phil Show*, he admitted in another interview, "I would've been sweatin' blood each week trying to make it work." Simms also got the sense that Phil relished his suburban home life and hobbies. He wasn't ready to retire, but neither was he interested in repeating the late nights and hectic pace of *SNL.* After all, he was forty-seven now—at least a decade older than anyone in the *NewsRadio* cast except for co-star Stephen Root, who was only a few years his junior—and uninterested in last-minute road trips or on-set drama. "There were more than a few times when things would come up and these younger cast members would be upset about something," Simms says. "And Phil was always the one going, 'Guys, we're very lucky and doing a great job. I've been through it all. Everyone just relax and try to enjoy every day.' So he was a good stabilizing influence."

Because *NewsRadio* marked the first time since his Chick Hazard days that Phil had played the same character week after week, director James Burrows had some initial reservations about his hiring. But after Burrows and Phil met, Simms says, concerns evaporated. Phil was definitely the right man for the job.

Set at the number two radio station in New York, WNYX-AM, *NewsRadio* features a cast of eccentric characters that includes (besides Phil's McNeal) a mega-rich owner (Jimmy James, played by Root), a neurotic station manager (Dave Nelson, played by Dave Foley), a beautiful and highly competent reporter (Lisa Miller, played by Maura Tierney), a goofball reporter (Matthew Brock, played by Andy Dick), a party-girl secretary (Beth, played by Vicki Lewis), a smart and gorgeous news anchor (Catherine Duke, played by Khandi Alexander), and a tough-guy maintenance man (Joe Garrelli, played by Joe Rogan).

"[Phil] knew everybody's name on the set from the boom operators to the grips to the newest people," Andy Dick said in 1998. "He would give me all kinds of advice. He called me the most of anyone when I was in rehab recently for thirty days. He called me all the time. I'm also in therapy, and on the set I would rehash my whole therapy session with Phil because I felt he could give me a second opinion. He would give me the emotional second opinion."

The set was freewheeling, laid-back, and atypically democratic. And ratings mattered not in the early going, only doing solid work. But it took several months for Phil, who toted around scripts with his scenes neatly tabbed, to fully gel with the cast and acclimate himself to a workplace that was as relaxed and team-oriented as *SNL* had been stressful and cutthroat. Even into his second season, he clung to a sort of battle mentality. "We had to kind of beat Phil up the first couple of years," Root says. "He came from *Saturday Night Live*, where you had to fight like a tiger to get your stuff on. Whereas you came into our thing and somebody went, 'Oh, that's funny. Why don't you use this, Phil?' And he'd go, 'What are you talking about? You're giving me jokes?' He was completely not used to that. So we really had to go, 'Phil, Phil, just go back to zero. We're all going for one goal here.' And then he got it and it was just the best."

When Vicki Lewis watched Phil perform, she "sensed in him a rage . . . I don't know many men who don't have that, but I could see that under the surface. He never raged *at* anybody, but he had a strong point of view and he could get frustrated and put his foot down. He seemed too smart to me and too logical to me, at times, to be an actor. And I think that's what made him particularly funny in the way that he was funny."

In the early days, Simms says, some of the actors complained that Phil seemed to be getting special treatment—because he *was* getting special treatment. But Simms says it had nothing to do with Phil's ties to Brillstein-Grey, which produced *NewsRadio* in partnership with Universal Studios, and came entirely from him. "Maybe I'm old-fashioned," he says. "We were a bunch of kids and he was a grown-up, and you show some respect. Also, I probably rewarded him a little more in ways, because you want to reward the guy who's calm and cool when people are flipping out about whatever the problem of the day is."

As a favor to director Tom Cherones, who arrived about halfway through season two and stabilized operations (until then different directors came and went, with a somewhat disorienting effect), Phil occasionally acted as bullhorn. "I don't like to shout," Cherones says, "but he would do it for me. So whenever anyone would be laughing and joking [between scenes], he would be the one to say, 'Stop playing, boys and girls! Let's do the work!'" Between takes, Phil doodled on Bill McNeal's desk blotter.

Like Simms, Lewis was also respectful of Phil's grown-up status and says he was never begrudged his absence from group shenanigans. When, for instance, several cast members and writers stayed up all night drinking and screwing off following an awards show or after a season wrapped, Phil was not part of their gathering. And when late morning came and they were all "sweating like rapists" and spontaneously en route to Las Vegas for more gleeful cavorting, Phil was nowhere to be found. When he did stick around, it was never for long.

Occasionally he used Brynn as an out—not just from after-hours antics, but in general—announcing in a wisecracking way that he had to "get home to the old ball-and-chain."

In keeping with his elder statesman status, he also gave Lewis investment advice. "This doesn't last," he told her when the show got rolling and actors began to buy clothes and cars and homes. "I was very young emotionally and it was my first sitcom, so I tended to revere him," she says. "And that kept me from being comfortable." Phil also "set a healthy boundary," whereas some of his colleagues' boundaries—Lewis's included—were less defined. "It was almost like the first time we had had fun in a group in our lives," she says. But the tight bonds that formed sometimes were detrimental to outside relationships. Bringing significant others around the set was awkward, Lewis recalls, "because they didn't fit in and nobody went out of their way to let them in."

While Phil began *NewsRadio* as a star of some renown thanks to his long stint on *SNL*, he was a dedicated ensemble player from the start. So were the rest of his cohorts, all of whom were quick studies that could hold their own in any given scene. Phil knew it and was delighted. He'd logged enough time as The Glue. "Not since *Taxi* has there been a show with so many performers capable of just waltzing out there and swatting one out of the park," he proclaimed not long after the show began airing. There's a lot of affection between the cast members, too, which is another thing you can't take for granted. Everyone seems to genuinely like and respect each other, so it's a very pleasant work environment."

Phil had a big hand in making it so. Playful and lighthearted, but with a comic's cynical edge, he kidded around with cast and crew alike, proclaiming, "This is the money shot!" or "Watch and learn!" Phil's *CB4* and *Greedy* co-star Khandi Alexander was often paired with him in the set's raised and glassed-in broadcast booth. Over time they developed an easy rapport in which shit-giving was frequent. "This has to be taken in the right tone," says Alexander, who is black, by way of introducing a Phil anecdote. "We were in the fishbowl and the whole show was going on, so we would stay in character and have our own show up there to keep us interested. And I remember one time in particular, Phil was just staring at me and it was driving me crazy. Like, 'What are you staring at?' And he just looked at me and went, 'You know, looking at you makes me long for slavery.'" At which point Alexander laughed like hell.

On another occasion, Phil—whom Alexander deems "the most childlike in spirit" of her cast mates—took her for a spin in his big white Mercedes. Even though the neighborhood around Sunset Gower Studios was sketchy, Alexander remembers, Phil was seemingly oblivious to the blight and blasted his Radiohead tunes through open windows with nary a care in the world. "You're like, 'Excuse me! Excuse me! You're white! Your car's white! It's a bad neighborhood! Get me out of here!'" she says, recalling her words of warning. "No connection. None." Phil just joked that he was safer with her along. "I just remember him being so rude!" Alexander says with a laugh. "Very Bill McNeal with a foxy black chick."

In early March 1996, *Los Angeles Daily News* TV critic Phil Rosenthal called *NewsRadio* (which had by then moved to a much tougher time slot between eight and nine P.M. on Sundays) "a hit waiting to happen" and declared that its cast was "quietly becoming one of television's top comedy ensembles." Although it was then ranked only thirty-ninth among prime time shows, it fared extremely well with the 18-to-49-year-old crowd that advertisers adore. Added Rosenthal, "Its stories are ordinary: Christmas bonuses, gossip, sloppy desks, office romance, and who's going to get that big promotion. And yet it always finds the inherent humor."

Simms recalls that Phil was a breeze on the set and took issue with his lines only once. And once again, as with James Downey at *SNL,* his pushback stemmed from content he considered religiously offensive.

"He was very apologetic and kind about it," Simms says, "and he said, 'I'd rather have a different line, because there's all sorts of different people in America [who] believe in stuff. And even though it's funny to us, to someone else that could be a really important thing.' So we changed the line." Phil's delivery, as usual, was right on target.

"I always find it kind of pretentious when actors talk about their instrument or their voice," Simms has said, "but he did seem like he had a logical approach to it and knew the eighteen different pitches of voice he could do and all that. It was almost like a robot, in the best possible way."

Later in March, a couple of weeks after finalizing his last will and testament in Beverly Hills (Brynn got everything in the event of her husband's death, their children if she failed to survive), Phil jetted east to host *SNL*. It was his first time back since exiting the show in May 1994, and he'd been looking forward to it "like a tiger looks forward to eating Siegfried and Roy." Hitting the ground running, he opens with a monologue that pokes fun at his Master of a Thousand Voices reputation. When Phil can barely get a word out without slipping into an impression, he grows despondent, bolts from the studio, and shuts himself in his dressing room. "Leave me alone!" Phil yells when Tim Meadows knocks. Then, talking to his reflection in the mirror: "Phil can't finish the monologue . . . because I don't know who Phil is . . . Who *are* you?"

Sketch-wise, he's all over the place like in days of old: as Charlton Heston, Frank Sinatra, Frankenstein, a cop, Cirroc the Unfrozen Caveman Lawyer, and name-dropping drama coach Bobby Coldsman ("This is something, this is nothing. This is *some*thing, this is nothing."). In a bit that was cut during dress rehearsal but appeared later on, Phil plays a seemingly docile codger named "Uncle John," who swills booze and snorts cocaine while recording a radio ad for his famous buttermilk pancakes. "I miss it very, very much," Phil said of *SNL* prior to his host appearance that month. "If *SNL* was done in L.A., I would never leave."

The next day, Fox aired an episode of *The Simpsons* titled "A Fish Called Selma," in which a jobless Troy McClure courts and then marries Marge's chain-smoking drag-of-a-sister Selma to improve his public image and revive his career. It was by far Phil's most significant McClure portrayal to date.

Selma: Is this a sham marriage?

Troy: Sure, baby. Is that a problemo?

Selma: You married me just to help your career?

Troy: You make it sound so sordid. Look, don't we have a good time together?

Selma: Yes, but—

Troy: Don't you have everything you ever wanted here? Money, security, a big hot flat rock for Jub-jub?

Selma: But . . . don't you love me?

Troy: [Sincerely] Sure I do. Like I love Fresca. Isn't that enough? The only difference between our marriage and anyone else's is, we know ours is a sham.

Selma: (Beat, Tentative) Are you gay?

Troy: Gay? I wish! If I were gay there'd be no problem. No, what I have is a romantic abnormality—one so unbelievable that it must be hidden from the public at all costs. You see—

Selma: Stop. You're asking me to live a lie. I don't know if I can do that.

Troy: It's remarkably easy! Just smile for the cameras and enjoy Mr. Troy's Wild Ride! You'll go to the right parties, meet the right people. Sure, you'll be a sham wife—but you'll be the envy of every other sham wife in town! So whad'ya say, baby? *She considers for a second and lights a smoke.*

Selma: Tell me again about Mr. Troy's Wild Ride.
Troy puts his arm around Selma. She smiles.

With Phil's career again on the upswing, Brynn decided to give acting another try—and not just with lessons. Betty McCann, Phil's primary agent at William Morris, tried to assist Brynn at his behest. They'd send her out on some auditions, McCann told him. But Brynn "wasn't very dependable," McCann says, "and she really didn't score anything. Her ego was going south." Inexplicably, McCann says, Brynn even failed to provide basic but essential tools of the trade such as headshots. "We needed pictures and she'd say, 'OK,' and then she wouldn't bring them over." (A friend says Phil hooked her up with someone who could provide them.) Puzzled, McCann called Phil: "Do you think Brynn really wants to do this?" He wasn't sure.

Steve Small, Phil's attorney friend from his graphic design days, thinks part of Brynn's frustration came from her need to be recognized as more than a mother and the wife of a star. Aside from acting, Phil told him, Brynn wanted to learn how to play the piano and sing. "She saw a path similar to his, where she would be recognized and as famous as him," Small says, "but I don't think he ever encouraged that or gave her the impression that he was behind her."

John Hartmann's take is based on a hard truth he proffers to students in the college courses he teaches about the business of music entertainment. "Brynn came to L.A. to be a star," he says, "and she got sucked down the black hole of broken dreams. She was in search of a path to stardom. And she urged and egged Phil to get her parts or introduce her to people or advance her career—which he attempted to do up until the point that he realized she wasn't talented."

So as to keep himself interested and his *NewsRadio* character interesting in episode after episode, Phil plumbed what he considered to be a much more complex personality than McNeal might have had in the hands of another actor—certainly more complex than that of dunderheaded news anchor Ted Baxter (played by Ted Knight) on *The Mary Tyler Moore Show*. McNeal wasn't stupid and clueless like Baxter, just intensely self-absorbed, willfully out of touch, and—as Phil described him—"rife with inadequacies." Phil's formula for playing such a creep? Simple: "I just take myself and remove any ethics and character. All of us are capable of a low ebb from time to time. It's just that Bill lives there."

SNL had been hectic and draining, and Phil found that *NewsRadio*—at least at the start—was no cakewalk by comparison. It was actually overwhelming and exhausting, much more so than he had anticipated. And when he finally got a breather, he found himself tending to other business he'd been forced to shelve while shooting. As he settled into a groove, however, he found the hours much more family-friendly and thought the workload slightly tougher than "a week of trout fishing."

Brynn vied for his attention as well, but Phil never gave her enough. Publicly, everything was always peachy keen between them—or at most harmlessly frustrating. "I'm a lucky man," Phil told the audience at 30 Rock during the opening monologue of his second *SNL* hosting appearance in less than a year, on November 23, 1996. (The monologue's running gag is his many commercial endorsements.) "But I'd be nothing without my lovely wife Brynn. Our anniversary's comin' up, and I want to buy her a diamond necklace, just to show her what's important to me. Family, friends, good times, Michelob . . . That should cover the necklace!"

Several months after their anniversary, in April, Brynn would turn thirty-nine. Career-wise, she had no prospects. Disappointment mounted. Not only did Brynn feel isolated and housebound, she began to suspect that Phil was cheating on her. Marriage counseling helped little, in part because Phil wasn't all that keen on it. Sometimes Brynn went solo. Their sex life was on the downslide, too. But somewhere, underneath it all, love lingered. Says Britt Marin, "Phil used to tell me that even though they had marital problems, he still loved her and he was hoping to work things out."

Chapter 14

Phil, circa 1990s. (Courtesy of the Hartmann family)

When Phil had appeared on *The Howard Stern E! Interview* show in November 1992—the same program on which he'd talked about his falling-out with Paul Reubens—Brynn joined him partway through. It wasn't the most comfortable chat (at one point Brynn sat, reluctantly, on Stern's lap and kissed him), but it was somewhat telling. Being his usual nosey self, Howard wondered whether Brynn loved Phil for his fame. She denied it. He also inquired, with comical indelicacy, if she'd ever "worked nude." She told him no, but mentioned her stint as a swimsuit model. That, of course, piqued Stern's interest, leading Phil to jokingly wish aloud that "I could show you my wife's body." Stern was all for it. Said Brynn, who'd been relegated to mere spectator, "I have no voice here."

Five years after that awkward exchange, whatever thrill had existed between Phil and Brynn was gone—or certainly on its way out the door. Increasingly, when Brynn tried to initiate sex, Phil rebuffed her. And lately, she was always the initiator. Steve Small says Phil could be both withdrawn and "tone-deaf" when it came to his interactions with Brynn. One time, while visiting Phil at a summer home he'd rented in Malibu (the waters off its beach had a modest-sized point break where Phil rekindled his interest in surfing), they were walking down the beach when Phil revealed that Brynn was mad at him. Small asked why, and Phil told him that after a female neighbor had dropped by to visit, Phil had turned to Brynn and said, "Wow, she has great-looking tits." Small was aghast and not at all surprised that Brynn had reacted poorly. Phil didn't get what the big deal was. "He was such a curmudgeon," Small says. "Everything was around Phil and she was kind of an accessory."

On another occasion Small got a phone call from Phil after Small had visited him and Brynn in Encino. Phil was audibly upset. "What did you say to Brynn?" he asked. At first Small was unsure what Phil meant. He then recalled a brief conversation he'd had with her after Brynn answered the Ponderosa phone one day and began asking questions about her husband. During their chat Small told her there was "a very small room inside Phil that no one would get to." It was merely a casual observation, he says, "but apparently it amped her up quite a bit to the point where he was upset with me for saying that. She was very fragile."

Britt Marin was later stunned to learn, though he isn't clear on how, that Brynn had become so suspicious of his and Phil's Catalina getaways that she'd hired (or so he was told) a private investigator to secretly snap photos of them as they lounged on and off the island. "I think Brynn thought that we were gay, which we were not," Marin says. Craig Strong and Randy Bennett, Phil's Chick Hazard business partners and each other's longtime life partners, got the sense that Brynn harbored disdain for homosexuals. Although Phil was known to impersonate a flamboyantly gay John Wayne on the deck of his boat; although he once described a dream he'd had about George Bush and Kirk Douglas getting it on; although he struck a stereotypically "gay" pose with fellow actor Kelsey Grammer for the cover of *L.A. Magazine* (excoriating letters to the editor followed)—not to mention the Coke ad that never aired due to his overly effeminate hairdresser shtick—Phil's views on sexual orientation were ostensibly more broadminded. "So much of television has to do with the politics of sexual relationships," he said in that *L.A. Magazine* story, published in May 1996. "The gay community has always had a delightful sense of sarcasm about sexual mores. Unfortunately, to a large segment of our society, gay people are viewed as sexual outlaws . . . God forbid a straight person should acknowledge that there are pleasures associated with their anus. That's a big, big door that people don't want to open."

"Phil had a very soft, feminine side to him," Strong says. "And I think [Brynn] may have thought that Phil had had [gay] relationships." After Phil and Brynn married, Bennett contends, "all the gay Groundlings were sort of pushed out of his life as much as possible. I think Brynn was threatened, and I know other people felt that way as well." And though it "upset Phil," Bennett says, "he was not going to confront her about stuff like that."

As for other women, Marin says none came to his attention in all the time he spent with Phil—which was a lot. In fact, Marin adds, Phil even was careful not to get overly familiar with female fans he met while out and about—including those who asked to board his boat at Catalina Island. If Brynn knew, he knew, she'd have a fit. "Phil never strayed," John Hartmann contends. "He was a very unique cat. 'Good' is the best word to describe him."

As Phil told Conan O'Brien that year—jokingly, as always, but with more than a hint of truth: "I am up to my elbows in a midlife crisis, let's be honest. I can't cheat on my wife; she's psychic. If I look at another woman, she comes home [and says], 'Who's Laura?' I go, 'I didn't get a name!' She's a Sagittarius, you know . . . . So I buy toys." (Coincidentally or not, Phil's pal Leno has long employed a similar line, once joking, "It's cheaper to have thirty-five cars and one woman than one car and thirty-five women.")

As John Hartmann and Floyd Dozier tell it, acquaintances of Phil and Brynn (a couple) once tried to make a quick buck—many bucks, actually—by framing Phil for having an extramarital affair. One night after dinner, according to Dozier's telling, these people suggested the four of them visit a nearby strip club called the Body Shop—the same establishment Phil had dropped by with Lynne Stewart after seeing *Platoon* in 1986. When Phil consented to getting a lap dance, the story goes, a hidden video camera supposedly caught all the sordid action from somewhere overhead. Not long thereafter, John says, Phil and Brynn arrived home to find a manila envelope nailed to their garage door. Inside was a videotape of Phil at the Body Shop and a note demanding $25,000 to stop its dissemination. "Phil had no problem with its being released," John says, because the blonde sitting next to Phil—the one who seemed to be enjoying herself—was Brynn. Nonetheless, Phil hired a private investigator ("He looked like Luca Brasi from *The Godfather*," Dozier says) that put the matter to rest and destroyed the master tape.

For a while, though, Brynn persisted in her as yet unfounded concern. When Victoria Jackson visited the Hartman home, likely in the latter half of 1997, she was pulled aside by Brynn and told something overly intimate, something she didn't want to hear: Brynn suspected Phil of cheating. "I thought it was very inappropriate, because I didn't really know them that well," Jackson says. "It was such a private thing. She's telling me something about [hearing] a woman calling on the phone, but the woman hung up when she would answer."

Although Stewart and Brynn were friends, and Stewart admired Brynn's humor, beauty, generosity, and energy, she'd heard from others about Brynn's "jealous streak." "[But] she was never jealous of me," Stewart says, "because she knew what good friends [Phil and I] were and that I had never had an affair with her husband, even when she wasn't married to him."

From talks with Phil and observations of him and Brynn together, Cassandra Peterson developed a much more critical opinion. Brynn, Phil told her, was angry and jealous "because she felt that he was blocking her career as a screenwriter." In his book *Jealousy*, San Francisco–area psychiatrist Eugene Schoenfeld describes the emotion:

> *Jealousy is not envy . . . Envy is somehow more passive than jealousy, wistful rather than grief-stricken, more pique than anger.*
>
> *Jealousy and envy are both unpleasant, but envy is like getting stung by a mosquito or, at worst, a bee. It hurts but it's not overwhelming. Jealousy can be like having a rusty jagged knife stuck in your gut and—depending on the circumstances—slowly twisted. You rarely hear of people killing because of envy.*
>
> *The components of jealousy are fear or anticipated grief, a loss of self-worth, a stirring of early feelings of insecurity, and anger directed at a loved one or whoever is diverting his or her attention. Usually one or two of these components are felt more than the others.*

Brynn would also make snide comments about her kids, Peterson says, and often put Phil down in public. "I saw that so many times. It just made me go, 'How could a guy like this be with a woman like this? I don't get it.'"

During Jackson's Encino visit, Brynn mentioned that she was fearful of losing Sean and Birgen in a divorce, and that she was attending Narcotics Anonymous meetings for cocaine abuse. She had "slipped," Brynn admitted through tears during an early 1997 phone call to her sister Kathy Wright in Wisconsin.

Kathy knew what "slipped" meant: a drug relapse, most likely with cocaine. Brynn had also started drinking again socially—beer, margaritas—in the months leading up to it, and drinking made her want to snort coke.

On May 11, 1997, Mother's Day, Brynn went out that evening after a holiday get-together and returned in less than pristine condition the next morning. Phil was furious and demanded she see her psychologist before checking into the Sierra Tuscon rehab clinic in Arizona. They fought like hell, but Brynn ultimately agreed to his demands and left the next day. Partway through her first week in treatment, though, she called Christine Zander to say she missed her kids and wanted out. Also, Brynn insisted she didn't need rehabilitating. After she returned home, Zander says, "I don't think cocaine was discussed anymore. Or her addiction."

On at least one occasion Phil expressed great concern about Brynn to his mother, Doris. "I've been out of my mind," he told her during a phone conversation Doris later recalled. "Brynn's been gone all day. She keeps phoning me and telling me she's coming home. She wouldn't come home. I didn't know where she was. Mother, I actually got down on my knees and prayed to God that she'd return safely."

"Where is she now?" Doris asked him.

"She's sleeping it off," Phil replied. "Mother, I've told her this and I'm going to tell her again. Now this is the honest-to-God truth: If she does this again, I'm out of here and I'll take the kids with me. She can have everything. I don't care. But I'm not going to live with someone who can't control drugs and alcohol."

Mostly, though, he kept details about Brynn's problems and their eroding relationship close to the vest, only hinting at turmoil in his typically joshing way and sugarcoating the bitterness beneath while focusing on lighter topics. "He liked to brag," says Jay Kogen. "He always used to like to brag about what he bought and what he had and brag a little bit about money and brag a little bit about parts he was doing . . . I think at a certain point he was interested in being perceived as somebody who was successful and doing good stuff and doing well. He would talk about how well his life was going, most of the time. Never anything negative, almost never anything problematic. Except very occasionally, if there was trouble in his marriage, he would say, 'Oh, it's not easy being married.' But very rarely."

Those in whom Phil fully confided were few. His ex-wife Lisa was one of them—unbeknownst to Brynn, who, Phil cautioned, could *never* know of their get-togethers. Despite its many problems—the arguing, the communication breakdowns—he was resigned to stay in his marriage, Lisa says. "She's freaking me out with all this plastic surgery," Phil exclaimed of Brynn. And yet, as a former Hartman nanny would later assert, Phil encouraged at least some of it because he "thought her face was too round and wanted her chin to be more square."

Much to Lisa's dismay, Phil seemed utterly—*stupidly,* she thought— unconcerned that Brynn owned a gun. "You are asking for it," Lisa warned. "You are crazy if you let her have a gun." Phil was blasé. Brynn would never do anything harmful with it, he assured. It was simply for protection because she was often home alone with the kids.

"Phil, do not let her have a gun," Lisa says she implored. "Take that gun away!"

Again, Phil brushed off her apprehension: "Nothing's ever going to happen."

Brynn was getting help in rehab, Phil told concerned parties, they were going to couples counseling (when Phil went) and everything would be fine. And they were indeed trying to make things right,

Ohara Hartmann says. "I don't know whether it was stubbornness or Catholicism or just love, but they worked hard at the relationship and she was unhappy. It was kind of mind-boggling to him. He was someone who loved life, and they had a lot of blessings."

Small thinks Phil's tone-deafness also came into play when dealing with Brynn's addictions. He had little understanding of her situation and "was confident that, through the strength of his personality, he could pull her through her dependencies." Which indeed demonstrates a poor understanding of the albatross addiction truly is. In his insightful book *Clean: Overcoming Addiction and Ending America's Greatest Tragedy*, author and journalist David Sheff writes:

> *The view that drug use is a moral choice is pervasive, pernicious, and wrong. So are the corresponding beliefs about the addicted—that they're weak, selfish, and dissolute; if they weren't, when their excessive drug taking and drinking began to harm them, they'd stop. The reality is far different. Using drugs or not isn't about willpower or character. Most problematic drug use is related to stress, trauma, genetic predisposition, mild or serious mental illness, use at an early age, or some combination of those. Even in their relentless destruction and self-destruction, the addicted aren't bad people. They're gravely ill, afflicted with a chronic, progressive, and often terminal disease.*

Brynn did not go with Phil when he returned to Brantford that July. The purpose of his visit—the first since he'd left as a young boy forty years earlier—was a gala celebration during which Phil and two other prominent Brantford natives (NHL player Doug Jarvis and scientist-inventor Dr. James Hillier) were immortalized on the town's new Walk of Fame. "Phil Hartman couldn't be here tonight," Phil joked during the presentation ceremony. "He's at a similar event honoring Jay Silverheels" [the actor who played Tonto on *The Lone Ranger*]. He also asked for impression requests from the crowd, which came to include Bill

Clinton, Charlton Heston, and (perhaps a first for Phil) boxer Mike Tyson. On a more serious note, Phil attributed his success to "a lifetime of love and support from my mom and dad, and it means so much to my family and myself to know that our name will be woven into the history of this town forever."

Back at *NewsRadio,* which started taping its fourth season late that summer, Phil quietly and selectively shared his domestic problems with Khandi Alexander and Vicki Lewis, the latter of whom was then living with her actor boyfriend Nick Nolte and dealing with his problematic drug use. When Phil arrived on the set one week with scratch marks on his face, their origin was only intimated to Lewis. But she knew. When he showed up oddly unshaven and unkempt because he'd slept on his boat, she knew then, too. "How do you do this?" he asked her. Like him, she had no answer.

Joe Rogan winced at the pattern of fighting and reconciling that Phil and Brynn seemed to follow. "He just kind of thought that every relationship got ugly and then you made up and then got ugly and then you made up," Rogan later said. After an especially nasty episode during which Phil had sought refuge on his boat, Rogan said, Phil's tone was disingenuously upbeat when he announced a reunion: "I'm back with my blushing bride!" Congratulations abounded, but Rogan thought, "Oh, fuck. That's not good. It's a disaster."

Lewis says Phil never wore his emotions on his sleeve and was very private about revealing any discord at home. The only reason she knew was because they shared "a similar horror." At a Golden Globes party one year, Lewis remembers, both of their mates began drinking when both were supposed to be sober. She and Phil exchanged worried looks. And late in 1997, at a *NewsRadio* Christmas party, Phil and Brynn got into a public squabble. "He was being lovely and she was being really loudly caustic about him," Lewis says. "Like, 'Oh, he's so *fucking* funny!' And it was shocking to see, because you saw a little window into how she could get."

On December 31, 1997, the Hartmans hosted a small New Year's Eve soiree at their home. Family and friends, including some of Phil's entertainment world colleagues, were invited. Comedic actor Andy Dick, who co-starred with Phil on *NewsRadio,* was among them. Even then Dick's struggle with substance abuse was no secret, and later that evening a close confidant of Brynn's saw her and Dick enter the master bathroom and lock the door behind them. This confidant feared the worst—that Brynn was inside doing drugs—and began banging on the door, screaming for Brynn to come out. She did not.

Roughly a decade later, in July 2007, Dick appeared on comedian Tom Green's Internet talk show *TomGreen.com Live.* When the issue of Phil and Brynn and drugs arose, he grew foggy in recounting "whether I gave Phil Hartman's wife cocaine." He also said this: "Look, if you're looking to . . . get drunk, you're gonna go to a bar. If you're looking for drugs, you're gonna go to somebody who you think does blow. She is somebody that, that night, wanted to get high. 'Oh, he must have it. Do you have any?' 'Yeah, maybe I do.' . . . I didn't know aaaaaanything about her past. I didn't know any of that."

The incident sparked a long-simmering feud with Jon Lovitz that would culminate in a 2007 fracas at the Laugh Factory comedy club in West Hollywood. According to Laugh Factory owner Jamie Masada, Lovitz "picked Andy up by the head and smashed him into [a] bar four or five times, and blood started pouring out of his nose." Lovitz himself gave a similar account in the media.

Starting in January 1998, Phil spent the next few months finishing the fourth season of *NewsRadio.* Brynn, too, was busy working on a project with her friend Sheree Guitar. They'd met in 1995 at their kids' school, where they both volunteered at the library. For the next few years, they worked together on a movie script called *Reckless Abandon.* The story of murder and mayhem that ensues after two women become ensnared in a drug smuggling ring, it contains circumstances and characters based very loosely on Brynn's life. A vicious drug dealer even is named Omdahl—Brynn's maiden name. When Brynn showed a draft to Phil shortly before her fortieth birthday in April, he gave it his stamp of approval and said he'd help shop it around. He even agreed to play one of the main characters (the husband who is killed by a drug gang while trying to find his kidnapped wife) if it was ever produced. Guitar says Brynn was "elated beyond belief."

But Phil's enthusiasm might have been manufactured. When he popped into Lewis's dressing room one day at *NewsRadio*, Brynn's script in hand, he was sheepish and apologetic. "Brynn wrote this," he told her. "Could you maybe read it and have your agent take a look?" Lewis agreed, but thought Phil seemed "embarrassed to have to ask. It was kind of like, 'Look, I don't know if it's any good. I'm trying to make her happy yet again.'"

At the beginning of April, around eight P.M., a neighbor who lived kitty-corner to the Hartmans called 9-1-1 to report that she'd heard five gunshots that seemed to emanate from their house on Encino Boulevard. Upon walking outside her own home, the neighbor also smelled gunpowder. Two female LAPD officers responded to the call but were unable to determine where the shots originated.

In keeping with his core philosophy, Phil maintained an attitude of gratitude while continuing to embrace what he knew was a charmed life. He had plenty of money, a slew of engrossing hobbies, a beautiful family, and an enviably solid career. He also knew his value like never before. "I am a name," he said, "and a name means that I'm well-known within the industry and respected as someone who can deliver." Julia Sweeney, for one, took note of his amplified swagger. "He was not humble anymore, I'll tell you that," she says. "He was more concerned about his career and what was going to happen next." Now that the work came to him, Phil was happy to point out it was simply a matter of choosing what would most effectively take him to the next level.

NewsRadio, he had concluded only three years into his stint, was not it. As ratings kept dropping, Phil decided he was ready to move on. "I wish I were still on *SNL*, frankly," he told one journalist. To another, he admitted, "I'm forty-eight and up to my eyeballs in midlife crisis. The first few years of Bill McNeal still felt fresh to me, because I was expanding and learning about the character. But after three years, we've pretty much explored the depth of this guy." If the show lasted and NBC made him an offer he couldn't refuse, Phil added, of course he'd stay on board after his five-year contract expired. But that would mean a huge pay bump, one "unjustified by my position as an ensemble player in a mid-pack series. I don't want to stay somewhere just to get a paycheck."

As season four of *NewsRadio* wound down, Phil claimed to have fielded some "enticing" offers that he'd been forced to decline because of his NBC obligations. He now also had several more films to his credit, including *Jingle All the Way* (with Arnold Schwarzenegger) and *Sgt. Bilko* (with Steve Martin), which Phil promoted on *The Oprah Winfrey Show* in Chicago. During his time on the set playing Sgt. Bilko's aptly named nemesis, Major Colin Thorn, Phil and Cathy Silvers (daughter of the original Bilko, Phil Silvers) had a heart-to-heart. On a lunch break one day, as she recounts in her 2007 book *Happy Days, Healthy Living*, Silvers joined Phil, Martin, Dan Aykroyd, and Chris Rock at a table:

> *Phil seemed sad that day and I asked him if he was alright.*
> *Phil replied, "I'm alright, Catherine—thanks so much for asking. How are you, my dear?" . . .*

"I am not so fine, Phil. My husband and I are probably going to divorce, and we have two kids. I thought we had a great marriage, but he just doesn't seem to get the Hollywood wife deal, I guess. I am kinda down, and here I am shooting a comedy and trying to be funny."

Phil admitted, "You know, Catherine, I am going through a similar thing at home. Brynn loves me and the kids and, God knows, she has everything in the world." He pulled out pictures of his boats and homes and cars and let us all look through them. "I have given her everything a woman could ever hope for, but she just isn't happy. I just don't get it, either."

Phil had played the president of the United States in director Joe Dante's 1997 HBO satire *The Second Civil War,* and now he was about to hit big screens yet again as the impatient and materialistic Phil Fimple in Dante's digitally animated feature *Small Soldiers.* "Both of the guys he played for me were assholes, there's no doubt about it," says Dante. "And it was something that obviously came easily to him, because he played that part in other pictures. What impressed me on this film, however—because he was surrounded by a lot of really good dramatic actors, like James Coburn and James Earl Jones—was how good a dramatic actor he was. I had thoughts of putting him in very serious roles."

Well aware of his status as an "intermediate level" celebrity, Phil still held out hope for a breakout part, be it dramatic or comedic. As he confided in a 1997 interview, he was "cautious of the fact that very few people in comedy have careers after age fifty. I think there's a notion in our society, and it may be valid, that people aren't as funny when they get older. It's a stigma still attached to the rebelliousness of youth. I do believe that sooner or later I'll get those great roles like Gary Sinise's part in *Forrest Gump* or Tommy Lee Jones's as Two-Face in *Batman Forever.*"

One early-stage project that had him jazzed was a feature-length Three Stooges film, with Phil in the role of Moe Howard—the sensible grown-up of the zany trio, naturally. "What's redeeming about this project is that those numbskulls never held a grudge," he said in *Canadian Cigar Lifestyles* magazine. "They expressed their hostility by beating each other silly and then moved on. Emotions were always expressed and then cleared like an Etch A Sketch."

NewsRadio wrapped season four in early spring of 1998. Its fate hung in the balance, to be determined when NBC announced a new fall lineup in mid-May. Having hopped time periods twice more (from Tuesdays to Wednesdays and back to Tuesdays) and sunk even lower in the ratings (to a dismal fifty-fifth place overall), it nonetheless remained popular among eighteen-to-twenty-four-year-olds. But it would need a much wider appeal to survive, and that appeal remained elusive. Phil attributed part of the show's lagging to its going head-to-head with Brett Butler's hit *Grace Under Fire*. "Our show is popular in the major markets," he said, "but all those trailer parks across America were tuning in to the 'Hillbilly Bride.'"

In a chat with the *Houston Chronicle*, Phil offered another theory. The "little freak show of very isolated individuals," he said, could "get raunchy, sexually ambiguous. There's no contesting the quality of it, but from a strictly marketing standpoint you can see that it has somewhat limited appeal. We have a hard-core, sort of cult following that I think will stick with us wherever we go. But the masses, I don't [think] they've picked up on it."

Phil was careful not to grouse publicly about his lot, however. He'd bitched openly in the past—about *SNL* and *NewsRadio*—and each time he had regretted the whiny-seeming candor of his comments. "This prime-time life has made me a multimillionaire," he said, "and I have a great career going. It's the equivalent of a wartime colonel complaining about the mission the general has sent him on. It's just not appropriate behavior." If *NewsRadio* went away, and he hoped that wouldn't be the case, it would "just open up other opportunities for me."

While he was still in network limbo, Phil dubbed an English-language voice part (that of black cat JiJi) for Disney's reissue of the Japanese film *Kiki's Delivery Service,* and reteamed with his *SNL* work wife Jan Hooks to play her kidnapping boyfriend Randy on the two-part finale of NBC's *3rd Rock from the Sun.* It was his second appearance on the prime-time comedy—co-created and written by former *SNL* scribes Bonnie and Terry Turner—since 1996. Brynn even got a non-speaking part as "Venusian #1." One night after work, Hooks, Phil, and Brynn went out for drinks. "You know," Brynn told Hooks, "if anything ever happens to me, you should marry Phil." Brynn was kidding, Hooks says. But it wasn't an entirely outlandish notion.

On April 23, Hooks received word that her father had died after a very brief illness. Phil was the first one to stop by her dressing room with words of consolation. He also sat with her quietly while she "screamed and sobbed." Only one week later, it was Phil's turn to mourn. On April 30, his father Rupert passed away at the age of eighty-three in Lake San Marcos, California, after a three-year battle with Alzheimer's disease. Seven of his children (Sarah Jane was not present) were at the hospital to say good-bye before he was removed from life support. It was the first time in a long while they all had gathered. Afterward, they ate and drank at the country club where Doris and Rupert had played countless rounds of golf. "We talked about how we were all going to be better about spending time together and being a family," Jane Hartmann says. Phil covered the tab.

The siblings assembled once again, on May 8, for Rupert's funeral mass at St. Mark's Catholic Church. All of them but Phil. "Is your brother coming?" some attendees asked Jane, who thought Phil might have stayed away to avoid upstaging their father. But Ohara Hartmann says work on *Small Soldiers* is what kept Phil from attending. "I was angry," Ohara says. "I was like, 'Why isn't he here?!'"

"But he paid for everything," she adds wryly. "If you pay for the funeral, I guess going is optional."

Phil also kept his word to Lovitz, who was then shooting a sitcom pilot for ABC. Phil had promised to act in it, and he didn't disappoint despite Lovitz's imploring that he not worry about showing up in light of Rupert's death. Phil not only showed up, he stayed late into the night for pickup shots. "I could just see him smiling at me with pride," Lovitz later recalled. "It just made me feel great. I remember that night feeling I was no longer his younger brother, [that] we're equals. It was such a comfort having him there."

Two days after Rupert's funeral, on Sunday, May 10—Mother's Day—Doris Hartmann spent the first of several nights with Phil and Brynn in Encino. With Doris's encouragement, Brynn went out and bought a $5,000 bracelet for herself. "Go ahead," Doris told her. "It's Mother's Day." Phil, she knew, probably forgot. But when Brynn showed off her purchase to Phil, he turned to Doris and said, "We need to take it back." Doris knew he meant it. Phil liked to spend money on himself but could be penurious when it came to spending it on others. Then again, Britt Marin says, Phil was about to buy Brynn a new Mercedes.

Unlike most of his previous summers since fame came, the summer of 1998 was going to be carefree and rife with relaxation. Phil made sure of that by turning down work and renting a house in Malibu's Latigo Canyon, which he'd done previously. Throughout May, he and Brynn went out with friends and even sang karaoke (the B52's "Love Shack") at a birthday party. They also had dinner with director Rob Reiner, during which Brynn supposedly brought up the subject of guns. According to Ed Begley Jr., who says he heard the story from

Reiner himself, Reiner (long a gun control advocate) asked Brynn if having a firearm at home was a good idea. She said it was—that it made her feel safer. They also spoke about the importance of listening. "I'm a really good listener," Phil remarked. Brynn shot him a look and countered, "No, you're not."

As Brynn told Christine Zander, she already had the thing she wanted most: to be married with children. But especially after moving back to L.A. in 1994, Brynn began to yearn for more—in particular, the acting career she'd forsaken to raise a family. "This is nothing he ever said to me, but I think Phil was the kind of guy that really wanted a wife to take care of things," Zander says. "He wanted to have a beautiful home and he wanted it to be kept well and he wanted a mother for his children. And Brynn filled those roles perfectly." Even so, Zander adds, "I don't think she felt enough attention and adoration and support for the things she wanted to do outside of the family in a career."

That May, Brynn reportedly tried to check into rehab again—this time at the celebrity-frequented Promises in Malibu—but there were no vacancies. (Zander, who talked to Brynn during this period, recalls no mention of Promises.) In the meantime, she booked a his-and-hers "Endless Courtship" spa package to enjoy with Phil at an establishment near their home. While friction between them seemed to be dissipating, things could still get tense. (As a friend later put it, "They were just trying to get through the month of May.") When Brynn got amped up and shaky, Phil stayed calm and collected, hardly ever raising his voice. That drove her nuts. "He would never tell me crap," says friend Wink Roberts, "but he was going into detail about how he would fight with Brynn, and how she would want to fight and argue right before he went to sleep. And a lot of times he would pretend like he was asleep, just to avoid the argument." Roberts asked him why he stayed in the relationship if it was so rocky. Maybe he needed to end it and redo everything and go get happy again. But

Phil wasn't hearing it. Rehab might work, he replied. And he loved his kids too much to be forcibly separated from them. He had no choice but to maintain an optimistic outlook.

As Phil described his situation to friend Steve Small, "I go into my cave and she throws grenades to get me out." Phil also told Small that he sometimes had to restrain Brynn. When things heated up, Sean and Birgen typically retired to their bedrooms and closed the doors.

"They had the worst combination of the drugs they used [as] the antidote to their difficulties," Julia Sweeney says. "For Phil it was getting more relaxed and more detached, and for Brynn it was more getting hyped up and more volatile." Their substances of choice, she says, only intensified the clashing between already opposite personalities. "She was definitely high-energy, and this is without doing coke," Sweeney says of Brynn. "She kind of had a nervous, brimming edge to her, and Phil was like, 'Hey, man, it's all gonna be fine.' And then when they got frustrated with each other, Phil would smoke pot and she would do cocaine. So just imagine!"

Lately, Brynn had grown more mercurial in her moods. When she was up, she was really up. When she was down, she was way down. She also had a temper that could flare without warning and that caused her to lash out. At other times she would go into her bedroom and lock the door, stewing in silence and not bothering to open it when someone knocked. It didn't help that over the past couple of months her drinking had increased both away from and at home—mostly beer and wine, though typically not in great quantities, the bottles and cans often left strewn about.

In early April, hoping to alleviate her growing unhappiness, she'd also begun taking the antidepressant Zoloft. Marketed by Pfizer since 1991, the so-called "selective serotonin reuptake inhibitor" is prescribed for depression and has also been used over the years to treat obsessive-compulsive disorder, anxiety disorders, panic disorders, post-traumatic stress disorders, and other psychiatric afflictions. A titration "starter" kit (dosage unknown) was given to Brynn in late March by Encino psychiatrist Arthur Sorosky (now deceased), who cared for Sean. Whether or not he warned Brynn to avoid drinking alcohol, as the precautionary statement on a typical prescription insert would have noted, is not clear, but she could tell from the start that it wasn't the right medication. It made her feel more nervous and agitated than usual, as though she wanted to jump out of her skin. From a medical perspective, she may have been experiencing a side effect known as akathisia, which outspoken psychiatrist Peter Breggin has described as "being tortured from within . . . like the screeching of chalk down a board, only it's going down your spinal column." Brynn also began suffering from nausea, diarrhea, and sleeplessness. Extended naps during the day to make up for restless nights did only so much good.

After one week, she stopped taking Zoloft and stayed off it for more than a month on the advice of a doctor because she had undergone a simple procedure on her nose (whether it was cosmetic or medically necessary is unclear). On May 24, Brynn called Sorosky to report her worsening symptoms, which included deepening feelings of depression. He recommended that she cut her original dosage in half. Whether she had begun taking Zoloft again at full dosage before that call or resumed at half dosage afterward is also undetermined.

Phil dealt with some inner turmoil of his own that month, much of it related to his father's recent death and Phil's augmented sense of mortality. In early May he gave an interview to the *Catholic News Service*. Strangely, in light of his long-lapsed Catholicism, he conveyed a seemingly renewed sense of religiousness—or perhaps he was merely tailoring his words for the publication as he tailored his act for a specific venue. "[O]ur faith prepares us for what lies ahead, and tells us that it's a mystery to us, and we tremble before that mystery," Phil told the writer. He also mused about the meaning of death, saying his "faith has guided me to believe it's a rebirth. We are set free from the mortal coil, and we'll see wonders beyond our imagination. We'll get close to the Creator. I've believed that all my life even when I've questioned other aspects of my faith. I'll be there with my father in heaven."

On or around May 25, Floyd Dozier went to spend an afternoon with Phil at his rented house in Malibu. While strolling down the beach and deep into a conversation about the nature of human existence, they came upon a dead seal that had washed ashore. Their talk then turned to dying and the hereafter. "He was very pensive that day," Dozier says.

Phil was pensive, too, when he spoke with Cassandra Peterson by phone during that same period. Peterson's dad had died not long before Rupert, and so they fell into a discussion about their late parents, their kids, and the fickle nature of life: one minute you're here, the next you're gone. "We got very heavy and very deep and talked and talked and talked," Peterson says. Before they hung up, Phil said something that Peterson remembers vividly "almost word for word": "If I die tomorrow, I would know that I have had a better life than anyone could have ever dreamed of having. It has so far outweighed my expectations. I've got a beautiful wife, two beautiful children, and I'm the luckiest man alive."

Despite recent sad events in his life and the challenges facing his wife (not to mention his marriage), there were many reasons to chin up. After briefly getting the axe, *NewsRadio* had been renewed for another season. *The Simpsons,* as usual, brought him nothing but joy— even when he failed to get a fat pay bump along with the regular cast members. "I've probably done fifty of the two hundred episodes," he said, underestimating by three, "but it's the one thing that I do in my life that's almost an avocation. I do it for the pure love of it." And actually, life on the home front was slowly improving as well, or so Phil claimed. Late in the month, when Steve Small called to check in and see how things were going with Brynn, Phil was upbeat. Couldn't be better, he told Small. Everything was working out.

Brian Mulhern got the same sense. Around May 26, he and Phil were on the phone discussing a movie screenplay they were writing together. Phil was also giving Mulhern a career pep talk, telling him to hang in and that a break would come eventually. His tone was bright. In the middle of their rap session, for a reason Mulhern could not discern, Phil began to laugh. When Mulhern asked him why, Phil said, "Brynn just flashed me!"

"They were joking around and being playful," Mulhern says. "He seemed like he was on cloud nine."

I have spent my life seeking all that's unsung.

—The Grateful Dead, "Attics of My Life"

Chapter 15

Phil on Catalina Island, 1990s.

May 27, 1998

U pon arriving in Newport early that afternoon to procure some boat supplies for their Boston Whalers, Phil and Britt Marin stopped to chat up a gorgeous woman sitting just outside Schock Boats. All of them watched a jellyfish bloom in the water nearby. Then they toured a few boats and talked with a saleswoman. When it came time to place their respective supply orders, the man in charge was temporarily off-site, so Marin and Phil ate lunch at the popular Cannery restaurant on Newport Boulevard while they waited for him to return. Marin paid.

Meanwhile, back in Encino, the Hartmans' nanny Lorraine picked up Sean and Birgen from school at Los Encinos Elementary. When she returned to the Hartman house at around three P.M., Brynn was there with the new housekeeper Gigi. She'd reluctantly fired the family's former maid, whom the kids liked, after the woman damaged portions of the kitchen (including the floor) and stuffed dirty clothes into a cupboard.

Around 4:30 P.M. Phil and Marin headed for home, and an hour or so later Phil dropped his pal off at Sunset and the 405. They made tentative plans to meet up the next day, Thursday, at Phil's summer rental house in Malibu. He and Marin would catch some waves in the morning followed by tennis in the afternoon. On his way back to the Ponderosa, Phil stopped off at West Marine boat store in Encino to buy a few more supplies.

Returning home around six P.M., Phil told Lorraine he was tired. He also asked Brynn where they were going that evening for their date night. They'd been trying to spend more quality time together, and date night was part of that effort. Informed the outing was actually scheduled for Thursday, Phil asked Brynn if it would be all right for him to swing by his hangar at the Van Nuys airport, where he kept his plane, Ferrari 355 GTB, and other toys. He'd be gone only about an hour. Brynn said fine. When he left, she confided to Lorraine that Phil had been elusive lately and who knew what time he'd return. Brynn then began sorting through and discarding old videotapes with the housekeeper. She may also have sipped from a can of beer. Afterward, she went to buy clothes for Birgen at an upscale children's boutique called Ragg Tattoo, located close by on Ventura Boulevard. Back a half hour or so later, she walked out to the pool to check on the kids and then went to exercise, either in the Hartmans' home gym in a room off the garage or at Bodies in Motion just minutes away and also on Ventura.

A while before Phil rolled in from Van Nuys around eight P.M., Brynn asked Lorraine if she could stay a bit longer than usual that night so Brynn could have drinks with a friend, Christine Zander (although Brynn didn't mention her by name), at Buca di Beppo restaurant just up the block. A UCLA student at the time, Lorraine was typically at the Hartman house from around three P.M. to seven P.M. Monday through Friday—sometimes later. But since Brynn had given her no advance warning, Lorraine declined because she needed to study for finals. Soon, though, she reconsidered and said she could stay. Brynn seemed pleased and gave Lorraine the OK to leave when Phil pulled in.

At around 7:30 P.M., Brynn emerged wearing dark jeans, black boots, and a pinstriped navy blue blazer. After saying good-bye to the kids, telling them she'd probably be home before their bedtimes, she headed for the garage and got into her dark-green Jeep Cherokee for the thousand-foot trip to Buca di Beppo.

Soon after Brynn exited, Phil entered. Lorraine told him Brynn had gone out with "a girlfriend," though she wasn't sure whom. They talked for about fifteen minutes, after which Phil took a dip in the pool with Sean and Birgen. They were all laughing when Lorraine left.

Just up the street, Brynn and Zander played catch-up at Buca di Beppo's small bar. They hadn't seen each other in a couple of months. Over the next two hours, Zander had two glasses of wine and Brynn two Cosmopolitans (fruity vodka martinis) with half a beer chaser. They ordered no food. During the course of their conversation, the 5'9", 125-pound Brynn groused about having gained weight recently on account of a temporary workout lull following her minor nose surgery. Eventually, talk turned to her flagging sex life with Phil. But while that part of their marriage wasn't great, Brynn told Zander that they were getting along better lately and becoming closer friends. Brynn also voiced disappointment about her career. She had just turned forty and, aside from a couple of barely noticeable TV shots, a blip on the big screen, and the unfinished movie script with Guitar, she'd never accomplished anything as an actor or a writer.

As they chatted, Zander twice left to use the restroom. The first time she returned to the bar, around 8:30, Brynn was just getting off the public phone. Zander heard none of her conversation and didn't ask with whom Brynn had been speaking, but the restaurant's assistant general manager thought Brynn looked unhappy during her conversation—and furtive, as though she wished to talk in private. He also thought she mentioned the name Mat (or Matt).

At some point toward the end of their hangout session, Brynn invited Zander to migrate elsewhere and keep the evening rolling. Zander declined. No problem, Brynn said. She'd call another friend to meet her. Using the public phone a second time, she rang her longtime acquaintance Ron Douglas. His answering machine picked up. Fifteen years earlier, Brynn and Douglas had been lovers and fellow drug users. Since then Douglas had cleaned up and was working as a stuntman. In contrast to the hard-partying days of old, his current relationship with Brynn had more of a brother-sister dynamic. On occasion, and with Phil's general knowledge of the situation, Brynn swung by Douglas's place to hang out. When that happened, Phil had only two requests: *Don't let her stay out too late. And if she asks for cocaine, don't give it to her.* Douglas agreed, though sometimes Brynn arrived with her own stash.

When she bellied back up to the bar, Brynn informed Zander that her "friend"—unnamed—wasn't home. Thinking this friend might be someone who'd provide Brynn with cocaine, Zander was relieved.

A short time later, Douglas checked his messages from a pal's house and called Brynn back at the restaurant. They made arrangements for her to drop by his place in Studio City.

Around 9:45 Brynn and Zander paid the bill and left. "I'll be back real soon," Brynn told the bartender on her way out. "And I'll be sure to bring Phil."

Paul and Phil in the backyard of their home on Dufferin Avenue in Brantford, Canada, early 1950s. *(Courtesy of the Hartmann family)*

Paul, John, and Phil, circa late 1950s or early 1960s. *(Courtesy of the Hartmann family)*

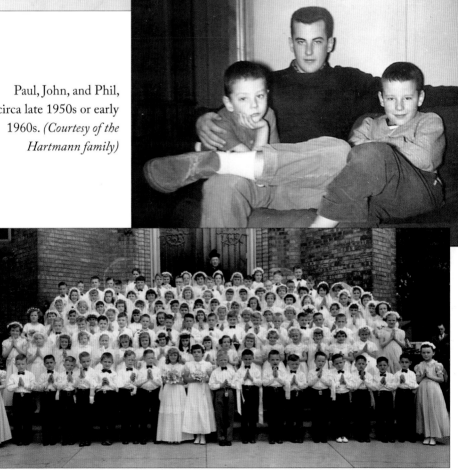

'hil's first communion class at St. Basil in Brantford, Ontario, Canada, mid-1950s. Phil is the rst boy in the front row, far left. *(Courtesy of the Hartmann family)*

Phil, Doris, and Paul, late 1950s.
(Courtesy of the Hartmann family)

Doris and Rupert on their wedding day, May 1938,
Niagara Falls. *(Courtesy of the Hartmann family)*

Phil, circa mid-1950s. *(Courtesy
of the Hartmann family)*

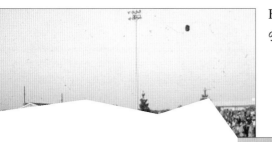

High school graduation, 1966. *(Courtesy of the Hartmann family)*

Westchester high school yearbook photo, 1966. *(Courtesy of the Hartmann family)*

Phil, with Gretchen, early 1970s. *(Courtesy of Sparkie Holloway)*

As best man at Sparkie Holloway's wedding, April 15, 1972. *(Courtesy of Sparkie Holloway)*

With Tom Maxwell from The Groundlings, 1977. *(Photo by Tracy Newman)*

As an early Chick Hazard, 1978. *(Courtesy of Paul Hartmann)*

With the band Poco, 1979. *(Henry Diltz)*

With actress Daryl Hannah at
Hartmann & Goodman, circa
1980. *(Henry Diltz)*

With Lynne Stewart, 1981.
(Photo by Tracy Newman)

At Crossroads of the World, circa 1980.
(Henry Diltz)

Chick Hazard (Phil) and Carmen Pluto (Victoria Bell), early 1980s. *(Photo by John H. Mayer)*

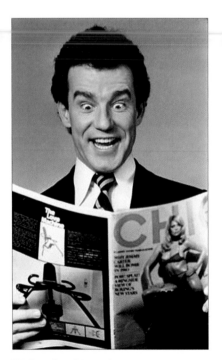

Phil, early 1980s. *(Photo by John H. Mayer)*

With the Chick Hazard cast, The Groundlings, early 1980s. *(Photo by John H. Mayer)*

Phil and Paul "Pee-wee Herman" Reubens rehearse, 1981. *(© Abe Perlstein)*

Paul Reubens, Phil, early 1980s. *(Courtesy of Lisa Strain-Jarvis)*

Phil and Lisa on their wedding day, December 18, 1982. *(Courtesy of Lisa Strain-Jarvis)*

On a road trip, early 1980s.
(Courtesy of Lisa Strain-Jarvis)

Early 1980s. *(Courtesy of Lisa Strain-Jarvis)*

August 1983. *(Courtesy of Lisa Strain-Jarvis)*

Phil and Lisa, December 1983. *(Courtesy of Lisa Strain-Jarvis)*

As Frank Sinatra, with Jan Hooks (Sinead O'Connor) and Sting (Billy Idol) in "The Sinatra Group," SNL, January 19, 1991. *(Photo by Alan Singer/ NBC/NBCU Photo Bank via Getty Images)*

As Cirroc the "Unfrozen Caveman Lawyer," SNL, January 16, 1993. *(Photo by Al Levine/NBC/NBCU Photo Bank)*

As Ed McMahon
with Dana Carvey's
Johnny Carson,
SNL, October 27,
1990. *(Photo by Al
Levine/NBC/NBCU
Photo Bank via Getty
Images)*

As Ed McMahon in "Carsenio" sketch, SNL, May 18, 1991. *(Makeup by Norman Bryn, www.makeup-artist.com;*
© *Norman Bryn, All Rights Reserved)*

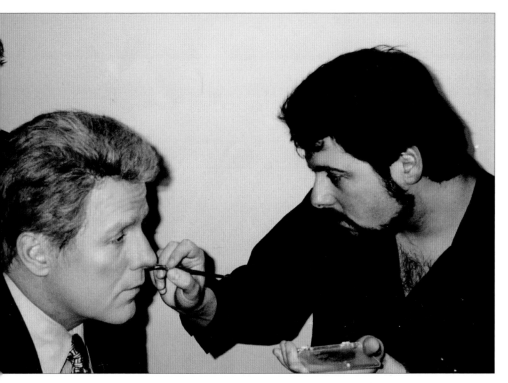

As Bill Clinton, with makeup artist Norman Bryn, 1993/94 season. *(Makeup by Norman Bryn, www.makeup-artist.com; © Norman Bryn, All Rights Reserved)*

As Bill Clinton, SNL, March 12, 1994. *(Photo by Alan Singer/ NBC/NBCU Photo Bank via Getty Images)*

Phil as con artist Lyle Lanley *(with Leonard Nimoy)* on *The Simpsons* in "Marge vs. the Monorail." *("The Simpsons"™ ©1990 Twentieth Century Fox Television. All Rights Reserved.)*

Brynn, Sean, and Phil, circa 1990. *(Courtesy of the Hartmann family)*

Phil, Doris, and Rupert, circa mid-to-late 1990s. *(Courtesy of the Hartmann family)*

Stephen Root as Jimmy James and Phil as the Blue Genie on the set of NBC's *NewsRadio*, 1998. *(Courtesy of Stephen Root)*

With Sean and Birgen in Malibu, circa late 1990s. *(Courtesy of Steven P. Small)*

Smoking a cigar on Catalina Island, 1990s. *(Courtesy of Steven P. Small)*

Near Catalina Island cave, 1990s.

About to catch some tasty waves, 1990s.

After parting with Zander, Brynn made her way to Douglas's Studio City home—phoning Phil three times while en route—and knocked on his door around 10:15 P.M. Douglas answered and invited her inside. They sat in his living room and talked. Brynn was cheery and a bit buzzed. When she asked for a beer, Douglas obliged with a can of Schaefer's. Brynn downed two more after it but, as far as Douglas could tell, she never seemed drunk. At one point in their conversation, Brynn told Douglas about the movie script she was writing. She also carped about her relationship with Phil, and about the precious little time he spent at home. He was always with his friend Britt, she said, and it made her feel like "dirt." To make matters worse, Brynn said, Phil smoked a lot of pot and was "out of it" much of the time. Douglas could tell she was starved for attention, so they goofed around on the piano and talked some more. The later it got, the more Douglas insisted she go home to her family—in part because he feared an angry call from Phil. But Brynn didn't want to leave.

Then, out of the blue, she asked Douglas if he believed in God. Douglas said yes, though he was surprised to hear such a question from Brynn, who had never broached the subject in all the time he'd known her. Perhaps she was prompted to ask it by Neale Donald Walsch's book *Conversations with God,* one of many she was then reading. Others included *Many Lives, Many Masters* by Brian L. Weiss, *Drinking: A Love Story* by Caroline Knapp, and *Making a Good Script Great* by Linda Seger.

At 12:36 A.M., still ensconced at Douglas's place, Brynn phoned her longtime friend Susan, whom she sometimes consulted when struck with the urge to use cocaine. Susan didn't answer; her phone was off. A couple of minutes later Brynn dialed Phil's private line at home but hung up in less than a minute, likely having gotten no answer. She then phoned 4-1-1—directory assistance—though it's unknown what listing she sought.

At approximately 12:45 A.M., two and a half hours after she'd arrived, Brynn finally left Douglas's house. He told her to call him when she got back to Encino, just so he knew she'd arrived safely. But she never did, using her car phone only for message retrieval as she drove out of Studio City. When Douglas rang her on the mobile line shortly after that, there was no answer. And since calling her at home risked disturbing Phil and the kids, he figured she was fine and went to bed.

Sometime after Brynn's return to Encino, likely around one A.M., it is possible that she and Phil argued. About what, no one knows. The troubling escalation of her drug and alcohol use? His paternal and spousal neglect? Whatever the case, Brynn was upset. "Sorry! Sorry! Sorry! Sorry!" she screeched from behind their closed bedroom doors. Perhaps weary of fighting or just weary, Phil lay down and went to sleep (or pretended to sleep) wearing red-and-white Dachshund-print boxer shorts and a purple T-shirt.

Chapter 16

Phil on his boat *Anika* off the coast of Catalina
Island, 1990s.

May 28, 1998—early morning

According to police, the most likely scenario for what then transpired is this: sometime in the next couple of hours, as Phil sleeps with his bent right leg exposed atop the sheet and cover and his left arm extended straight out beneath him, Brynn enters the master bathroom suite. There, on a closet shelf, is the metal lockbox in which she and Phil keep their firearms and gun supplies. Extracting his Smith & Wesson .38, she returns to where her husband lies. From her side of the bed, she takes aim and fires the first shot. A second and a third follow. One strikes the right side of Phil's neck, just lateral to his chin. Another enters through his posterior right forearm, exits out the anterior, and re-enters his right lower chest. Both are fired from no more than eighteen inches away, the latter causing a fatal wound. The most damaging shot, also fatal, is fired at point-blank or nearly point-blank range and enters just above the bridge of Phil's nose, passing through his skull and brain before it comes to rest. Death is quick, perhaps instantaneous. Incongruously, he seems to be smiling, as if in the middle of a sweet dream.

An hour or so later, probably after drinking more alcohol and possibly after snorting cocaine (though she may have done so earlier), Brynn phones Douglas. It is 3:25 A.M. She tells him Phil isn't home, but that he left a note: "I'm going out for the night. I'll be back—Phil. Love you." Brynn doesn't want to be alone, she tells Douglas, who dismisses the idea of her returning to his house. It's too late, he says, and she can't leave her kids unsupervised. Drink a glass of milk, he advises, take some aspirin, and go back to sleep. Irritated, he tries to do likewise.

Twenty minutes later Douglas hears his doorbell ringing repeatedly, along with banging on his front door. Still aggravated and now bleary-eyed, he walks downstairs and peers out the window. Brynn is outside in a long-sleeved pullover T-shirt, white pajama bottoms, and light-colored argyle socks—no shoes. Her hair is still down, long and straight, and she clutches her Prada purse. When Douglas opens the door to ask her what's going on, he catches a strong whiff of alcohol on her breath. She's drunk—he can tell. And Douglas is angry—she can tell. "Don't yell at me!" Brynn says on her way inside. "Phil yells at me all the time."

Stumbling into Douglas's house, Brynn attempts to sit on the living room sofa but slides off onto the floor. Crying, she blurts out something about having killed Phil. Douglas thinks little of the hysterical statement, assuming she and Phil merely had another fight. Besides, Brynn is obviously inebriated. Still on the floor, she looks as though she is nodding off. Douglas tells her she smells like a brewery and chastises her again. Brynn says her stomach hurts, that she's sick, and passes out. Guessing she might have taken an overdose of pills, Douglas wakes her. When he does, she runs to the bathroom and vomits. This happens several times:

nod off, run to the bathroom, vomit. Douglas decides he should keep her awake until she sobers up. To that end, he serves her water and hot tea.

At Brynn's requests, Douglas calls the Hartman home several times. There is never an answer and he leaves no messages. During one of his calls, Brynn starts to root around in her purse. For what, she does not say. Then it tumbles out onto the floor: the Smith & Wesson .38. Douglas is incredulous, asks her what she's doing with it. Brynn picks it up and doesn't respond. *Give it to me*, he demands, and Brynn complies. Upon opening the gun's cylinder and spinning it around, he sees what appear to be all six cartridges in their chambers. Which means, he assumes, that no bullets have left their births. A feeling of mild relief sweeps over him and he stashes the piece in a kitchen drawer. "See?" Brynn says. "I told you I killed Phil!" Douglas remains doubtful.

A little before six A.M., not long before her kids usually awaken and after two and a half tortured hours at Douglas's house, Brynn finally seems sober enough to drive home. But she agrees to do so only if Douglas follows her back. He should bring the gun, too, she tells him. Fetching it from the drawer and checking its cylinder again while staring down the barrel, Douglas notices something he hadn't before: two of the bullets are missing. (In fact, as he'll later learn, three are gone.) Hoping Brynn might only have fired warning shots into the air, he puts the gun inside a tan plastic SAV-ON shopping bag and rushes out behind his frantic friend. He doesn't want to, but feels he has to. Placing the concealed weapon in his trunk, he gets behind the wheel of his black Lincoln Town Car and starts the engine.

Around six A.M., as Douglas tails Brynn back to Encino, she phones her good friend Judy. "Oh, God!" Brynn exclaims when Judy answers. "I think I killed Phil!" Hysterical and sobbing, she is speeding and driving erratically; traffic laws mean little. She blows red tri-light signals at two intersections.

"Where are you?" Judy asks.

"I don't know!" Brynn replies. "I don't know!" "My life is over!"

Trying to pinpoint her location, Judy asks Brynn to read off a couple of street signs. Sepulveda and Ventura, Brynn tells her. She is close to home. Judy hangs up, gets dressed, and drives over to 5065 Encino Boulevard.

Minutes later Brynn arrives there and pulls into the garage. Douglas finds a street spot nearby. He retrieves the .38 from his trunk and follows Brynn through the garage entrance. Once inside, he trails her down a long hallway to the master bedroom at the north end. Peering in, he sees Phil's motionless body on the bed and soon notices the bullet wound in his head.

"Oh, my God, he's dead!" Brynn screams. "I told you I did! I told you I did! I killed him! I killed him! I don't know why!"

Douglas just stands there for a moment, the horror before him sinking in. Things seem to be moving in slow motion. Out of her mind with grief and panic, Brynn makes another call—to her friends Steve and Marcy. She tells Steve what she told Douglas and Judy: "I killed Phil!" Steve tells Marcy. They, too, drive over from their house just three blocks away.

Now Douglas is in the hallway outside the master bedroom. There is a phone nearby. He picks up the receiver and dials 9-1-1.

Police dispatcher: Emergency operator 614.
Douglas: Yeah, hi, this is 5065 Encino Boulevard. And, um, I
    was called over to the residence. I think there's been a shoot-
    ing here.
(Douglas speaks in an unsteady monotone.)
Police dispatcher: OK, do you see a victim?
Douglas: Yes.
Police dispatcher: OK, hold on for the paramedics, OK? One
    moment.
Douglas: OK.
Police dispatcher: I want you to stay on the line.

Douglas: OK.

Fire dispatcher: Fire Department emergency operator, how may I help you?

Douglas: Yeah, hi, there's been a shooting at 5065 Encino Boulevard.

Fire dispatcher: How many people are shot?

Douglas: Just one, and um . . .

Fire dispatcher: Do you know what part of the body?

Douglas: I think around the head and the neck. I just got here.

Fire dispatcher: The person who shot him, is he still around?

Douglas: Yeah, she's his wife.

Fire dispatcher: [T]he wife shot him and they're both there?

Douglas: Yeah.

Fire dispatcher: Is she hurt at all?

Douglas: I'm not sure. I'm trying to calm her down. OK?

(The police dispatcher comes back on the line.)

Police dispatcher: Hello, sir?

Douglas: Yeah.

Police dispatcher: Did, uh, was this on purpose or was this an accident or what, sir? Do you know what happened?

Douglas: I have no idea . . . She was drunk. She said she killed her husband and I didn't believe her.

Police dispatcher: OK, are they both there right now?

Douglas: You're right. Now, can you trace this address because I'm not sure?

Police dispatcher: All right, where's the weapon now?

Douglas: It's in my hand because, um, she brought it to my house.

Police dispatcher: What's your name, sir?

Douglas: My name's Ron, Ron Douglas.

Police dispatcher: All right, sir, we're going to get the officers on the way.

While Douglas is on the phone, Brynn closes her bedroom's double doors and locks them. Douglas tries to get in but cannot. He is still holding Brynn's bagged gun and wants nothing more than to escape this nightmare. Unfortunately, the front door dead bolt is locked and he can't find a key. Brynn continues to wail.

Apoplectic in her shattered state, at 6:21 A.M. she calls her sister Kathy in Wisconsin. First she tries Kathy at home, but there is no answer, so Brynn dials her work number. Kathy's assistant answers, senses that something is deeply wrong, and immediately alerts her boss. Kathy comes on the line.

"Phil is dead!" Brynn says.

"What do you mean, Phil's dead?" Kathy wonders aloud. "What happened?"

Brynn is unable to speak. Kathy tells her to take a breath.

"I don't know!" Brynn exclaims. "I'm sick! I don't remember!"

Then: "Tell the children that I love them."

"I know you love them," Kathy says, and asks if Brynn called 9-1-1. The answer is unclear. Distraught like Kathy has never heard her before, Brynn emits a series of bone-chilling shrieks.

When she calms down enough to speak, Brynn mentions that she called Marcy and Ron. She also tells Kathy about Douglas.

"You mean Ronald McDonald?" Kathy asks, using a nickname Brynn bestowed upon him long ago.

Yes, Brynn tells her. Ronald McDonald.

Kathy asks if anyone else is in the house. She needs to talk with someone besides Brynn to better assess the situation and to make sure Sean and Birgen are looked after. Brynn's crying and screaming persist. Then she says, "I've got to go. I gotta go," and hangs up.

At 6:32, Brynn's bedroom phone rings. She answers: "Hello?"

"Hi, this is the police department, um, is Ronnie home?"

"Yes," Brynn says, "come in."

"Ma'am?"

"Yes?"

"Is there someone who's been shot there?"

"Yes."

"How many people are inside the house?"

"Help me."

Crying, Brynn hangs up.

The police call back.

"Ma'am?"

"Hello? Hello? Hello? Hello?"

"Ma'am, how many people are inside the house right now?"

"I don't know."

"OK, thank you."

This time the police disconnect.

Parking on Encino Boulevard near the Hartmans' front gate, Marcy rings the buzzer a few times but gets no response, so she tries calling Brynn with her cell phone.

Brynn answers: "Hello?"

"It's Marcy. Open the gate."

"Over the gate," Brynn says in a panicked tone. "Over the gate."

The call ends.

Steve succeeds in opening the gate latch. He and Marcy walk up to the front door, through which they can hear a woman screaming. Inside, wanting desperately to split the scene, Douglas keeps searching in vain for a key. As he does, Steve and Marcy see him through a window. He stares at them and they at him—strangers.

"Who are you?" Marcy asks from outside.

"Ronnie."

"Let us in."

"I can't open it," Douglas tells them. "It's a dead bolt. I need a key."

"Get it from Brynn," Marcy says.

"No," Douglas replies. "I can't. Is there another way in?"

Marcy looks behind her and sees that police have arrived. One of the uniformed officers motions to them. She and Steve retreat from the house.

Probably rousted by the ruckus, nine-year-old Sean makes his way to where Douglas is standing. (He will later recall that Douglas got him from his bedroom.) They have to get out of there, Douglas says. Fortunately, Sean knows where his parents keep a key for the back door. He retrieves it and they exit. Toting the gun bag in one hand, Douglas ushers the boy outside toward the rear gate and hands over Brynn's weapon to a couple of waiting officers from the LAPD's West Valley division. Sean is placed in their protective custody. Douglas also gives the officers a quick rundown of events and informs them that six-year-old Birgen remains inside, possibly asleep.

Once Douglas and Sean are out, several officers make their way into the house through the open west center door. They pass through the kitchen and into the hallway that leads to the bedrooms. Two officers crouch down on opposite sides of the hall. Three more get into similar "positions of advantage," focusing their attention on the home's north side, where the master bedroom is. From behind its doors they can hear a female's moaning and muffled screams.

Brynn is again on the phone with Kathy.

"Take care of my children," she tells her sister.

Kathy asks what Brynn means.

"Just let them know how much I love them," Brynn says, inconsolable and sobbing. "Tell Mom . . ."

She cuts her sentence short as officers announce their presence. One of them calls her by name: "Brynn!"

"I gotta go," Brynn tells Kathy for the second time, and hangs up.

From Wisconsin, Kathy's husband Mike calls Los Angeles 9-1-1. He is told that officers have already been dispatched to the Hartman house.

Brynn is done making calls.

Settling into her king-sized bed with Phil's body, she props herself up against the headboard with a pillow. In her right hand is the Charter Arms .38-caliber five-shooter she has owned for years and fired countless times. Inserting its two-inch barrel into her mouth, she squeezes the trigger. A fatal bullet passes through her brain and lodges in the headboard. Her head slumps toward Phil and her shooting hand drops to the right, almost touching him. Her index finger is still on the trigger.

Although one of the responding officers hears a single gunshot emanate from the master bedroom at around 6:38 A.M., he cannot be sure of its origin or target. The response team, therefore, proceeds to clear the other bedrooms, including Birgen's. Once she is taken from the home and handed off to a female officer who carries her to safety, officers devise a diversionary tactic in order to extricate Brynn with as little risk as possible to her, Phil (whose precise condition at this juncture is unknown to anyone but Brynn), or themselves. It proceeds as follows: Two officers leave the residence and set up outside Brynn's bedroom window. Its curtains are drawn. "Los Angeles Police Department! Come out with your hands up!" the lead officer, Sergeant Daniel Carnahan, shouts two or three times. There is no response. Using a found brick, one officer hurls it through the glass while simultaneously, inside the house, another forces entry into the bedroom. He is accompanied by uniformed backups.

They encounter a grisly scene. Phil and Brynn are both dead—that much is quickly ascertained. But no one knows why. Outside, just beyond the crime scene perimeter, concerned neighbors mill about worriedly. As media outlets get wind of the developing story, an onslaught commences.

Chapter 17

Etching on façade of Church of the Recessional,
Forest Lawn Memorial Park in Glendale, California, 2012.
(Photo by Mike Thomas)

The circus arrived quickly. Television, print, and radio reporters staked their claims outside the Hartman house, firing questions at LAPD media relations chief Lieutenant Anthony Alba. Along with squad cars and a police van mobile command center, yellow police tape with bold black letters that read POLICE LINE DO NOT CROSS blocked the immediate area from cars and pedestrians. A brilliant sun and news helicopters hovered overhead.

As details began to emerge, Phil's friends and family members—and even those who merely knew him casually or not at all except through his work—sat in shock before their televisions and phoned each other in tears. Jon Lovitz held an impromptu gathering at his home, where he expressed utter incredulity and angrily wondered aloud why this horrible fate had befallen his friend. Others, too, were in a state of drop-jawed, red-eyed incredulity.

Starting around nine A.M., a couple of hours after Phil and Brynn were pronounced dead and forty minutes before their deaths were called in by a West Valley detective, the L.A. coroner's office began getting phone calls from media outlets seeking details about the case. At 10:20 A.M., two members of the coroner's office—investigative chief Daniel Akin and investigator Craig Harvey—were summoned to the scene. Prior to their arrival, West Valley handed over jurisdiction of the Hartman case to the LAPD's Robbery/Homicide division, to be co-led by veteran detective Thomas Brascia. He and his colleague, Detective David Martin, formulated an investigative team that processed the crime scene and coordinated with the coroner's office.

But it wasn't until 2:26 P.M.—roughly six hours after they arrived on Encino Avenue—that Akin and Harvey were allowed inside the house to begin examining and ultimately removing Phil's and Brynn's bodies. Brascia attributes the delay in part to a "transition of investigative responsibility" and says protocols were set up in ensuing years to allow the coroner quicker access. But Harvey, today the chief coroner investigator and chief of operations, questioned the extended holdup then as he questions it now. "Unfortunately, far too many LEA [law enforcement agency] investigators seem to believe that a death scene is 'frozen' in time and therefore they can take all the time they want to deal with that scene," he explains. "That is only partially true. There are aspects that are frozen to the extent they are not disturbed. However, the human body and biological evidence are changing as the clock ticks.

"The proper management of a death scene is a difficult concept to grasp for some folks. The body, as the most fragile 'item of evidence' at a death scene, needs to be addressed quickly and evidence collected. Then the body should be removed from the scene and placed under refrigeration. The body's value to the death scene is not so important that a sketch or photo would not suffice so that [it] could be removed."

Still, he concedes, the six hours that elapsed prior to initial examination probably didn't affect the results of his postmortem work in the Hartman case—though "really, we will never know."

As more media arrived on the scene, friends and casual acquaintances of Phil's and Brynn's were plumbed for information. After Alba's initial press conference, Commander David Kalish gave another one later in the day to update investigatory developments. *Yes, it was a murder-suicide. Yes, they were still questioning friends and family.*

On the day Phil died, Pakistan—neighboring India's longtime foe—claimed it had conducted five nuclear tests. By late in the day, news of Phil's tragic death had superseded that alarming announcement on many newscasts across the nation. Numerous friends and some family members learned about Phil's horrible fate along with millions of others.

JOHN HARTMANN:
Nobody could have expected it. I didn't even believe it when I first heard it. And I went down there instantly from the phone call that announced it to me to prove that it wasn't true. But I heard the radio guys talking about it, and guys on radio don't say things that way unless they're true. By the time I got to the house, I was concerned about the children and I accepted that [Phil and Brynn] were gone.

I knew it was a murder-suicide before I got there. I was not allowed in the house that day because it was a crime scene. But I went straight to where the children were [the West Valley police station] and started to take care of them. That was the issue.

PAUL HARTMANN (FROM CANADA'S *NATIONAL POST*):
I had gone to town to get some plumbing parts and I was enjoying the ride, but when I pulled up to the house, there was my wife in the

driveway. She had this look on her face that made me want to turn the car around. . . . I went inside and turned on the TV and there was my brother John, in front of Phil's house, with a police lady. They were wheeling two people away.

NANCY HARTMANN MARTINO:

Mom would have reacted poorly to Phil's death. Thank God, when he was killed, she was with me up at our ranch in [California's] Anza Valley. If she'd have been home alone, turned on her TV and seen that, I don't know what would have happened.

LEXIE SLAVICH (JOHN HARTMANN'S EX-WIFE):

I was moving to Northern California to start my business. And Ohara and [her then-boyfriend] Patrick were driving with me in my Accord, and the [moving] truck was behind us. The minute we pulled out of my parents' home in Loma Linda, Arizona, that's when I came across the news. As we headed into the mountains we couldn't get any reception on our cell phones. But John's wife Valerie finally reached us when we were approaching Phoenix. I answered the phone and said [upbeat tone], "Hi, Val!" And she said, "I can tell from your voice you haven't heard the news. Brynn shot Phil and then killed herself." Ohara was driving and I just blurted out, "Brynn shot Phil and then killed herself!" And Ohara just freaked out. I said, "Pull this car over!" John wanted me to put [Ohara and Patrick] on an airplane to have them take care of Sean and Birgen, and I said, "We are not separating. We're driving straight to L.A."

OHARA HARTMANN:

I could tell right away that it was really bad news. Naturally, my first reaction was that something had happened to my dad or brother. I tensed up. My mom turns to me while I'm driving and says, "Brynn shot Phil and killed herself. They are both dead." I remember breathing in so deep. I knew it was real, but I had no concept of how to process that information. Valerie told my mom that the kids were asking for my boyfriend and I, so we needed to get to L.A. as soon as we safely could. My boyfriend was in the moving truck, so I had to flag them down to pull over on the highway. When I did, I shared the news with him.

Now that I was safely out of the car, I remember just running out into the desert and running in circles and crying and screaming. It felt like the whole world had just fallen. I could not believe that two people who were such a big part of my life were suddenly gone. I couldn't believe my cousins were now orphans. My heart hurt in a way it never has before or since that moment.

SPARKIE HOLLOWAY:
I'd seen a helicopter hovering over his house and went, "I wonder what that is." I didn't have the [TV] sound on. And then the first call I got was from work. I worked Fire Department dispatch and they had somehow leaked it back to the Fire Department dispatch that this was Phil. They all knew Phil was my friend, so I got a call at home: "Hey, Sparkie, turn on Channel 4. Somebody's shot and killed Phil.' And I turned that on. Phil was the best man at my wedding and there was another guy named Wally Montgomery who worked Robbery/Homicide. He called to tell me that they were investigating a homicide, and it was Phil. Then I had to sit and watch that stupid news coverage. They were talking about some other man in the house. And I'm going, "What the fuck is this? What are they doing? Do they have to keep talking, because none of this is going to be true. It's all bullshit."

MARK PIERSON:
We were all crying off and on for weeks. But I think Jon Lovitz, as much as anyone. Jon really knows that Phil opened doors for him and he wouldn't be where he is today without Phil. Phil was Jon's biggest benefactor.

JULIA SWEENEY:
The day he died, I felt a lot of compassion for [Brynn]. Because I had just gotten out of a relationship a couple of years before that with a very passive guy who was making me crazy with his passivity. And I could see how someone [like that] could make you go crazy. And I don't even do drugs. I can only imagine how I would be if I was also doing drugs. That doesn't make it right, but [it's like], "Say something to me! Why aren't you talking to me? Don't look down! Or just say what you're thinking about right now! Just talk to me. But don't shut down when I'm upset."

I really empathize with her, even though it was completely her fault and such a disaster how it came out. I also empathize with her about when she realized what she did. The bravest thing she did was kill herself. I thought it was a loving thing to do for Phil.

MIKE SCULLY (*THE SIMPSONS*):
The day it all happened was a day we were scheduled to have one of our Thursday morning table reads, which are always at 10 A.M. And I found out literally at 9:55 what had happened to Phil. I think it was [writer] George Meyer who came into my office and told me the news. He had just heard it on the radio. It was just such a shock; you couldn't believe it. And everyone had already arrived for the table read. I decided to cancel the table read and I went down [to the room], and most of the people had not heard yet. So I got up to say something before the read. Frequently the showrunner will get up and welcome everybody, maybe do one joke and then you get started. That day I stood up and said I had an announcement to make and I could see it in people's faces: They were kind of expecting a joke. And then when I tried to explain what it was, it was really horrifying to see the look of shock and disbelief that fell over people's faces. They just couldn't process what they were hearing; it was such a shock to all of us. And then

we just quietly left the room. It was a very sad, shocking day on the show.

ALAN CRANNIS (FORMER GROUNDLINGS BOX OFFICE MANAGER):

Phil always took the time to come into the Groundlings box office and say hi to everyone. "How's everyone doing? How are things shaping up? What's the show look like?" And he always took it upon himself, after the show, to thank me, to thank the lighting guys, the tech guys, the people who walked onstage and moved the props. That's the reason why—and this sticks out so strongly in my mind—during that very confusing time when we all first learned about his death, and up to the memorial service that was held at the [Groundlings] theater in his honor—I started getting phone calls from former lighting technicians, former stage managers. All of these other people who, like me, were in the shadows nonetheless remembered how nice Phil always was and wanted to pour their hearts out about what a tragic loss it was.

VICKI LEWIS:

When he was killed and I was still in that relationship [with Nick Nolte], I would ask Phil, "How do I guide my way out of this?" In those moments of despair and loneliness and fear, I don't know why I went to him but I did. And I felt like he was there. The day that he was murdered, I was asleep and Nick came in to tell me that he was killed, and I knew he had been killed. And I sat up before Nick said anything and I said, "It's Phil." I just knew. And so I do sort of always have him there, like a Christmas tree ornament in my mind.

JAY LENO:

Not much shocks you after a while, but I remember going to work and having the radio on and hearing "Comedian Phil Hartman was shot by his . . ." What?! You know, in the movies, when people react violently to something they hear on TV or they look shocked? I always thought that looked kind of crazy. It really did that to me. I remember stopping the car and pulling over and going, "What?" Grabbing at the radio. "We'll be right back after this . . ." And I thought, "Jesus." It was so shocking and it made absolutely no sense. When you do this job you don't really get to know people outside the show because you're never outside the show, so I would always see Phil in a professional capacity. And he always brought such life to everything and always brought a funny take and a funny way of doing it. It's one of the great sadnesses of my life.

ED BEGLEY JR.:

I had a reaction that was quite immediate. I went, I think that same day or perhaps the next day, to get rid of a shotgun I'd had for years just for home protection. That opinion changed that day with Phil. I went, "Not even a shotgun. It's not worth it." I didn't want a gun in the house after that. And let me be clear: This wasn't for fear that my wife would use it. I just wouldn't want to get up in the middle of the night to go after an intruder and then have a friend be at the back door [instead]. So I took it to the North Hollywood police station. I walked in without it and said, "I have an unloaded shotgun in the car that I want to turn in. I understand you'll take it if I surrender it and the ammo. I want to get rid of this gun. I don't want it in the world."

When John arrived at the police station to be with Sean and Birgen, he was up front with Sean about what had transpired: "Mommy and Daddy" were dead. Upon hearing those horrible words, John told Larry King in 2004, Sean "immediately whimpered, then he cried out. It was like a fire rising up in his face and into his eyes."

That night, as the two of them lay in bed, Sean told his uncle: "I think Mommy did it." John agreed, but cautioned that they should wait for an official report from the police.

Phil's family and closest friends were tight-lipped from the start. On the emphatic counsel of John Hartmann, everyone ultimately agreed that silence was the best course of action. "Greg Omdahl [Brynn's brother] wanted to go on *Larry King* that week," John says, "and I said, 'What're you gonna do? Say she was a nice girl? She was a cheerleader in high school? What do you think's gonna happen on that show? You're not doing it.' And I had no authority, no power in this scenario other than pure meanness. But I would not let anybody talk to the media in either family."

"You couldn't go home," John adds. "There were people in your driveway. And this awful, ugly idea that they have a right to know is absurd. I've spent my life in the media, so I know these things, whereas the guy in Peoria whose son kills twelve people in school doesn't know that they don't have to go on TV the next day and expose their pain. I did not want to see Birgen and Sean one day go seeking the heritage of this, the legacy of this, and find my mom crying, my brother hating their mother on TV, and all that stuff. And I absolutely hammered everybody to the floor."

Instead, a press release was issued that effectively stated: *This hurts too much to talk about. Please leave us alone.*

And so, while former nannies and mere acquaintances, bartenders, and law enforcement officials told what they knew, and even what they didn't, Phil's siblings, mother, and kids went into temporary seclusion on two floors of a Woodland Hills hotel whose access was restricted by a round-the-clock security detail. Although the families stayed on separate floors, they met in a common area for meals. Sometimes things got tense. During one gathering, Doris and Brynn's mother Connie had a showdown of sorts. "It was insane," John says. "And I went insane. I think everybody went insane. My mother went insane. Brynn's mother went insane . . . Brynn's mother tried to defend her, but my mother didn't tolerate that and told her right to her face in front of everyone how she felt about it." Paul Hartmann, too, was deeply upset and began enlisting support among his siblings to keep Sean and Birgen in California. But Phil's will appointed Kathy and Mike Wright as the kids' legal guardians, and contesting California law in this matter would very likely prove futile. At John's urging, the issue was dropped.

When it came to retaining some measure of ongoing financial support for Doris, however, things got contentious. Phil had been sending checks to her and Rupert for years, but his last will and testament included no provision for their continuance. "It was like our family had no control over anything, and I think John really felt that," sister Jane Hartmann says. "There was nothing left for my parents, and that was a *huge* ordeal."

"I demanded that she be protected," John says of his stern efforts on Doris's behalf. "I said, 'Don't make me play hardball with you. I've spent my life fighting record companies on behalf of artists, and if you think I care more about you than I do my mother, you'd better not challenge me.' And they did, and I let 'em have it. And I let 'em have it in a vicious, vicious way. And so they don't like me. I knew there'd be a price, but what do I care? In all honesty, I was never close to them. They're good people and they did a brilliant job with the children as far as I'm concerned—under horrid circumstances."

At the time, using his will as a guide, various publications placed the value of Phil's estate at only $1.2 million. But attorneys say that number almost certainly represents just a fraction of his assets not held in what's called a revocable trust (used to avoid a probate court hearing and for tax-saving purposes). The amount would rise as assets—including Phil's house, cars, boats, motorcycle, and plane—were sold off in the ensuing months. According to instructions in his will, there were to be distributions for living expenses and schooling, with the remainder paid to Sean and Birgen in equal portions starting when each turned twenty-five and ending ten years later if and only if a bachelor's degree was obtained from "a four-year university accredited by the Western Association of Schools and Colleges or some comparable nationally recognized organization."

In general, though, civility ruled during the strange and strained converging of clans. "I wanted to be mad," says Phil's older sister Martha, who fought the urge to ask Brynn's parents, "Why did your daughter have to do this?" "We treated them all with respect. Of course, they were scared to death. They didn't know what they were coming to."

Outside, journalists and paparazzi were ready to pounce. A couple of them even made their way over to Catalina Island, where Debbie Avellana—Phil's acquaintance from Armstrong's restaurant—did her best to evade their most tabloid-ish inquiries. Namely, this one: Was Phil leading a gay lifestyle? Avellana scoffs now as she scoffed then. "Like you could pull off something like that around here, where the houses are five feet apart and you know how many times your neighbor pees," she says. "There is no walk of shame here. We're proud."

As John Hartmann later described the increasingly surreal atmosphere in which he and his family were forced to exist, "Reporters descended on our world like locusts, and they were insatiable. We became a form of prey and were forced into hiding to conceal our tears and protect the dignity of our family at a very difficult time. We were all dazed in the first days following the tragedy and any statement would have projected only anger and pain . . . There was no flavor that would turn that pill sweet."

On the day Phil was murdered, his former Groundlings co-star Phyllis Katz got a call from her friend in New York wondering if Katz had heard the news about Phil. She had not. She turned on her television— and left it on for hours, until Katz could take no more. Not knowing where else to go, she drove to the Groundlings Theatre on Melrose with the hope that some of Phil's other former cast mates might have the same notion. They did not. So Katz just sat in the office, wondering what to do next. Then the phone rang. It was Laraine Newman, who was calling from the gathering at Jon Lovitz's house. As she and Katz talked, they devised a plan—at Newman's suggestion—to honor Phil at an invite-only Groundlings send-off. Word soon went out.

Starting late afternoon on Wednesday, June 3, the Groundlings Theatre began filling up. Paparazzi were stationed outside on Melrose but barred from entering. Before long all of the venue's ninety-nine seats were occupied by family members (including John and Paul Hartmann and Paul's wife Christie), friends, and former colleagues. Lorne Michaels and Steve Martin sat together. Marcia Clark of O. J. Simpson trial fame was there, too. "Tom Maxwell and I were standing in the lobby," Katz says, "and the doors opened and all these people came in. And there were people who hadn't spoken to each other in years, people who had had arguments, people who left the Groundlings disgruntled and had said, 'I'm never going into that building again!' All of these things were forgiven and forgotten, because people were there to say good-bye to Phil."

As Craig Strong remembers the proceedings, "It was typical Groundlings: over-the-top funny, over-the-top drama, over-the-top egos trying to outdo one another with their stories about Phil." Strong also recalls some "bizarre stuff" from Paul Reubens, one of many speakers. Randy Bennett has the same memory. "He and Phil were always on and off, and he was trying to say something about this [being] his fault and that he was a terrible friend. On the one hand it was like, 'Oh, Jesus, Mary and Joseph!' And on the other hand it was so tragic. It was so heartbreaking that he had let this enormous friendship go by the wayside."

Mark Pierson shared some memories, as did Maxwell, who mentioned Phil's ever-changing looks during their time together on Melrose. One year he was a surfer dude talking about "bitchin' waves," the next he was a cowboy driving a pickup truck. And one day, when

Maxwell offhandedly suggested he and Phil get the hell out of town, join the Merchant Marines, and travel to South America, Phil thought for a few seconds and replied in all seriousness, "Yeah. Let's do it."

Lovitz also spoke. According to Strong, he made a point of telling everyone that he thought Phil had been sleeping when Brynn shot him—that he had died without feeling any pain. Others have expressed the same hope. "From the wounds on Phil, it went fast," investigating detective Dave Martin told members of the Hartmann family some weeks later. "Phil was dead instantly. *Instantly*. And my theory is that from the position in his bed, he was probably sleeping and he never knew what happened." The brutal truth, though, is that no one knew—and no one knows—which shot came first. Not the detectives, not the coroners—no one but Brynn.

The next morning, June 4, 1998, friends and relatives of Phil and Brynn (including their children, Sean and Birgen) arrived at the imposing gates of Forest Lawn Memorial-Park and Mortuary in Glendale, California. The final resting place of George Burns and Gracie Allen, Jimmy Stewart, and Humphrey Bogart—and, more recently, pop star Michael Jackson—it is so legendary a locale that even Pope John Paul II dropped by during his visit to L.A. in 1984.

A media throng had already formed and photographers tried to capture images of the mourners. And though they were barred from tailing the funeral procession, a couple of them tried and failed to sneak in. (Security was so tight, in fact, that John Hartmann's ex-wife Lexie was detained until her identity could be confirmed.) After passing an initial checkpoint, cars and limousines were allowed to proceed up a tortuous main road, past lush landscaping and rows upon rows of flat grave markers, to Forest Lawn's venerable Church of the Recessional, where Phil and Brynn would be memorialized. Built in 1932, the handsome 150-seat stone structure is situated on a precipice that overlooks the Los Angeles skyline. A replica of the tenth-century Parish Church of St. Margaret in the Sussex, England, village of Rottingdean, where the novelist and poet Rudyard Kipling once resided, it is also a popular wedding spot—one that takes its name from Kipling's poem "Recessional."

> *God of our fathers, known of old—*
> *Lord of our far-flung battle-line*
> *Beneath whose awful hand we hold*
> *Dominion over palm and pine—*
> *Lord God of Hosts, be with us yet,*
> *Lest we forget—lest we forget!*

Cresting a hill where the church stands, the limousines took turns pulling into a white tent that shielded disembarking passengers from telephoto lenses in helicopters overhead—and wherever else prying eyes might lurk. The Hartmann and Omdahl families, along with other invited guests, sat in dark-wood pews under an arched wooden ceiling. Displayed up front, backlit by a tripart stained-glass window, were large photographs of Phil and Brynn as well as urns containing their ashes

"The dust had not settled and there were a lot of intense feelings going around," John says. "It was pretty awkward. But I think, by then, the families had more or less accepted their roles, and they were tough. You can't walk away and you have to deal with it. It was very strained, and I think it might have seemed very bizarre to the [outside] observer."

As they trickled in, attendees received limited edition copies of a hand-drawn program made by John's current wife Valerie. Printed on thick stock, with a parchment insert, each one of a hundred was numbered in pencil—a special keepsake from this sorrowful occasion. On its cover, four porpoises encircle the earth. Inside the earth is a blue sea from which leap four more porpoises in perfect alignment. In a blue sky whose horizon melds with the sea, four stars twinkle. Four: Phil, Brynn, Sean, Birgen.

A Service of Memory for Phil and Brynn Hartman, it reads in large font on front. On back is a passage from John 13:34: "A new commandment I give unto you, that ye love one another."

On the left inside page in script font:

A SERVICE OF MEMORY

FOR

PHILIP AND BRYNN

HARTMAN

Philip Edward Hartmann

1948–1998

Brynn Hartman

1958–1998

Mourners also received prayer cards with a portrait of Phil on one side and a famous passage from University of Oxford divinity professor Henry Scott Holland, titled "Death Is Nothing at All," on the other. Someone had sent the uplifting words—delivered by Holland during a May 1910 sermon following the death of England's King Edward VII—to Doris after Rupert's passing, and she thought them an apt tribute to her middle son.

Death is nothing at all.
I have only slipped away to the next room.
I am I and you are you.
Whatever we were to each other,
That, we still are.

Call me by my old familiar name.
Speak to me in the easy way
which you always used.
Put no difference into your tone.
Wear no forced air of solemnity or sorrow.

Laugh as we always laughed
at the little jokes we enjoyed together.
Play, smile, think of me. Pray for me.
Let my name be ever the household word
that it always was.
Let it be spoken without effect.
Without the trace of a shadow on it.

Life means all that it ever meant.
It is the same that it ever was.
There is absolute unbroken continuity.
Why should I be out of mind
because I am out of sight?

I am but waiting for you.
For an interval.
Somewhere. Very near.
Just around the corner.
All is well.

Omitted was this final portion: "Nothing is hurt; nothing is lost/ One brief moment and all will be as it was before/How we shall laugh at the trouble of parting when we meet again!"

The ceremony, rife with elements of the Catholic Mass that Phil had long ago ceased to attend ("Connie Omdahl and I *insisted* on having a priest," Phil's sister Nancy says, referring to Brynn's mother), began with a song performed by famed rock musician and Phil's acquaintance of many decades Graham Nash, whom Phil had come to know during his tenure at Hartmann & Goodman. Strapping on an acoustic guitar, Nash began to play his poignant solo composition "Simple Man." Written as a lover's lament, it was suddenly imbued with new meaning at this funeral for a friend.

I am a simple man
And I play a simple tune
I wish that I could see you once again
Across the room, like the first time.

I just want to hold you,
I don't want to hold you down
I hear what you're saying
and you're spinning my head around
And I can't make it alone . . .

During his homily, Friar James Cavanagh assured gatherers that Phil and Brynn were together and at peace in heaven. Not everyone believed it.

As part of John Hartmann's eulogy, in which he directly referred to the tragic events of May 28, he read a poem he'd penned the previous week after things calmed down a bit and there was time to think. In it, to the puzzlement of some, he referenced the Bear Clan of Native American mythology (the Omdahls), wolves (the Hartmanns), and a three-legged dog (John himself). Its first stanza set the tone:

There lays a puzzle upon the bed
Where a pair of bloods have run out red.
She placed her rubies upon his head

> *To eclipse the life and light he shed*
> *The night our shooting stars fell dead.*

Helping to close the ceremony as he'd begun it, Nash again took up his guitar, stood at the chapel's center, and sang the well-known Crosby, Stills, Nash & Young hit "Teach Your Children." It was quite a difficult performance, Nash says, even for a veteran of the stage. He chose the song "because it epitomized the idea of passing along information to [Phil's] kids and from his kids."

> *Teach your children well*
> *Their father's hell did slowly go by*
> *And feed them on your dreams,*
> *The one they picked, the one you'll know by.*

> *Don't you ever ask them why*
> *If they told you, you would cry,*
> *So just look at them and sigh*
> *and know they love you.*

Afterward, other family members were invited to speak. Greg Omdahl did so, and Nancy Martino made brief remarks as well. During Paul Hartmann's remembrance, he foreswore future use of the surfer slang "killer waves." He and Phil had caught them plenty of times at California's choicest spots, but the term was now too colored with dark meaning. More prayers followed before the memorial came to a close; mourners filed out into the sunshine and eventually made their way back down the long and winding road. Some of them would converge again at other tributes to Phil in the weeks and months ahead.

Chapter 18

Phil in his dinghy near Catalina, 1990s.

On Monday, June 8, the L.A. coroner's office released its toxicology report on Brynn. Phil's body was clear of harmful substances, but based on stomach, urine, and blood analyses, Brynn's contained cocaine, alcohol (a blood level of .11 percent) and two components of Zoloft—desmethylsertraline and sertraline—in what the coroner's chief investigator, Craig Harvey, described in the media as "therapeutic levels." "Between the cocaine and alcohol, the two of them most definitely intensified the other's effects," he told CNN. "The Zoloft is kind of a wild card."

John Hartmann has a different view that he says was informed by the L.A. coroner himself, who told him "cocaine was not even a factor. Although I think he doesn't understand cocaine, because cocaine is downright evil. He said it was the Zoloft and the alcohol. There are heavy admonitions on Zoloft: 'Do Not Mix with Alcohol.' And he said when it hit her brain it exploded, she didn't know what she was doing, she didn't know why she did it, and I accept that as true." But L.A.'s then–chief forensic toxicologist (and now forensic laboratories chief) Joseph Muto calls that conclusion "unfounded."

Also found at the Hartman home were numerous prescription medications in Brynn's name: phentermine (an appetite suppressant), methocarbamol (a muscle relaxant), Daypro (an anti-inflammatory), Augmentin (an antibiotic for bacterial infections), diazepam (the same as Valium, for anxiety), minocycline (an antibiotic), cyclobenza-prine (another muscle relaxant), and Zovirax (an antiviral).

As Muto informed police some days later, according to investigative reports, the level of Zoloft found in Brynn's system when he examined her was "very low." So low, in fact, that had this not been a high-profile case, he probably wouldn't have bothered to report the results. Asked about this remark more recently, however, Muto is genuinely confounded. "I would never say that something wasn't worth mentioning if it weren't a high-profile case," he says. "Whatever we find is worth mentioning."

In May 1999, about a year after Phil and Brynn died, Zoloft maker Pfizer would be named in a wrongful death lawsuit brought by Brynn's brother Greg Omdahl on behalf of Sean, Birgen, and Phil's and Brynn's estates—of which, in their respective wills, Omdahl was named executor. Arthur Sorosky, the doctor who gave Brynn samples of the antidepressant, was sued as well. In Pfizer's case, the pharmaceutical giant was accused of marketing a drug that, Omdahl's lawyers claimed, contributed to Brynn's erratic behavior (part of the torturous and potentially suicide-related condition akathisia from which she might have suffered, but which then did not appear in precautionary statements on Zoloft package inserts) and ultimately violent actions.

"Brynn Hartman did not have a major clinical depression," the suit alleged in part. "She was dealing with some situational 'stressors' in her life and may have thought she needed a 'pick-me-up,' and one might argue that she had a chronic, low-grade condition like dysthymia; but she did not have major clinical depression. And, yet, as a result of Pfizer's aggressive over-promotional activities, she was given Zoloft."

Describing akathisia in a July 1999 article on *Salon.com,* Peter Breggin, psychiatrist and outspoken opponent of various psychiatric drugs, explained that it could drive someone "into extreme states of irritability, anger, and frustration. People can become more depressed and more despairing; their impulse control loosens and they do stupid things. So the violent impulses that an ordinary person would control come pouring out or even appear for the first time."

According to police records, Muto explained that the high level of cocaine in Brynn's urine could indicate use over a day or day and a half prior to her death. The level of cocaine in her blood also signified a recent ingestion. And while the postmortem amount in her system was not inordinately high, Muto said at the time, it would have been "extremely high" were the results backed up (extrapolated) four to five hours. Today, though, Muto insists that extrapolating the levels of cocaine in Brynn's system makes absolutely no sense to him. "You can't even do that," he says. "How do I know what she was doing? That's speculation." There is, he adds, no way to tell when Brynn used cocaine (it has a short half-life but can linger in the urine for days) or how much she ingested, and thus no way to determine how high she might have been at the time she killed Phil.

And so, despite her personal issues and possible motives, definitive reasons for why Brynn took her husband's life and then her own remain frustratingly elusive.

Ten days after *SNL* aired a June 13 tribute to Phil that included some of his greatest sketches and was assembled by Robert Smigel, Hartmann family members met with LAPD Robbery/Homicide detective Dave Martin, who filled them in on investigation details and addressed their concerns. On the subject of Ron Douglas and the extent of his involvement, Martin shot down reports that painted Douglas as being "some type of real villain . . . When I talk to him, I don't get that impression." Paul went so far as to laud Douglas for stepping up in a very tense situation and getting Sean out of the house. Shortly after that meeting, the Studio City stuntman was dropped as a suspect. He had simply been in the wrong place at the wrong time.

Brynn, of course, was a key topic as well. Although Paul and Doris wondered what role the emotion hatred might have played in her shocking actions, Doris also called Brynn "the most gracious little lady that I had ever met."

She was far less kind about the voracious media.

"I think they're taking a lot of care for an eighty-year-old mother to hear that her son's [had] his head blown [off], you know? Especially when we just lost Dad [four] weeks before. We didn't need that. I think the media should really be called on the carpet by the police. They have no business . . ."

Paul interjected. "It's freedom of the press, Ma. It's part of the Constitution. Can't fight that."

"Oh." Doris seemed surprised.

"It's OK, Mom," John said. "That's part of the system."

"Well, I just think it's *wrong* and I think someone should fight it," she replied.

"You can't change the Constitution," Paul emphasized. "Freedom of the press is freedom of the press."

"But you don't have to participate," John added.

"We didn't," Doris said.

"We're not in the papers, we're not on TV," John continued. "Because we didn't play the game."

"And you think it's all right?" Doris asked. "Now, what if I had fallen with a heart attack in shock? Would you have been upset about it?"

"Yes, I would," John told her. "And I'm upset about the whole thing, Mom. But you've gotta understand that we have to deal with realities . . . It's over now, at least. You're going to hurt for a long, long, long, *long* time. But at least we don't have to go through court and [Brynn] being tried in front of us [as] the kids are crying out . . . So it's been handled the way it should be. The police cannot control the press. It is a Constitutional right that you get the benefit of every day—believe me. If we didn't have freedom of the press, we'd have big trouble like they do in places where they don't. It's like a double-edged sword. When they print nice things about Phil, it feels good. When they print horrible stuff, it feels bad. Now, they thrive on the horrible stuff. They sell more papers if it's horrible."

"That's because people have this thing about misery loves company," Paul said. "People are miserable, and when they see more misery than they're experiencing [themselves], it makes them feel good. It's a real simple thing, you know?"

"Mom, you just have to ignore it," Mary urged, "because its all bull . . . Let's focus on the positive and the good."

John agreed. "We have to move forward and have a life. That's what Phil would want us to do."

The biggest tribute to Phil was held on July 14 at L.A.'s Paramount Theatre, a former 1920s movie palace. Scores of friends, acquaintances, family members, and colleagues gathered to pay homage, including First Brother Roger Clinton and his Secret Service bodyguards. Several people who were especially close to Phil personally or professionally shared funny and touching memories of him. Jon Lovitz, the emcee, went first and humorously shot down rumors that Phil was gay. He also spoke of working with Phil on *SNL,* Phil's curiosity and enthusiasm and the fact that he was never jealous or envious. Next to the term "joie de vivre" in the dictionary, Lovitz remarked, was a picture of his late friend—the man he called his "idol" and "mentor."

"The day after Phil died, I looked up at the sky and there was a rainbow around the sun," Lovitz said. "And it was so unusual they talked about it on the radio. An expert said it was sunlight reflecting off of ice crystals in the air, and I knew it was Phil. And he may be gone, but he's still my friend."

Lovitz then addressed Phil's children directly: "Sean and Birgen, they're still your parents and they can still hear you, and I still feel him inside of me."

As he continued, Lovitz spoke of a girlfriend's twelve-year-old son, Charlie, who had died of cancer. When Lovitz had guest-starred on *NewsRadio* in 1996, he told Phil about the boy and how excited Charlie was about life despite his grave illness. "Are you afraid to die?" Charlie was asked. "No," he replied, "I'm just glad I could be here." When Phil heard that, Lovitz remembered, he "burst out crying and tears just flew out of his eyes. And he's like, 'Yeah, that's what I'm talking about. That's how I feel about life.'"

Lovitz went on to read Henry Van Dyke's poem "Gone from My Sight," which employs sailing as a metaphor for dying. It reminded him of Phil, he said, and was helping him through his grief.

I am standing upon the seashore. A ship at my side spreads her white sails to the morning breeze and starts for the blue ocean. She is an object of beauty and strength. I stand and I watch her until at length she hangs like a speck of white cloud, just where the sea and sky come to kneel with each other. Then someone at my side says, "There, she is gone."

Gone where?

Gone from my sight, that is all. She is just as large in mast and
hull and spar as she was when she left my side. And she is just
as able to bear her load of living freight to her destined port.
Her diminished size is in me, not in her. And just at the
moment when someone at my side says, "There, she is gone,"
there are other eyes watching her coming and other voices
ready to take up the glad shout, "Here she comes!

Purposely or not, Lovitz omitted the poem's three concluding
lines:

And that is dying . . .

Death comes in its own time, in its own way.
Death is as unique as the individual experiencing it.

Following a montage of his best comedy moments, Jan Hooks—
Phil's waltz partner in their "Love Is a Dream" sequence and his co-
star in so many other sketches—took to the stage and, choking back
tears, addressed Phil through a letter she had written.

"My dear sweet Sandy," she began, calling Phil by a nickname
she'd given him at *SNL* based on the color of his hair. "How I wish
I could have one more dance with you." Hooks thanked him for his
steadfastness as an acting companion, praised his consistent commitment to character, and marveled at his grace under pressure.
She lamented his violent death, too, but felt confident he was at
peace.

When Paul Simms's turn came, he talked about Phil's smiling
fortitude in the face of mildly rigorous stunts he was made to perform, such as painting his entire body blue and being suspended from

wires as though he was floating in outer space. One of those stories elicited a laugh from either Sean or Birgen, Simms says, which made him feel a bit better.

Jay Leno spoke of his and Phil's Jack Benny banter—backstage at *The Tonight Show,* in restaurants, or wherever they happened to encounter one another: "Oh, *Jay!*" "Oh, *Phil!*" He recalled, too, the time they talked about their deceased fathers and the way Phil could save even the worst sketches from fizzling. "There are certain people you want to grow old with," Leno said, "and he was one of those people."

During John Hartmann's turn at the microphone, he spoke of his and Phil's joint birthday blowouts (they were both born in late September) and the time he almost shot out young Phil's eye with his new Red Rider BB gun. Of emigrating from Canada and farting contests in their boyhood bedroom. And, as ever, he did not shy away from darkness, prompting one friend to remove Sean and Birgen from the room.

While Brynn might not have been "the very best wife or the very best mother," he said, neither should she be defined as a killer. On the contrary she should be praised for her "grace." As for what it all meant—the tragedy of May 28, the shattered lives in its wake—John was matter-of-fact.

"Nothing. It means nothing. It's just what happened one day in the West. They were victims of the same accident. There is no one to hate and no blame to be laid. *I beg you to forgive her.* So put this incident in your past and close the door. Forget—if you can."

Doris Hartmann closed out the tribute, thanking her children for their support and the various people who had helped Phil throughout his life and career. "My whole family basked in the limelight and grace of Phil's life," she said. "It was wonderful. Now the light is out and an awkward night has fallen on our time. And we will *never* be the same."

As she left the stage, singer-songwriter Jackson Browne—there at the request of his old acquaintance John Hartmann—sat at a piano and played his melancholy ballad "For a Dancer." He wrote the song for a friend of his who died in a fire, Browne has said. The friend was a dancer, an ice skater, a tailor, a painter, and a sculptor—a real Renaissance man. "He had this great spirit," Browne recalled, "and when he died, it was a tragedy to everyone that knew him."

Keep a fire for the human race
Let your prayers go drifting into space
You never know what will be coming down

Perhaps a better world is drawing near
And just as easily it could all disappear
Along with whatever meaning you might have found

Don't let the uncertainty turn you around
Go on and make a joyful sound!

Into a dancer you have grown
From a seed somebody else has thrown
Go on ahead and throw some seeds of your own

And somewhere between the time you arrive
And the time you go
May lie a reason you were alive
But you'll never know.

As mourning for Phil continued in the months after his death, some business realities had to be dealt with as well. First and foremost, NBC and the folks at *NewsRadio* had to figure out whether to continue the series or pull the plug. At the network's hit comedy *3rd Rock from the Sun,* Phil had appeared in the season finale and was due to return for the next season's opener, but his part had to be rewritten and recast. Over at *The Simpsons,* creator Matt Groening and other show honchos—stunned and heartbroken when they heard the awful news—decided to honor Phil by retiring his characters. Lionel Hutz and Troy McClure, in particular, would be sorely missed. Since Groening had also cast Phil in his new Fox animated series *Futurama*—for which Phil had come in to audition about a week before his death, even though Groening and executive producer David Cohen told him it was unnecessary—shifts would have to be made there, too. The show's character Zapp Brannigan, to be voiced by Phil, was taken over by *The Ren & Stimpy Show*'s Billy West and performed in the same arch style Phil had originally intended. Another character, Philip J. Fry (also voiced by West), is Phil's namesake. A planned sequel to the Sony PlayStation game Captain Blasto, which hit stores in early May and features Phil's voice in the title role, was scrapped as well.

On the film front, Joe Dante's animated–live action hybrid *Small Soldiers* was due out from Dreamworks on July 10. Already in the can, with Phil in the central role of toy soldier–beleaguered suburban dad Phil Fimple, its TV promos were recut to exclude Phil so as to avoid associating real-life tragedy with make-believe comedy. A temporary *Small Soldiers* ride at Universal Studios was also revamped to exclude Phil's audio portion. His co-star, Kirsten Dunst, tearfully rerecorded her portion.

NBC and *NewsRadio*, however, were in the biggest quandary of all. By that point the show's ratings had plummeted, and now its lynchpin was gone. A week or so after Phil died Simms invited the cast and various other show staffers over to his Bel Air home. There, they swapped Phil stories and—with a nudge from show producer Brad Grey—Simms spoke to the group. "Well," he began, "Phil's dead." Wincing soon gave way to laughing. Simms also conversed privately with Grey, assistant producer Julie Bean, and director Tom Cherones about how best to handle the shocking turn of events. "Tom, to his credit, was very forceful," Simms says. "He said, 'We've got to keep doing the show. It's not about people's jobs. It's not about the money.' He basically said, '[Brynn] killed Phil. We can't let her kill the show, too.' And that sort of meant something to me."

It soon became clear that the most logical actor to replace Phil on *NewsRadio* was Lovitz. Not only had he guest-starred a couple of times, he was Phil's close friend. "It would have felt too weird, somehow, to bring in someone who was a brand-new person," Simms says. "At least with Lovitz, we felt like there was still some connection to Phil. Somehow it made sense in the bigger picture." According to Simms, during a gathering at the home of musician and Phil's friend David Foster shortly after Phil died, Dennis Miller cracked, "Lovitz, it looks like you finally got some work now that Phil made room for you." Lovitz, Simms recalls, was aghast.

Simms's next and even greater challenge was to craft the first episode of *NewsRadio*'s fifth season, wherein Bill McNeal's absence would need to be explained. "I don't think anyone ever wants to write a so-called very special episode of TV," he says. "And it was an impossible one to figure out how to write." Wanting to avoid sappy-maudlin at all costs, Simms jokes that he went for "an enlightened version of maudlin."

During the shooting of "Bill Moves On," it was difficult for cast members to fully contain their still-raw emotions, which of course risked killing the comedy. Likewise, during the writing process, Simms knew he couldn't wallow in melancholy or moroseness. So he decided to extinguish McNeal in one of the most common ways possible: a heart attack. "At least in the fictional world, we could make it so that he died peacefully," Simms says.

At the start of the episode, which aired September 23, station manager Dave Nelson (played by Dave Foley) frets that his eulogy for Bill had gone on way too long and just plain sucked. He is not disabused of these notions. For inspiration, Simms drew directly from his own angst over having to speak at Phil's Paramount tribute in July. Simms was also very mindful that each character should have a spotlight moment to say what Bill—and by association, Phil—really meant to him or her. He solved that by having Foley read funny letters McNeal had penned to each of his colleagues. "I remember when I was writing it, thinking, 'This is half writing and half wish fulfillment,'" Simms says. "I sort of put into Phil's character's mouth [Phil himself] sort of comforting everyone from beyond. It felt like even though his character had gone, his voice was still there one last time."

That summer, Paul Hartmann set off for the San Francisco area to visit renowned psychiatrist Eugene Schoenfeld, whom he'd tracked down through one of Phil's friends. Formerly known as "Dr. Hippocrates" when he wrote a widely circulated newspaper column about sex and drugs from 1967 to 1979, Schoenfeld is a veteran physician and bestselling author who provides expert-witness testimony about the effect of drugs in civil and criminal cases.

Aside from offering Schoenfeld the chance to hang out with some of his brother's remains, an opportunity Schoenfeld accepted, Paul asked the doctor to analyze Brynn's toxicology report. After doing so, Schoenfeld opined that Zoloft could have been a culprit in the deaths of Phil and Brynn.

He has since changed his mind and now thinks the Pfizer settlement was likely an attempt by the company to stave off more negative press. Schoenfeld has also altered his original opinion about the effect of Zoloft on Brynn's actions. In short, it had little if any impact. "The toxic mix was the cocaine and alcohol," he says. "And a very bad mix is alcohol, cocaine, guns, and emotional turmoil." The author of *Jealousy: Taming the Green-Eyed Monster,* Schoenfeld has studied many cases where that beast raged out of control and wrought havoc. "Jealousy feeds on itself," he writes. "The more jealous we are, the more insecure we feel. The more insecure we feel, the more liable we are to experience jealousy . . . Jealousy is essentially a protective reaction based on survival instincts. A solid sense of self-esteem allows us to distinguish between true and false threats of loss."

Which isn't to dismiss Zoloft's potentially serious side effects or the impact it may have had (even at very low levels) on Brynn's behavior.

Not long after his first visit with Phil and at Paul's request, Schoenfeld scattered some of Phil's ashes under the Golden Gate Bridge. Phil's remains would make their way to several other spots before the year was through.

Chapter 19

Phil, Catalina Island, 1990s. (Photo by Steven P. Small)

September 24, 1998

Nearly four months after his death on what would have been Phil's fiftieth birthday, thirty or so close friends and family members boarded a sixty-four-foot yacht, *Mantis,* at Dana Point to scatter his ashes in the waters of Emerald Bay off Catalina Island. Part of Brynn's remains came along as well.

In the preceding months, Paul Hartmann had kept part of Phil's remains on his farm in Aguanga, California, and divided the rest among several of Phil's friends for scattering at his brother's favorite spots around the country. From his catamaran, Wink Roberts sprinkled Phil along the Malibu shore. More of Phil went to former Rockin

Foo band member Ron Becker in New Mexico and to the top of California's Mounts Whitney and San Jacinto.

The sea was choppy and the sky overcast as *Mantis'* mostly cheery throng of travelers sped toward their destination, about twenty-six miles slightly northwest of the mainland. "You couldn't be somber about Phil," Clif Potts says. "Because when you talk to each other about Phil, you're always laughing about something he did. The predominant point was not that he got shot. It was what his life was and how cool it was when he was around."

Besides six of Phil's seven siblings (Sarah Jane was not present) and his deeply aggrieved mother Doris, several Groundlings made the trip. Among them were Laraine Newman, Phyllis Katz, Jon Paragon, and Lynne Stewart. Cassandra Peterson was unable to attend, but her husband Mark Pierson was there. Close friends Potts, Sparkie Holloway, Britt Marin, Floyd Dozier, and Wink Roberts took part in the celebration, too. And it *was* a celebration, one that John Hartmann likens to "a floating Irish wake."

Everyone wore purple-and-white leis fashioned from what Paul recalls were fragrant plumeria flowers, and a lovely set of coconut tatas was passed around (with its complementary grass skirt) for clowning purposes. As Catalina came into view off the port bow, Paul's wife Christie pressed the coconuts to her chest and belted a bit of "Bali Ha'i" from Rodgers & Hammerstein's musical *South Pacific.* Inside and out, laughter and smiles abounded. Classic rock tunes from Pink Floyd and the Grateful Dead played over the motor's loud whirring. A large American flag fluttered and snapped in the wind. On the ledge below a salt water–dappled cabin window, encircled by flowers and another lei, rested a framed photo of Phil as the seafaring not-so-ruffian Captain Carl from Pee-wee days. Stewart, as Miss Yvonne, posed lovingly by his side. Another glossy, of Phil handsomely be-suited and hosting *Saturday Night Live,* adorned an interior wall.

Perched at the stern, his thatch of unruly graying hair and matching beard swirling in the breeze, Paul Hartmann animatedly held forth about matters cardiologic. "If you're depressed, angry, or sad," he explained to several listeners, "you're sending a stress signal to the heart." The responding signal, he went on, hits the brain center that controls production of DHEA—the so-called and controversial youth hormone. Aside from counteracting the process of aging, Paul explained, it also helps maintain the heart's elasticity. "People who are chronically angry or carry animosity toward [others]," therefore, "turn their hearts into leather." But he claimed behavioral health types had devised a simple preventative measure called *freeze framing.* "Every time you get into a negative thought cycle, like depression or anger or animosity toward a fellow worker, you stop yourself consciously for one minute and you think about a loving experience or a time and place in your life where you were very happy and joyous."

For Phil, Catalina *was* that place—"a happy place." At Catalina, he was fully himself. At Catalina, professional pressures dissipated. At Catalina, discord gave way to harmony.

Upon its initial docking at Catalina's isthmus, *Mantis* picked up several other passengers—including Jon Lovitz, John Hartmann, and John's wife Valerie, who had helicoptered over and then driven from Avalon. After they climbed aboard, champagne corks popped and bubbly flowed. If one was so inclined—as Phil almost certainly would have been—God's herb was available for recreational toking. And the cuisine was top-notch: a catered feast of salmon (full name: Salmon Rushdie) and herbs-and-olive-oil-marinated chicken breasts and fresh fruit.

Shoving off from the isthmus, Phil's gang then motored through smooth waters to where he'd again be at one with the ocean, as he had been while surfing and scuba diving and snorkeling and sailing. He was arguably even more content in the water than he was onstage, and so it made perfect sense that he should rest in peace where he'd been most *at* peace. But there was one small hitch: Although Phil had asked Marin to scatter his ashes in the shallows around Indian

Rock, doing so required the use of a dinghy, which was disallowed for liability reasons. Adjacent waters had to suffice.

"Before we send Phil on his final journey, we'll pass this basket around," Phil's sister Mary announced over the soothing strains of a pan flute. She cradled a small, square wicker-like container nestled in a light-blue cloth. In it, beneath a layer of flower petals, was Phil's white-ish pulverized remains. Those who wished to do so, Mary said, could hold the basket and memorialize him aloud or silently. Paul went first.

"Today," he began, "we are here to spread the ashes of Philip Edward Hartman." His tone was steady and his manner relaxed as he recalled surfing with Phil, their hours spent laughing in the same bedroom on La Tijera, Phil's workaholic ways, and his "sensitivity" to friends.

"I loved Phil and I will always love him," Paul concluded. "And I'll miss him really a lot."

It was Lovitz's turn next, but he could not speak. Staring down at the dust that had once been his cherished friend and idol, he quietly said, "I don't know. These are his ashes, but it's not him." Others spoke, some through tears, of God and the universe and how "Phil is a spiritual being now." John—descended from his solitary perch on the boat's upper deck—thanked Phil for giving him two especially useful books: *Zen Macrobiotics* and *Yoga, Youth and Reincarnation.* Both, he said, had changed his life and "made me a better man." Wink Roberts fondly recalled sailing with Phil, and Sparkie Holloway garnered grins and giggles with his story about Phil's Lyndon B. Johnson impressions in high school.

At last it was time to perform the act for which they'd all gathered. Again, Paul took the lead. Standing on a platform at the stern, his bare feet submerged in seawater, Phil's baby brother—the one he'd squired to Disneyland and jealously watched ride his first-ever wave all the way to the beach—was again calm and collected. "Well, Phil," he said, regarding his brother's ashes, "we're going to release you into the elements." Paul then added, with a pirate-y growl, "And like Captain Carl, who longed to go back to the *briny blue*, so is Phil." And with that, it was man overboard. Seconds later rays of sunshine pierced the overhead gloom.

Back on deck and clasping a wooden cube containing Brynn's ashes, Paul spoke in a tone that was devoid of animosity, anger, or sadness. "I forgive Brynn and I send her love and I wish her well on her journey. And I pray for her." He then passed the cube to Brynn's visibly pained friend Judy, who offered a brief tribute of her own before reuniting husband and wife. Some grumbled about the comingling.

A short while later, its mission accomplished, *Mantis* headed home. As her passengers talked—about Phil, about life—the Grateful Dead's 1970 album *American Beauty* blasted start to finish a couple of times over. "Well, another successful crossing!" Paul declared in a goofy voice before letting loose a maniacal high-pitched laugh.

The journey back, like the voyage there, was not a solemn one.

Epilogue

Phil at Catalina/Indian Rock. (Photo by Mark Pierson)

September 24, 2013—Phil's 65th birthday

D escending from Banning House Lodge, a venerable bed-and-breakfast perched high on a hill in the less touristy section of Catalina Island called Two Harbors, Phil's confidant and fellow outdoorsman Britt Marin and his guest rented a bright yellow Malibu II double kayak at a harbor-side shack, stashed scant supplies, dragged their rig into the blessedly calm ocean, and pushed off to scatter Phil's mortal remains in fifteen to twenty feet of water around Indian Rock in Emerald Bay—just as Phil had requested. Not surprisingly for Southern California at that time of year, it was a brilliantly sunny day with temperatures in the mid-to-upper seventies. Perfect.

Along with several other friends and family members, Marin had been given a small portion of Phil's ashes—contained in a light-colored wooden cube—by Paul Hartmann during the first scattering ceremony in late September 1998. But they had been in his possession long enough, Marin decided; the fulfillment of Phil's wish was years overdue. And so, with a purposeful dearth of fanfare and the desire only to do right by his pal, here he was.

After gliding over schools of bright-orange Garibaldi fish and by harbor seals, whose rear flippers protruded from the water as if the creatures were standing on their heads, and after a series of semi-comical efforts to pry open the sealed-tight box in which Phil's dust resided (a screwdriver was finally procured from a grim-faced fellow at Camp Emerald Bay, where Phil had first encountered Catalina as a Boy Scout, and many whacks against a hard buoy finished the job), Marin's kayak approached Indian Rock. The incessant squawking of pelicans and seagulls perched on the natural monument's numerous craggy outcroppings provided a sound track of sorts as Marin carefully and reverently sprinkled bits of Phil over kelp forests and in three other spots until his ash supply ran dry.

Filling the box with seawater to rinse out any remnants, he slowly poured its contents back into the briny blue and held it suspended upside down until every last drop had drained. Pausing for a moment, he gazed at the empty vessel that had contained Phil and was therefore part of him by association, and said, "Wish fulfilled." A few minutes later, with his kayak unsteadily parked along the rock's jagged perimeter, Marin disembarked with Phil's makeshift urn, positioned it on a small ledge near a wispy shrub, climbed back down, and paddled away.

Now, for as long as wind and waves and curious wildlife will allow, Phil can gaze out over crystalline waters that preserve his spirit in death as they renewed it in life. And no doubt he likes it there in Emerald Bay.

It is, after all, a happy place.

Acknowledgments

Like many of my best ideas, the notion to write a biography of Phil Hartman came from someone else—namely, scribe and former stand-up comedian Vince Vieceli. A former comic and co-author of the recently published "Stand-Up Comedy in Chicago," Vince e-mailed me one day in late 2010 and said he'd like to read a book about Phil. "That's a great idea," I replied, "and a subject I love. Phil was tops." So a massive thank-you goes to Vince for getting my creative juices flowing again after a frustrating dry spell.

Soon thereafter, I made contact with Phil's older brother John Hartmann—a sharp guy and spry yoga master who can perform the full-on splits, as he did for my benefit at the bar of Monty's steakhouse in Woodland Hills, California. When I first told John of my desire to chronicle Phil's life, his response was highly encouraging: in essence, "go for it." The ball rolled on from there. Several of Phil's other siblings generously joined the fold as well: his younger brother Paul and sisters Nancy, Jane, and Martha. John's daughter Ohara was a phenomenal ally, too. Thanks to all of them for recalling countless and sometimes-painful memories, and for abiding my deluge of e-mails confirming facts and fleshing out details. Their participation made a big difference.

Phil's first wife, Gretchen Gettis Blake, and his second wife, Lisa

Strain-Jarvis, were kind and invaluable sources, offering up numerous recollections, handwritten notes, photos, and moral support along the way. I am in their debt. Phil's loyal friends Floyd Dozier, Britt Marin, John Paragon, Mark Pierson, Clif Potts, Wink Roberts, and Sparkie Holloway provided crucial assistance as well.

Since this project's very early stages, Senior Philologist Emeritus Angel Rosenthal, Ph.D. (that's a doctorate in Philology, fyi)—who has kept close tabs on Phil for many years and knows more about him than anyone else I've ever met—was always selfless with her time, knowledge, and archives. I can't thank her enough. The efforts of my former agent at Writers House, Ken Wright, helped make this book a reality. I'm indebted to Ken for his years of work on my behalf and wish him all the best in his gig as vice president and publisher at Viking Children's Books. Alec Shane picked up where Ken left off and hasn't missed a beat. Besides being a responsive and knowledgeable agent, he's trained in martial arts, and I like knowing that someone who represents me can literally kick ass if circumstances warrant. At St. Martin's Press, my excellent and always supportive editor Marc Resnick (who *literarily* kicks ass) was pumped about this project from the get-go and nimbly shepherded it from start to finish. Thanks also to editorial assistants Kate Canfield and Jaime Coyne, jacket designer Rob Grom, copyeditor Steve Roman, production editor Eric C. Meyer, publicists Angie Giammarino, Katie Bassel, and Kelsey Lawrence, and attorney Mark Lerner. During research trips to L.A., my superlative sister-in-law Teresa Holzbach and the rocking Celina Denkins saved this writer-on-a-budget many greenbacks by putting me up in their secluded abode, where I slept well, ate well, and was made to feel extremely welcome. Big love to both.

Over at *The Simpsons,* Antonia Coffman was immediately enthusiastic about the book and nothing but accommodating in every way despite her incredibly busy schedule.

Who's next? So many. Biography making, as you might know, takes a village—at least. Here, then, are scores of other residents whose contributions aided me in ways great and small: Richard Abramson, Anthony Alba, Khandi Alexander, Gary Austin, Debbie Avellana, Hank Azaria, Andy Bandit, Sara Baum, Tobe Becker, Gerry Beckley, Ed Begley, Jr., Victoria Bell, Randy Bennett, Tom Brascia, Les Brown, Norman Bryn, Megan Callahan, Eric Carlson, Nancy Cartwright, Carmen Chandler, Tom Cherones, Michael Clark, Craig Clough, Kathy Constantine, Paul Cotton, Doug Cox, Alan Cranis, Joe Dante, John Davies, Henry Diltz, Jim Downey, Victor Drai, Jessica Driscoll, Richard Duardo, Jonanthan Eig, Tom Farley Jr., Gillian Flynn, Joe Furey, Joel Gallen, Susan Gamble, Tom and Henry Gammill, Rob Glushen, Art Golab, Harlan Goodman, Paula Grey, Sheree Guitar, Larry Hagman, Charna Halpern, Jack Handey, Rich Hein, Mac Holbert, Carol Holloway, Jan Hooks, Sarah Immelt, Victoria Jackson, Al Jean, James Kaplan, Jann Karam, Phyllis Katz, Dawna Kaufmann, Jay Kogen, Mark Konkol, Linda Krohn, Robert Kurson, Jay Leno, Vicki Lewis, Neal Marshad, Jamie Masada, Tom Maxwell, John Mayer, Betty McCann, Edie McClurg, Scott Michaels, James Andrew Miller, Jay Mohr, Chad Moore, Jaye P. Morgan, Brian and Kevin Mulhern, Angela Munoz, Marianne Murciano, Joel Murray, Graham Nash, Laraine Newman, Tracy Newman, Claire Nicholson, Kevin Noonan, Bob Odenkirk, Nicole Panter, Cassandra Peterson, Tim Cahill Pickart, Bonnie Pietila, Helga Pollock, Phil Proctor, Mike Reiss, David Rensin, Michael Rofe, Stephen Root, Lauren Roseman, Tom Schiller, Josh Schollmeyer, Michael Scott, Mike Scully, Rosie Shuster, Jim Signorelli, Sarah Silverman, Paul Simms, Bob Sirott, Steve Small, Robert Smigel, Brian Stack, Tim Stack, Hanala Stadner Sagal, Bill Steinkellner, Lynne Stewart, Craig Strong, Chad Stuart, Julia Sweeney, John Thomas, Judy Thompson, Joanne Toll, Michael Varhol, Steve Warmbir, Anna Weinstein, Rusty Young, Christine

Zander, Bill Zehme, Ari Zudkewich, Bill Zwecker and Alan Zweibel. If there's anyone else I should have thanked and didn't, please forgive the omission.

As ever, I'm grateful to family members who've long championed this book and my work in general—including my sisters Lisa and Sarah, brothers-in-law, cousins, aunts, uncles, and grandparents.

To my wife, Sandy—the remarkable multi-tasking mother of our two daughters and the most awesome spouse I've ever had (OK, the *only* spouse I've ever had): Despite the fact that I'm sometimes slightly frustrating to live with, you have made me a better man. I love you. Grace and Audrey, I love you too—equally and unconditionally and more than you could ever imagine. Thanks for putting up with all of my time away from home: the late nights, the traveling, the innumerable lost weekends. I do what I do for you. And a little bit for me, because I like it, but mostly for you.

This book is dedicated to my parents, Sam and Paula Thomas, whose perpetual generosity, rock-solid values, and boundless dedication to their kids (and grandkids) are qualities I admire greatly and try to emulate. They are role models nonpareil.

In closing, a huge tip of Chick Hazard's rakishly cocked fedora to Phil Hartman for keeping me entertained, intrigued, and inspired along the way. Hope I did him proud. Also: bread good, fire bad.

Bibliography

BOOKS

Balbirer, Nancy. *Take Your Shirt off and Cry: A Memoir of Near-fame Experiences.* New York: Bloomsbury, 2009.

Bryn, Norman. *Makeup & Misery: Adventures in the Soap Factory.* Cos Cob, CT: Classic Creature Craft, 2009.

Cartwright, Nancy. *My Life as a 10-year-old Boy.* New York: Hyperion, 2000.

Farley, Tom and Tanner Colby. *The Chris Farley Show: A Biography in Three Acts.* New York: Viking, 2008.

Gaines, Caseen. *Inside Pee-Wee's Playhouse: The Untold, Unauthorized, and Unpredictable Story of a Pop Phenomenon.* Toronto: ECW, 2011.

Griffin, Kathy. *Official Book Club Selection: A Memoir According to Kathy Griffin.* New York: Ballantine, 2009.

Hirshenson, Janet, Jane Jenkins with Rachel Kranz. *A Star Is Found: Our Adventures Casting Some of Hollywood's Biggest Movies.* Orlando, FL: Harcourt, 2006.

Kerr, Cherie. *I've Asked Miller to Say a Few Words: New and Exciting Ways to Improve Speaking and Presentation Skills Through the Use of Improvisational Comedy Techniques.* Santa Ana, CA: ExecuProv, 1995.

Mohr, Jay. *Gasping for Airtime: Two Years in the Trenches of Saturday Night Live.* New York: Hyperion, 2004.

Rensin, David. *The Mailroom: Hollywood History from the Bottom Up.* New York: Ballantine, 2003.

Schoenfeld, Eugene. *Jealousy: Taming the Green-eyed Monster.* New York: Holt, Rinehart, and Winston, 1980.

Shales, Tom and James A. Miller. *Live from New York: An Uncensored History of Saturday Night Live*. Boston: Little, Brown, 2002.

Silverman, Sarah. *The Bedwetter: Stories of Courage, Redemption, and Pee*. New York: Harper, 2010.

Silvers, Cathy. *Happy Days Healthy Living: From Sit-com Teen to the Health Food Scene*. Berkeley, CA: North Atlantic, 2007.

NEWSPAPER AND MAGAZINE ARTICLES

"Actor's Killer Was Drunk." *New York Times*, 9 June 1998.

Allis, Tim. "Taking a Bite out of Bill." *People*, 25 January 1993.

Arnold, Christine. "Olympic Festival: Fun, Frivoligy." *Miami Herald*, 25 June 1984.

Baker, Kathryn. "Phil Who? The Funny Guy on SNL." Associated Press, 4 August 1987.

Bianculli, David. "A Reubens Masterpiece: Pee-wee DVD Is a Classic." New York *Daily News*, 17 November 2004.

———. "'Second Civil War' First-Rate." New York *Daily News*, 14 March 1997.

———. "'SNL' Co-star Remembers Her Hartman." *New York Daily News*, 02 June 1998.

Blankstein, Andrew, and Solomon Moore. "Police Reviewing Brynn Hartman's Script." *Los Angeles Times*, 4 June 1998.

Braxton, Greg. "Without Their Anchor." *Los Angeles Times*, 23 September 1998.

Busch, Anita M. "Paramount Points to 'Coneheads' for 1993." *The Hollywood Reporter*, 12 September 1992.

Cagle, Jess. "Merry Hartman Merry Hartman." *Entertainment Weekly*, 11 March 1994.

Canby, Vincent. "'Pee-wee's Big Adventure,' a Comedy." *New York Times*, 9 August 1985.

Carter, Bill. "A Hard Job to Accept: A Slain Buddy's Show." *New York Times*, 7 October 1998.

———. "'Picking up the Flag': Lovitz Honoring Fallen Friend." *New York Times*, 12 October 1998.

Cerone, Daniel H. "Ham Radio." *TV Guide*, 30 March 1996.

———. "A Mandate for Mimicry." *Los Angeles Times*, 14 November 1992.

Chang, Donald. "Welcome Back, Phil: Actor's Homecoming 'a Little Emotional,'" *Brantford Expositor*, 7 July 1997.

Churchill, Bonnie. "The Importance of Voices and Toys." *Ultimate TV News*, April 1998.

"Coroner: Hartman's Wife on Drugs, Drunk." CNN.com, 8 June 1998.

Covert, Colin, and Jeff Strickler. "Move Along, Minnesotans, It's Only a Movie Superstar." *Minneapolis Star Tribune*, 12 April 1996.

Crane, Robert and Phil Hartman. "Phil Hartman's Guide to the Holiday Office Party." *Playboy*, December 1998.

Crosby, Sherry Joe and Eric Leach. "Storybook Lives End in Tragedy; Phil Hartman Dead, Wife Kills Self in Home." *Los Angeles Daily News*, 29 May 1998.

Dahlin, Andrea. "Groundlings Revue." *The Hollywood Reporter*, 27 April 1979.

Downey, Mike. "Nothing Funny about Death of This Funny Man." *Los Angeles Times*, 29 May 1998.

DuFoe, Terry, Tiffany DuFoe and Becky DuFoe. "The Return of Elvira, Mistress of the Dark: A VideoScope Sneak Peek at Her Haunted Hills!" *The Phantom of the Movies' Videoscope* 40, 2001.

Ehrenstein, David. "More than Friends: How Sitcoms Became the New Gay Art Form." *Los Angeles Magazine*, May 1996.

Esterly, Glenn. "A Tale of Two Comics." *TV Guide*, 16 December 1995.

"Family Members Hold Private Memorial for Hartmans." CNN, 5 June 1998.

Fantle, David and Thomas Johnson. "The Many Faces of Phil Hartman." *Canadian CIGAR Lifestyles*, Spring 1998.

Fitzpatrick, Robert. "The Olympic Arts Festival." *Festival Program*, Summer 1984.

Fleming, Charles. "Death in the Valley." *TV Guide*, 18 July 1998.

Fowler, James E. "A Lady and Her Ukulele: 'Saturday Night Live' Veteran Victoria Jackson Will Perform Songs from Her New Album at Pages." *Los Angeles Times*, 24 February 1995.

Fox. "The Groundling Revue." *Variety*, April 1979.

Freeman, John. "'NewsRadio's' McNeal Livin' It up as Despicable Cad." *San Diego Union-Tribune*, 8 March 1996.

Fretts, Bruce. "Tuesday Night Comedy Club." *Entertainment Weekly*, 31 March 1995.

Froelich, Janis D. "Saturday Night Lives: Current Cast Is as Good as Originals of 15 Years Ago." *St. Petersburg Times*, 29 September 1989.

"Frosty Phil." *Smoke Magazine*, Winter 1996.

"'Funniest Man on TV' Spoofs Commercials." Associated Press, 30 September 1992.

Galle, Deborah. "Movie Magic Wears Thin on Some: Filming of 'Houseguest' in Sewickley Area Has Some Merchants Angry, Others Amused." *Pittsburgh Post-Gazette*, 29 June 1994.

Gamble, Susan. "Doris Hartmann Dies of 'Broken Heart.'" *Brantford Expositor*, April 2001.

———. "Festival Honours Hartman." *Brantford Expositor*, 20 May 2000.

———. "For Phil's Family, Gala Mixes Joy and Sorrow." *Brantford Expositor*, 14 July 2000.

———. "Hartman: A Really Nice Guy." *Brantford Expositor*, 29 May 1998.

———. "Hartmania!: Phil Hartman's Homecoming." *Brantford Expositor*, 26 July 1997.

———. "Media Descends on City for Hartman Story." *Brantford Expositor*, 29 May 1998.

———. "On Our Walk of Fame: City Honors Hillier, Jarvis and Hartman." *Brantford Expositor*, 24 July 1997.

———. "Stars Come out to Honor Hartman." *Brantford Expositor*, 14 July 2000.

Garchik, Leah. "An Hour with Phil Hartman." *San Francisco Chronicle*, 10 August 1998.

"Gary Essert, 54, Dies; Film Festival Founder." *New York Times*, 18 December 1992.

Gendel, Morgan. "Another Groundling Hops to 'SNL'" *Los Angeles Times*, 30 September 1986.

———. "Lorne Michaels: Live from New York—Again." *New York Times*, 7 September 1985.

———. "Olympic Festival's First Gold." *Los Angeles Times*, 11 April 1984.

Gertler, T. "The Pee-wee Perplex." *Rolling Stone*, 12 February 1987.

Groening, Matt. "Phil Hartman (1948–1998)." *Simpsons Comics* 37, June 1998.

Gross, Jonathan. "PeeWeePhenom." *Toronto Star*, 24 January 1987.

Haddad, Dana. "Branham Gets Ball and Cameras Rolling." *Los Angeles Times*, 16 September 1993.

Hamilton, Nancy. "What Is a Groundling?" *L.A. Weekly*, 6–12 July 1979.

Harmetz, Aljean. "Olympic Arts Festival Opens in L.A." *New York Times*, 2 June 1984.

"Hartman on 'SNL' Split: 'I Got off the Titanic'" *Chicago Tribune*, 17 April 1995.

Hartmann, Paul, and Ben Kaplan. "First Person: A Brother's Quest to Enshrine Phil Hartman on Canada's Walk of Fame." *National Post*, 26 March 2010.

"Hartman's Departure Spawns Variety Show." Tribune Media Services, 31 July 1994.

"Hartman's Friends, Fans Ask: 'What Went Wrong?'" CNN, 29 May 1998.

"Hartman Reflects on Loss, Life." *Catholic News Service*, May 1998.

"Hartman's Wife Reportedly Confessed." Associated Press, 29 May 1998.

Hiestand, Jesse. "Hartman Children Attend Memorial." *Los Angeles Daily News*, 5 June 1998.

Howell, Peter. "Jingle All the Way (review)." *Toronto Star*, 22 November 1996.

I Ching Classic of Changes: The answers to many questions. The-iching.com 2005–13.

James, Christine. "Phil-osophy." *Sneak Preview*, Autumn 1996.

Johnson, Reed. "Comedic Career Seemed on Verge of the Big Time." *Los Angeles Daily News*, 29 May, 1998.

Johnson, Ted and Janet Weeks. "Phil Hartman: Many Voices, Many Laughs." *TV Guide*, 13 June 1998.

Johnson, Tom and David Fantle. "Reel to Real: Phil Hartman." *Hollywood Online*, 29 September 1997.

Karp, David. "Malibu Cuts the Tape." *Los Angeles Times*, 24 May 2000.

Kaufman, Joanne. "Grodin Goes for the Gags." *Chicago Tribune*, 15 May 1986.

Kay, Laura Smith. "Phil Hartman." *People Online*, 28 May 1998.

Klein, Joe. "A Postmodern President." *Newsweek*, 17 January 1994.

Kroll, Jack. "Champion Drama." *Newsweek*, 2 July 1984.

Kushman, Rick. "'Night' Was the Life." Scripps-McClatchy Western Service, 7 March 1997.

Lloyd, Robert. "Live from the '80s, It's 'Saturday Night'" *Los Angeles Times*, 11 November 2005.

Lowell, Sondra. "Groundlings 'Hazard' at Full Length." *Los Angeles Times*, 8 June 1984.

Mahoney, John C. "The Groundlings Unveil 'Revue,'" *Los Angeles Times*, 27 April 1979.

Marder, Keith. "At Home with TV's Phil Hartman." *Los Angeles Daily News*, 6 April 1997.

Marion, Michael-Allan. "Hartman Gala Turns Brantford Into . . . Comedy Central." *Brantford Expositor*, 14 July 2000.

Mashberg, Tom. "As Clinton Goes, so Goes Phil Hartman; The Transition." *Boston Globe*, 29 November 1992.

"Maybe He Can Learn Hillary." *Newsweek*, 16 November 1992.

McDaniel, Mike. "Phil Hartman Brings Back the Titanic on 'NewsRadio'" *Houston Chronicle*, 11 May 1998.

McKay, Gardner. "The Groundlings Leave Ground." *Los Angeles Herald Examiner*, April 1979.

Melton, Mary. "Comedy Central: Will Ferrell, Lisa Kudrow, Phil Hartman, Laraine Newman, Pee-wee Herman: Before They Became Household Names, They Were Groundlings, Members of L.A.'s Great Improv Company, Which Celebrates Its 30th Birthday This Month." *Los Angeles Magazine*, 1 October 2004.

Mooney, Joshua. "When a Movie Star Dies." *Toronto Star*, 10 June 1998.

Moore, Solomon, Greg Braxton and T. Christian Miller. "Murder-suicide Claims Actor, Wife." *Los Angeles Times*, 29 May 1998.

Moss, Stanley. "Interview with Phil Hartman." *Bomb*, Winter 1991.

The Movie Guys. "10 Questions with Phil Hartman." *Scope*, 30 May 1998.

Newton, Jim, T. Christian Miller and Solomon Moore. "Final Hours of Hartmans Detailed by Police Sources." *Los Angeles Times*, 30 May 1998.

"Obituary: Rupert Hartmann." April 1998.

O'Neill, Ann W. and Andrew Blankstein. "Police Release 911 Tape in Phil Hartman Case." *Los Angeles Times*, 3 June 1998.

O'Neill, Ann W. "Hartman Had Made Wife Sole Beneficiary." *Los Angeles Times*, 3 June 1998.

"Pakistan Reportedly Detonates Nuclear Devices." CNN.com, 28 May 1998.

"Pfizer Slapped with Suit over Actor's Death." *American Druggist*, 216.7, 1999.

Phillips, Michael. "Thanks for the Side-splitting Memories." *Los Angeles Times*, 27 September 1999.

Proudfit, Scott. "Phil Hartman: Tragic Irony." *Backstage West/DramaLogue*, June 1998.

Quill, Greg. "Second Civil War a Classic TV Tragicomedy." *Toronto Star*, 14 March 1997.

"Remembering Phil Hartman." *Entertainment Weekly*, 12 June 1998.

Rensin, David. "The Playboy Interview: Lorne Michaels." *Playboy*, 1 March 1992.

Reuters, Canadian Press, and Associated Press. "Hartman Killed." 29 May 1998.

Riccardi, Nicholas. "The Damage Undone: Neighbors Who Lost Homes Together Break Ground to Reclaim Their Former Lives." *Los Angeles Times*, 23 May 1995.

Rice, Darcy. "100 Flavors of Vanilla." *Orange Coast*, August 1996.

Rohan, Virginia. "Hail to the Chief: NBC Pays Tribute to Phil Hartman, Sketch Player without Peer." *The Record* [Bergen County, NJ], 12 June 1998.

———. "Out of the Bottle—Along with Many Amusing Characters, Phil Hartman of 'NewsRadio' Unleashes the Rare Exception." *The Record* [Bergen County, NJ], 24 February 1998.

Romano, Lois. "A New Life for Phil, as Bill." *The Washington Post*, 28 April 1993.

Rosenthal, Phil. "Savvy 'NewsRadio' a Hit Waiting to Happy." *Los Angeles Daily News*, 6 March 1996.

Russell, Candice. "Silly 'Houseguest' Wears out Welcome." *Sun-Sentinel* [Broward and Palm Beach, Florida], 6 January 1995.

Ryan, Mike. "The Movieline Interview: Jon Lovitz." 22 December 2010.

Sarkisian-Miller, Nola. "A Posh Spot North of the Boulevard." *Los Angeles Times*, 12 November 2006.

Schwed, Mark. "In Phil's Spirit." *TV Guide*, 26 October 1998.

Scott, Cathy. "A Mother's Day Present, Live from NY." *The Vista Press*, May 1992.

"7551 Sunset Blvd., Los Angeles, CA: Thee Experience: Performance List March–December" 1969. *Rock Archaeology* 101, 1 November 2010.

Smith, Chris. "Comedy Isn't Funny." *New York*, 13 March 1995.

Smith, Reginald. "Simi Valley to Exact Toll for Filming Its Scenery." *Los Angeles Times*, 24 December 1986.

Snierson, Dan. "Man of a Thousand Voices." *Entertainment Weekly*, 12 June 1998.

"'SNL' Co-star Looking for Studio." Tribune Media Services, 9 October 1991.

Span, Paula. "Passing the (Blow) Torch." *TV Guide*, January 1993.

Staff. "No Raise . . . no Big Deal." *Houston Chronicle*, 11 May 1998.

Staff. "People and Places." *The Baltimore Sun*, 15 September 1998.

Stein, Joel. "The Most Happy Fella." *Time*, 8 June 1998.

Sterngold, James. "Comedian Phil Hartman Is Shot to Death in His Home." *New York Times*, 29 May 1998.

Strickler, Jeff. "Nice Guy Phil Hartman Loves Playing Weasels." *Minneapolis Star Tribune*, 26 November 1996.

Surovell, Hariette. "Interview with Andy Dick." *Cover,* Summer 1999.
———. "You Don't Know Dick." *Salon.com,* 22 September 1998.
Tansey, Joel. "Honoring a Brother." *Brantford Expositor,* 24 May 2008.
"Ten Questions with Brian Mulhern." Rhodeislandcomedy.com, September 2011.
Thomas, Trevor. "The Groundlings." *Drama-Logue,* 3 May 1979.
Thompson, Bob. "The Jerky Guy." *Jam Showbiz,* 1 December 1996.
———. "'No Spikes, No Sudden Downfalls': Slow and Steady Wins the Race for Phil Hartman." Associated Press, 22 August 1995.
Thompson, Charles G. "My Restaurant Stories: Los Angeles in the '80s." 100 Miles.com, 4 August 2010.
Tresniowski, Alex. "Beneath the Surface." *People,* 15 June 1998.
"2 Boroughs May Host Disney 'Houseguest'" *Pittsburgh Post-Gazette,* 19 April 1994.
Vancheri, Barbara. "Comedian Sinbad Is the City's 'Houseguest.'" *Pittsburgh Post-Gazette,* 9 May 1994.
———. "Hartman, Sinbad Play It for Laughs in 'Houseguest.'" *Pittsburgh Post-Gazette,* 28 May 1994.
———. "Remembering a Most Welcome Guest in Our City." *Pittsburgh Post-Gazette,* 30 May 1998.
Van Derbeken, Jaxon, and Tyra Lucile Mead. "Comic Phil Hartman Slain in L.A./Wife Blamed in Murder-Suicide." *San Francisco Chronicle,* 29 May 1998.
Waters, Rob. "My Antidepressant Made Me Do It!" *Salon.com,* 19 July 1999.
Weinstein, Alisa and Jamie DeLange. "Woman on the Verge." *Us,* August 1998.
Wilkinson, Peter. "Who Killed Pee-wee Herman?" *Rolling Stone,* 3 October 1991.
Wilner, Norman. "Phil Hartman 1948–1998." *Toronto Star,* 4 July 1998.

WEB SITES

The *Saturday Night Live* Archives: http://snl.jt.org
Saturday Night Live Transcripts: http://snltranscripts.jt.org
Saturday Night Live episodes and clips: Hulu.com, Netflix.com, NBC.com (now only on Yahoo.com)

AUDIO/VIDEO

A&E Biography: Phil Hartman. April 12, 2004.
Audio recording of Hartmann family meeting with LAPD Robbery/Homicide detective Dave Martin. July 23, 1998.

Audio recording of tribute to Phil Hartman at Paramount Theatre, Los Angeles. July 14, 1998.

Chick Hazard at Groundlings Theatre, private video collection, December 1983.

E! True Hollywood Story: Phil Hartman. September 6, 1998.

Headliners and Legends: Phil Hartman, NBC. June 15, 2000.

The Howard Stern Interview: Phil and Brynn Hartman, E! Entertainment, November 27, 1992.

Late Night with Conan O'Brien, NBC. November 1996.

The Late Show with David Letterman, various clips, CBS. Early through mid-1990s.

Later with Bob Costas, NBC. February 14, 1992.

Later with Greg Kinnear, NBC. March 2, 1994.

Lovitz, Jon. *Second City Presents . . . with Bill Zehme.* Directed by John Davies. Brad Gray Television and John Davies Prods. Bravo TV, 2002.

NewsRadio: The Complete Series (Seasons 1 through 5), 1995–99.

Marin, Britten. Private home video collection. Early through mid-1990s.

The Pee-wee Herman Show: Live from the Sunset Strip's Roxy Theatre, Reubens-Callner Prod. 1981.

Pee-wee's Playhouse, Season 1 (six episodes), 1986. Paul Reubens/Herman World Inc.

Phil Hartman's Flat TV. Electric Paintbox, 1989, 2002.

The Simpsons. Select episodes (seasons 2 through 9), 1990–98.

SNL Collection: *The Best of Phil Hartman.* Broadway Video/NBC Home Entertainment.

SNL Collection: *The Best of Dana Carvey.* Broadway Video/NBC Home Entertainment.

SNL Collection: *The Best of Jon Lovitz.* Broadway Video/NBC Home Entertainment.

OTHER SOURCES

Autopsy Report, Brynn Hartman, Los Angeles Department of Coroner, 29 May 1998.

Autopsy Report, Phil Hartman, Los Angeles Department of Coroner. 29 May 1998.

California State University, Northridge, academic records.

Certificate of Death—Brynn Hartman, County of Los Angeles Department of Health Services. 2 June 1998.

Certificate of Death—Phil Hartman. County of Los Angeles Department of Health Services. 2 June 1998.

Contract between NBC Entertainment and Phil Hartman for written contributions to *Saturday Night Live*. 14 November 1985.

Court records. Hartman, Philip Edward vs. Change Name, September 21, 1992.

Court records. Los Angeles Superior Court. Hartmann, Philip Edward vs. Strain Lisa Lynn, November 14, 1984.

Federal Aviation Administration, Airmen Certification Branch.

Forensic Laboratory Analysis Report. May 29, 1998.

GSR (gunshot residue) Data Sheet, Forensic Science Center, County of Los Angeles, 28 May 1998.

Inventory and Appraisal: Estate of Philip Edward Hartman, Superior Court of California—Los Angeles. 31 August 1998.

Investigator's Report—Los Angeles Department of Coroner. 28 May 1998.

Investigatory records, Los Angeles Police Department. 28 May 1998 to 14 April 1999.

Letters from Doris Hartmann to Phil Hartman. Circa 1985.

Letters, notes—private collection of Lisa Jarvis. 1981–84.

Letters—private collection of John S. Holloway. 1968–69.

Phil Hartman ash scattering ceremony, private video collection. 24 September 1998.

Santa Monica College, Admissions and Records.

Toxicology Report for Brynn Hartman, Los Angeles Department of Coroner. 8 June 1998.

U.S. Citizenship and Immigration Services, Los Angeles, CA.

Will of Philip Edward Hartman. 11 March 1996.

Yearbooks: Orville Wright Junior High and Westchester High, 1962–66.

Index

healed himself before he needed to be attended to with heart bypass surgery.

SEVEN GENERATIONS

Imprints can also be associated with the psychological characteristics that we inherit from our parents. In Nancy Friday's book *My Mother, Myself*, she discovers she is reliving her mother's life despite doing everything in her power to do exactly the opposite. We often end up fighting the same battles and following the same life paths that our mothers and fathers did. If your grandmother and your mother were involved with abusive men in their lives, you might be predisposed to the same sort of relationship. Even the Bible states that the sins of the father will be inherited for seven generations. These sins are not judgments against innocent descendants but are negative energies that are passed along from one generation to the next. Psychologists believe that the subconscious motifs and behaviors we inherit from our parents might be encoded into the circuitry of the brain, and that the only way we can reprogram these circuits is through psychotherapy. I'm convinced that these negative patterns and habits ar encoded in the Luminous Energy Field as well and that the Illun nation Process can accomplish in one session what can often t years to heal through psychotherapy.

Talk psychotherapy often is not enough to achieve healing chology believes that once you become cognizant of hitherto scious "complexes" and "drives," you can become free noxious influence. Shamans, on the other hand, believe t lectual cognizance barely scratches the surface and is not bring about healing. Knowing that she was sexually abuse will help a woman to understand her reluctance to trust understanding alone will seldom allow her to particip mate relationship. We all understand that we should forty-five I also faced the loss of everything I loved. My earlier books had placed me in high demand as a speaker and teacher. Four days out of every week I was on the road lecturing on energy medicine and shamanism. I had very little time left for my family. Despite valiant attempts to preserve my marriage, including therapy and counseling, it fell apart. My wife and I separated, and shortly thereafter my six-year-old girl was thrown from a horse and had to undergo emergency surgery to repair a ruptured liver. I was leading an expedition to the Amazon jungle when this happened, visiting with a renowned medicine man — Don Ignacio. The shaman was a great seer, and when I explained to him what had happened in the last six months of my life, he described a dark mass over my heart.

"It's the grief that I'm feeling," I told him.

"No," he said as he gently placed his hand over my heart. "It is your grandfather's misfortune." He then went on to describe how my father's father had destroyed another man's career and incurred his wrath. This "curse" had been transmitted to my father, to my brother, and then on to me.

"You can heal this by battling adversaries in the world the rest of your life," Don Ignacio explained, "or you can heal your heart and the outer world will follow."

That evening Don Ignacio helped me to heal my heart. He cleared the dark nebula over my heart chakra and the generational imprint etched in my Luminous Energy Field. I flew back to the United States the following morning. My daughter was released from the pediatric intensive care unit a few days later and has recovered completely. It was too late to save my marriage, but my relationship with my children has grown and thrived. Today we have a great friendship. They have taught me how to be a great father. Since then I've become aware of how an imprint can be passed down from one generation to the next. When we heal these imprints within us, we heal them for our parents and children as well. I believe I've spared my son the need to go into major life crisis at the age of forty-six to heal his male lineage going back several generations. How do I know for sure? I know that I survived with my family intact, even though my marriage ended. Unlike my father, it did not take me twenty years to recover.

REIMPRINTING

For us believing physicists, the distinction between past, present, and future is only a stubbornly persistent illusion.

ALBERT EINSTEIN

The shaman is interested in draining the toxic emotional energy around an imprint and then erasing the imprint itself. The early stages of the shaman's training consists of a deep clearing or "scouring" of her Luminous Energy Field. The shaman no longer identifies with her personal history. Thus the Navajo medicine woman is able to say, "The mountains am I, the rivers am I." Shamans may have suffered loss, hunger, pain, and abuse, but they understand that above all they are travelers on a great journey through infinity.

This is the goal of healing through the Illumination Process. I am not very interested in working within my client's stories, the way the psychotherapist is. I am interested in assisting clients to realize that they are not their stories, not actors in a script written by their mother or father or by the culture or time they happen to be living in, but storytellers. To do this I have to access the underlying imprint in the Luminous Energy Field. It is very difficult to access these imprints directly. It's like trying to watch a movie by pulling the videotape out of its housing. We can only get to the film through the interface, in this case the VCR and the television screen.

The interface between our material world and the Luminous Energy Field is the chakras. In a sense, these spinning vortexes of energy can be thought of as sitting on top of the equals sign in Einstein's equation $E = MC^2$. The chakras employ energy to organize the physical matter of the body to create illness or health and to shape the world immediately around us. Through the chakras we are able to cross over from the world of matter into the sphere of energy.

PART II

THE

LUMINOUS

WORLD

The mystery schools of the past taught the secrets of our transcendent nature. These schools were founded by visionaries from the fertile crescent between the Tigris and Euphrates Rivers and by shamans from China and Tibet. Their teachings persist today. Many people have studied the Kabbalah, the I Ching, Tantra, and Tibetan Buddhism. In addition, there are excellent healing practices taught by Reiki masters and other practitioners of energy medicine. We have available to us a wealth of spiritual practices, including yoga and meditation, that can greatly assist us in our path.

Similar mystery schools existed in the Americas among the Maya, the Hopi, the Inka, and other native groups. They described the nine gates or passages a person undergoes in the course of becoming a sage.

Each of these gates corresponds to one of the chakras. The Inka shamans I studied with identified nine chakras. Each of these centers represented a gate the sage passes through in his self-realization. Seven of these centers are in the body. The other two reside in the Luminous Energy Field. In these two chakras the shaman enters a transpersonal reality.

The following chapters describe the anatomy of the Luminous Energy Field from a shaman's perspective. They include exercises for awakening our ability to see into the invisible world of energy. I call these seeing practices the Second Awareness, to differentiate them from the ordinary awareness of everyday life. They are powerful and practical methods for learning to perceive the spaces in between things and the luminous reality around us.

Chapter 6 presents the concept of sacred space. My mentor used to tell me to open sacred space and get out of the way. He was referring to the immense spiritual assistance available to us from healers in the invisible world. After learning these practices I discovered I did not have to do everything by myself. Explore the techniques in Chapter 6 to create spaces where Spirit can touch the body and infuse it with wisdom. Above all, experiment with the practices in this part of the book. The shaman's journey is a process of discovery. Ultimately, the experiences you have in these domains are your most reliable source of knowledge.

CHAPTER 4

THE CHAKRAS

Last night I tracked the cekes, the luminous filaments from my second chakra. We were in a lush valley overgrown with eucalyptus and pines. After dinner we went for what I thought would be a short stroll, but Antonio kept taking me farther into the forest. The moon was nearly full, and when the clouds parted we could find our way quite easily. When the moon was covered we were thrust into near total darkness. We arrived at a clearing where he asked me to sit on a boulder and connect with a tall pine a dozen yards away. I closed my eyes and imagined reaching out to the tree.

"Not with your head, niño," he said.

I hate it when he calls me "child," and he knows it. I'm convinced that's why he does it when he disapproves of what I'm doing.

"With your belly," he said. "Extend a tendril of light from your cosco [second chakra] to the tree."

When I did this I could feel a visceral connection with the pine, as if we were touching. I could sense the texture of the bark and even go into the tree itself. When Antonio asked me to open my eyes I could see the light filament extending from my belly.

"Now uncouple from the tree and connect to your earliest memory. Try to remember back to when you were a toddler, before you could walk, and link the filament to this boy," he said.

I must have spent the next hour trying to do it. I could tell

Antonio was growing impatient. "You are thinking," he said. "Stop thinking. Just do."

And then I got it. I could feel the skin of this boy the way I had felt the skin of the tree. I could taste what he tasted and sense how big the world felt. All of my senses were active and nearly on overload. It was no longer the me that I knew who was touching and feeling, but another, older, equally as familiar, younger me.

Then Antonio asked me to follow that luminous fiber, to track along the cord itself, allowing the images and feelings to flood into me. I imagined that I was walking along this cord as I walk on a trail, and espied images of my childhood and adolescence I had not thought about in decades: the Halloween costume my parents made me wear when I was five, the crush I had on my third-grade teacher, the time our dog died. The strangest thing. I was not only seeing the images, but the emotions were deluging me. I saw every painful and joyous moment of my life. Then Antonio tapped me on the shoulder.

"Next time," he said, "we are going to connect with who you are becoming ten thousand years from now."

JOURNALS

ACCORDING TO THE BELIEFS OF THE HOPI OF THE SOUTHWEST, "man is created perfect in the image of his Creator." In *The Book of the Hopi*, Frank Waters notes the belief that "the living body of man and the living body of the earth were constructed in the same way. Through each ran an axis, man's axis being the backbone, the vertebral column, which controlled the equilibrium of his movements and his functions. Along this axis were several vibratory centers which echoed the primordial sound of life through the universe." References to the chakras are found among the Hopi, the Inka, and the Maya, as well as many other aboriginal cultures around the world.